Developing Healthy

MESSIANIC

CONGREGATIONS

SAM NADLER

WORD OF MESSIAH MINISTRIES
CHARLOTTE, NC

ACKNOWLEDGMENTS

I am thankful to all who made this book a reality:
Editing: Laurel James
Book layout: Tim James
Proofreading: James & Kim Rogers, Ann Thomas, Mary Parker, & Shari Belfer
Transcribing: Shari Belfer & Joy Drauden

But of course, I give all praise to Messiah, who has called me into this work
and allows me and these others the great privilege in His service
to see Messianic congregations established worldwide.
All to the praise of His glory!

CONTENTS

APPENDICES: SUPPLEMENTAL MATERIAL

CHART INDEX

ABOUT THE AUTHOR

Dr. Sam Nadler is a Jewish believer in Yeshua who has a passion to communicate the Good News of Messiah with his people, and see discipled Messianic believers raised up as a testimony of God's faithfulness both to Israel and on behalf of Israel.

To further this goal, Sam leads Word of Messiah Ministries which plants Messianic congregations worldwide, providing coaching, support and assistance for leaders at every stage of the process. Sam also regularly conducts "Developing Healthy Messianic Congregations" conferences, providing practical biblical training designed to equip Messianic leaders and congregations to succeed, grow, and reproduce.

Raised in New York City according to Orthodox tradition, Sam searched for what the Messiah of Israel alone can provide: atonement and new life. After accepting Yeshua in 1972, Sam has been in full-time service for Him.

Sam Nadler understands the role of leadership from the inside. He served as a leader in the early days of Jews for Jesus, establishing JFJ's New York City branch. Beginning in 1979, Sam served with Chosen People Ministries. Recognizing the great need for new Jewish believers to be grounded and rooted in their faith through Messianic discipleship, Sam began personally planting as well as supervising the planting of several congregations in the Northeast United States. As God's grace became evident, in 1989, Sam was asked to lead Chosen People Ministries' worldwide organization.

In 1996, God led Sam and his wife, Miriam, to establish Word of Messiah Ministries, an organization focused on providing Messianic discipleship, developing Messianic leaders, and planting Messianic congregations worldwide for the furtherance of the Good News. WMM also provides teaching and exhortation to the greater Body of Messiah concerning the calling of all believers to make Israel jealous for Messiah (Romans 11:11). Sam received a doctoral degree from Southern Evangelical Seminary and has authored several books on Messianic theology, evangelism, and discipleship including *Messianic Foundations, Messiah in the Feasts of Israel, The Messianic Answer Book,* and *The Feasts of the Bible Curriculum,* as well as devotional commentaries on the books of Jonah and Ruth.

WHAT OTHER PLANTERS & LEADERS ARE SAYING ABOUT SAM'S COACHING:

―――――◇―――――

The material in this book has been used in Sam Nadler's leadership coaching ministry for over 30 years, and is also the basis for Sam's "Developing Healthy Messianic Congregations" conferences. Please contact Word of Messiah Ministries if you are interested in more information about Sam's leadership coaching or would like to schedule a conference in your area.

Michael Vowell, congregation planter, Calgary, Canada
Despite church planting training at *Moody* and *Dallas Theological Seminary* and experience here in Canada, nothing has been able to help and guide me like Sam's coaching ministry. Let me say it another way: Sam's coaching has caused our Mosaic Fellowship to thrive, reaching new believers and making new disciples for the Messiah... God has used Sam and his coaching ministry and our congregational plant is making a measurable impact on the Jewish community of Calgary.

Dr. Michael Herts, leader of *B'nai Avraham*, Hampton, VA
Dr. Sam Nadler with *Word of Messiah Ministries* has been the most instrumental of all the resources available to me as a congregation planter. His consistent mentoring took us from a God-given calling to a congregation about to be fully birthed. His focus on evangelism and disciple making, affirming a statement of faith, and developing a set of values that guide a congregation has saved us from many of the pitfalls that other congregational plants face. His individual mentoring, prayer, and encouragement has kept me on track when challenges seemed overwhelming. *B'nai Avraham Messianic Fellowship* would not be successful today if we did not have Sam's guidance.

Larry Rose, elder at *Eitz Chaim*, Dallas, TX
We are pleased to report that your work at *Eitz Chaim* has produced fruit. Our discipleship program will utilize your *Messianic Discipleship* book. Much has happened since you were here, mainly through the work of the Spirit that opened a dialogue within leadership to re-think our focus and vision. We are presently revamping our services, activities and printed materials to reflect a clearer focus on the Gospel. I cannot adequately express our appreciation for your work here, and how instrumental you were in our

decisions. We had a visitor accept Yeshua last Shabbat, which was the first saved in many years; we believe it is evidence of the first fruits from the seeds you planted.

Scott Brown, former leader of *Son of David*, Rockville, MD
Sam was the first to give me what I really needed. He rifled solutions to me, which advanced me toward my goal. By God's grace, Sam Nadler's coaching made the difference between success and failure in my ministry.

Vladimir Pikman, leader of *Beit Sar Shalom*, Berlin, Germany
Sam's leadership training and coaching helped me to have better priorities for my family and ministry. I now understand and am able to accomplish the Great Commission in a more effective, wise, and comprehensive manner.

Jonathan Sacks, leader of *Hope in Messiah*, Bowling Green, KY
Over the past several years, the Lord has used Sam Nadler to help us identify and implement congregational systems that have helped us minister more effectively. Implementing, reviewing, and modifying systems for making contacts, disciples, members, and leaders is essential for our congregation to fulfill its calling and vision to be fruitful in making disciples in our area and beyond.

Jamie Shapiro, leader of *Adat Yeshua*, Albuquerque, NM
Sam's "Developing Healthy Messianic Congregations" conference was excellent and very comprehensive. I've been in Messianic ministry since 1982, and wish I had the opportunity to go through a course like this 20 years ago. I see these conferences as being very helpful for leaders starting out in ministry, as they detail every area of ministry they will encounter. This type of training on establishing and developing healthy congregations is invaluable. I have not seen this kind of training before in the Messianic movement, and wish I had known about Sam's ministry earlier.

Allan Moorhead, leader of *Arrowhead Messianic Cong.*, Peoria, AZ
All of my leaders who attended Sam's conference were ecstatic afterwards. They each received information that was very useful and helpful for them and are already implementing ideas that they learned. Sam's teaching is excellent, he knows the material well, and you can tell he has a passion and love for Messianic Congregations and desire to help them succeed. The information about discipleship and follow-up was particularly valuable, as was Sam's new book, *Developing Healthy Messianic Congregations*.

FOREWORD

As an early pioneer in the Messianic Congregational movement myself, I was very eager to review Sam Nadler's manual on developing healthy Messianic congregations. I reviewed his earlier version for The King's University course I was teaching a few years ago and found this first version very usable, balanced, detailed, practical, etc. So, when Sam planned to offer his highly spiritual yet practically down-to-earth seminar in Phoenix, Arizona in January 2016, I was pleased to not only invite the entire Phoenix Minyan of Messianic Jewish leaders to participate, but to also pay my own as well as a rabbinic staff member's registration for a meaningful refresher.

One of the special features of Sam's seminar was the use of the revamped and highly upgraded manual *Developing Healthy Messianic Congregations*. This book seems to have nearly double the content of the original version, is incredibly well-organized, filled with wisely chosen practical counsel, and chock full of pragmatic advice on what are invaluable insights into Messianic congregation planting. While I sat the weekend listening to Sam Nadler offer a room full of Messianic start-ups incredibly sound instruction, I recognized that his seminar carefully punctuated the manual and that the two combined to afford the aspiring Messianic Congregation planter rock solid spiritual and practical guidelines for success.

Not all can attend one of Sam Nadler's vital seminars. But for anyone planting or intending to plant a Messianic congregation, *Developing Healthy Messianic Congregations* is a critically important acquisition. And in its new and extended format, it has proven to be of even greater value.

Raymond L. Gannon

Raymond L. Gannon, Ph.D.
Vice President of Academic Affairs, Messianic Jewish Bible Institute

PREFACE

I wrote this book because it is my desire and goal for *"all Israel to be saved."* That is, for the Jewish people as a whole to come to personal faith in Messiah Yeshua (Romans 10:1, 11:26), and I believe that a healthy, functional Messianic congregation is the most effective long-term testimony of the Good News to the greater Jewish community.

In the book of Jeremiah, God has made a gracious commitment to preserve the Jewish people as an identifiable nation:

"Thus says the Lord, Who gives the sun for light by day, and the fixed order of the moon and the stars for light by night, Who stirs up the sea so that its waves roar; The Lord of hosts is His name; "If this fixed order departs from before Me," declares the Lord, "then the offspring of Israel also will cease from being a nation forever." Thus says the Lord, "If the heavens above can be measured and the foundations of the earth searched out below, then I will also cast off all the offspring of Israel for all that they have done," declares the Lord." – Jeremiah 31:35-37

A Messianic congregation is an expression of this unbreakable promise of God, serving to effectively testify that Yeshua is the faithfulness of God to both Israel and the nations. In a healthy congregation, as new Jewish believers are discipled to understand and live out their Jewish identity in Messiah, the same God who promised that He would not *"leave nor forsake"* our people is seen in the eyes of the Jewish community, and to all who are watching, as the same faithful Lord who said, *"I am with you always, even to the end of the age"* (Matthew 28:20).

As Gentiles are saved through the evangelistic work of Messianic congregations, they will grow in the same faith and by the same discipleship as Messianic Jews. This makes their own communication of the Good News more clear and meaningful to the Jewish people and to all people. As Jew and Gentile together, believers in a Messianic congregation testify of God's ongoing faithfulness to Israel and the nations. Despite all that the enemy has attempted to do, the Jewish people have been kept by God. In Messiah, we, as a remnant people, are restored to God's service and testimony. The existence of Messianic congregations testifies to God's triumph!

We are blessed to live in a time where more and more people are embracing the need for there to be a present-tense Jewish testimony of the Good News. As a result, we are seeing new Messianic congregations springing up in Israel, the United States, and around the world. But what does it take to start a Messianic congregation? What does a healthy congregation actually do? Keep reading!

This book is designed to be used as a practical guide in the planting and establishing of healthy communities, walking you step by step through the stages of the planting process, presenting an in depth look at a healthy congregation's essential systems and responsibilities, and guiding you in how to plan and prepare for growth as the Lord would give the increase. My hope and prayer is that this book be used to develop strong Messianic leaders and congregations, who will in turn establish new Messianic leaders and congregations, so that many more will come to know and honor the Name of Yeshua HaMashiach, the Messiah of Israel.

Sam Nadler
January 12, 2016

INTRODUCTORY CONSIDERATIONS

WHY CONGREGATIONS?

Community Matters: God's love revealed

Notes:

Then God said, "Let Us make man in Our image, according to Our likeness; and let them rule over the fish of the sea and over the birds of the sky and over the cattle and over all the earth, and over every creeping thing that creeps on the earth." God created man in His own image, in the image of God He created him; male and female He created them. God blessed them; and God said to them, "Be fruitful and multiply, and fill the earth, and subdue it; and rule over the fish of the sea and over the birds of the sky and over every living thing that moves on the earth." – Genesis 1:26-28

THE MYSTERY OF RELATIONSHIPS

God, by His very nature, is relational. In Genesis 1, we see that before God created, He communicated! God's statement, *"Let Us make man in Our image,"* reveals that the Triune nature of God was at work in our creation. The very nature of God is meant to help us understand that God is love, and as the Father loves the Son, so we are to love one another. As people created in God's image, we are not godly if we are not loving. *"By this all men will know you are My disciples if you have love for one another."* (John 13:35)

Understanding the fact that we are all created in His image helps us to understand the function of a healthy congregation. We bear witness to the image of God in us as we care for one another in community, not settling to live as "lone rangers." As we read on through Genesis chapters two and three, we see that the cornerstone of a community is the marriage relationship and, from that, the family. "Congregation" is merely a word we use for families that meet together on the basis of agreed-upon values. Therefore, it is absolutely vital that the marriages and families which make up our congregations develop and become strong.

THE HISTORY OF SYNAGOGUES

Notes:

So how did the model of synagogues, or congregations as we know them today, come to be? The word "synagogue" is not found in the Torah. This is because synagogues were not established until the Babylonian captivity. Before that time, there were towns, villages, and cities overseen by elders who followed Torah and led their communities on the basis of Torah. At this time, everyone in each town was under the same regulations and legislation.

The first congregations began as the Jewish people returned from Babylon with little temples which later became our "synagogues." Though the model of congregations was not established until this point, we see that they were affirmed by Messiah:

"As was His custom, He went to synagogue on Shabbat." - Luke 4:16

We follow Yeshua's custom, even though it is not the custom of many. God's Word teaches us that congregational fellowship must be a high priority in our lives. We see in Hebrews 10:25 that we are to be, *"not forsaking our own assembling together, as is the habit of some, but encouraging one another; and all the more as we see the day drawing near."*

We prioritize community because we follow Yeshua. He validated the whole congregational idea and showed it to be meaningful through His life and practice.

THE INTEGRITY OF THE BODY

"As He is, so are we in the world" – 1 John 4:17

As we seek to have congregations that reveal the Lord, we need to establish God-centered communities, remembering that He is the Head and we are the Body. The living Head is revealed through a healthy Body. Thus, the health of a congregation is vital in order to demonstrate the love of Yeshua to those inside and outside the community. This becomes the congregations' testimony that God is alive and well, and is in their midst.

WHY MESSIANIC CONGREGATIONS?

Calling Matters: God's faithfulness revealed

In the believing community today, a Messianic congregation is the exception and not the rule. Though many believers appreciate the existence of Messianic congregations, many others do not understand the purpose of their existence. Therefore, an apologetic is necessary. Why would we plant Messianic congregations?

The planting of Messianic congregations has to do with our calling; the calling to demonstrate the faithfulness of God.

Yeshua is God's faithfulness to Israel and the nations. He alone is the fulfillment of the promises made to our fathers (Genesis 12:3, Romans 15:8). Although the greater Jewish community today may strongly disagree with this statement, it is vital that we communicate this biblical truth in a way that is relevant to them. A Messianic congregation, by its very existence, whether small or large, traditional or not so-traditional, is a demonstration of God's faithfulness to Israel.

Sharing Messiah with unbelieving Jewish people is vitally important. The work, however, does not end there. If a Jewish person comes to faith in Messiah, but then is not discipled in how to live for the Lord as a Messianic believer, they will become a dysfunctional member of the Body of Messiah and will present an ineffective testimony back to their own people. There are many Jewish believers in churches; however, due to lack of Messianic discipleship, they are often sadly not easily identifiable as being Jewish. In light of the fact that much of the greater Body of Messiah is unprepared to provide discipleship for new Jewish believers, Messianic congregations are necessary, for discipleship is a congregational matter. A community of rooted and grounded Messianic believers, who are lovingly reaching out and making disciples, clearly communicates God's faithfulness in Messiah, and provides a living testimony to unbelieving Jewish people.

The primary concern of our people today is not, "What does Isaiah 53 mean?" but, "Will there be a Jewish people?" As Messianic congregations, we are the identifiable remnant of Israel. A healthy Messianic congregation testifies, "Yes! *Am Yisrael Chai B'Shem Yeshua*" (The people of Israel live in the Name of Yeshua).

Notes:

_____

_____

_____

_____

_____

_____

_____

_____

_____

_____

_____

_____

_____

_____

_____

_____

The Messianic movement is all about Him, and Messianic congregations are all about Messiah. This is who we are, Who we testify of, and Who we glorify!

PAUL'S THEOLOGY & MESSIANIC CONGREGATIONS

Notes:

When we look at those whom God first used to spread His Good News to Israel and the nations, we see that He sent Peter, ignorant in many ways, to the Jewish people, and Paul, a highly educated "Hebrew of Hebrews" (Philippians 3:5) to the nations. Why? The Jewish community already had the background; they simply needed to hear the news that Yeshua the Messiah had come. However, when the Good News was brought to Gentile communities, an entire theology had to be communicated in order to bridge the gap and help the Gentiles to understand God and His redemptive plan. In the book of Romans, we see how Paul lays out the entire counsel of God to the Gentile congregation in Rome.

We see the theme of the book in Romans 1:16-17:

"For I am not ashamed of the Good News, for it is the power of God for salvation to everyone who believes, to the Jew first, and also (equally - CJB) to the Gentile. For in it the righteousness of God is revealed from faith to faith; as it is written, 'But the righteous man shall live by faith.'"

Paul's focus here is on the righteousness of God revealed in the Good News of Messiah. Through chapters one through eight, he goes on to cover the counsel of God regarding condemnation, justification by faith, reconciliation in Messiah, sanctification through the Holy Spirit, and glorification.

Chapters nine through eleven then deal with the mystery of Israel: the sovereignty of God in Israel past, the responsibility of man in Israel present, and the sovereignty of God in Israel future. Here, we will consider the calling of both Jewish and Gentile believers as seen in Romans chapter eleven.

THE JEWISH REMNANT OF ISRAEL

Romans 11:1-10

Romans 11 begins with a question:

"I say then, God has not rejected His people, has He? May it never be! For I too am an Israelite, a descendant of Abraham, of the tribe of Benjamin." – Romans 11:1

Why did Paul feel the need to bring up this point? As he preached the Good News, there were so many Gentiles being saved that some questioned whether God had moved on from Israel and chosen the Gentiles instead. So Paul made it clear that God would never reject His people, giving the proof of himself as a present-tense Jewish man. Today, Jewish believers demonstrate this same present-tense faithfulness of God as they keep a present-tense Jewish testimony.

THE GENTILE WITNESS TO ISRAEL

Romans 11:11-24

"I say then, they did not stumble so as to fall, did they? May it never be! But by their transgression salvation has come to the Gentiles, to make them jealous." – Romans 11:11

Gentile believers also have a vital role to play in demonstrating God's faithfulness: by making Israel jealous for their own Messiah. Though some may object to this idea, thinking that God is playing favorites, God's Word shows us that this couldn't be further than the truth! We are all on the same team; there is only one Body of Messiah, and only one calling which we share. Paul's ministry to the Gentiles was to help them understand this calling.

Paul goes on to remind the Gentile believers that they have been grafted in, and warns them not to become arrogant against the natural branches, for just as they were grafted in, God is able to graft the natural branches in again (Romans 11:23)

"For if you were cut off from what is by nature a wild olive tree, and were grafted contrary to nature into a cultivated olive tree, how much more will these who are the natural branches be grafted into their own olive tree?" – Romans 11:24

Notes:

_____

_____

_____

_____

_____

_____

_____

_____

_____

_____

_____

_____

_____

_____

_____

_____

Regardless of the number of wild branches, the fact remains that it is still Israel's olive tree. When Gentile believers act as if they have replaced the Jewish people, this is a huge problem. Paul was concerned about this, as he understood that the salvation of Israel is instrumental to the second coming of Messiah. Jewish believers today are the remnant, holding down the fort until the rest come in; national revival is coming!

THE NATIONAL REVIVAL OF ISRAEL

Romans 11:25-32

"and so all Israel will be saved; just as it is written, 'The Deliverer will come from Zion, He will remove ungodliness from Jacob.' 'This is My covenant with them, when I take away their sins.'" – Romans 11:26-27

Gentiles are not an afterthought to God; their witness to Israel is intrinsic to the very calling of God regarding the second coming of Messiah, the hope of Israel and the nations! The second coming is tied to the repentance of Israel, (Matthew 23:39) and it will be the *"sheep nations,"* the Gentiles who understand their calling, (Matthew 25:32) who will bring the Good News to them. Sadly, history has hidden this from the eyes of most of the greater Body of Messiah, but today we see many who are coming to terms with this awesome calling of God upon their lives.

In Messianic congregations, as Jews and Gentiles worship together as two witnesses before God, it is an acceptable testimony that God is faithful to Israel and the nations (Deuteronomy 19:15)! Together we live for the redemption of Israel, the hope of the world.

THEOLOGY SHAPES WHAT WE VALUE

As we consider these key issues, recognize that our theology matters very much, for what we believe shapes what we value. For instance, if a person truly believes that Messiah's second coming is tied to the repentance of Israel, they will value bringing the Good News to the Jew first. That which an individual or congregation values most will determine their direction and focus in life. Our actual values reveal our actual faith and will either help or hinder our witness for Messiah.

Values are incredibly important, for every person also evaluates life on the basis of the values they hold. As we evaluate people and situations, we will either validate or invalidate them based on our values.

People have all kinds of values by which they continually evaluate, validate, and invalidate. Just as one unbelieving congregation may compare themselves to another on the basis of how many *mitzvot* their rabbi keeps, Messianic congregations can also invalidate others as they place a high value on things such as the Jewishness of their community, the size of their congregation, the length of their service, etc. Sadly, in the Messianic world, this type of "one ups-manship" can be common.

However, these things should not be so amongst us! We must allow sound biblical theology to shape our values. As a result, we will value each other, evaluating according to godly values, not external issues.

DEBUNKING MESSIANIC MYTHS

From my experience in working with Messianic congregations, I have seen many issues arise as people evaluate and invalidate other individuals or congregations on the basis of non-biblical values.
Here, I hope to debunk several myths which, if not properly addressed, can hinder a congregation plant or greatly stunt the growth of an already established congregation.

Myth 1: "I am a congregation if I say so."
Often, what is said to be a Messianic congregation is in reality a Bible study. Without a clear understanding of what a Messianic congregation is, a person may declare any gathering with a Messianic expression of faith to be a congregation. So what constitutes a congregation? A congregation is a congregation not because of the size of the group, but because of the group's mutual commitment and loving accountability in Messiah (Hebrews 10:24-25). A congregation has a four-fold purpose which can be described using the acrostic "WIFE": A Messianic congregation is a **W**orship Center, **I**nstruction Center, **F**ellowship Center, and **E**vangelism Center (See page 104 for more information about these roles). Being a "center" for these things implies a level of clear commitment and accountability which is not found in other gatherings.

Notes:

_____

_____

_____

_____

_____

_____

_____

_____

_____

_____

_____

_____

_____

_____

_____

_____

_____

_____

_____

_____

_____

_____

_____

_____

_____

_____

_____

_____

_____

_____

_____

Myth 2: "Messianic congregations shouldn't do evangelism."
Regrettably, many groups of believers, whether in Messianic congregations or churches, do not reach out in sharing their faith. This lack of outreach indicates a spiritual weakness and disobedience to God's Word, as all believers are under a mandate to proclaim the Good News (Acts 1:8). Evangelism, therefore, must be part of the DNA of a Messianic congregation. Even at the very beginning stages of a new congregation plant, the leadership must teach and equip the core group to personally share their faith, inviting pre-believers to services, etc.

Myth 3: "Our service needs be centered on the Torah to be messianic."
Traditional Orthodox services are Torah-centered; everything in the service happens either before or after the Torah is read. As Messianic congregation leaders and planters, we faithfully utilize Moses as we proclaim Messiah, for all the Torah speaks of Him (John 5:39). However, in our use of Torah, Messianic congregations must always be Yeshua-centered, for Messiah is the very substance of everything we do. Our worship is in His name or else it is false worship. Apart from Him we can do nothing (John 15:5).

Myth 4: "Messianic congregations are under the Mosaic Covenant."
Because we utilize the Torah of Moses, as well as all of the Tanakh, in order to express our faith, some presume that this means we are declaring ourselves to be under the jurisdiction, or rule, of the Mosaic Covenant. We must be careful to explain that this is not the case. We are under the authority of the New Covenant. This critical distinction has numerous implications. For example, if we were still under the Mosaic Covenant, Yeshua could not intercede for us as High Priest, as He does not qualify to be such a priest under the Torah (See Hebrews 7-8). It is only because of the New Covenant that we are truly saved and have the benefits of His ministry. Through the New Covenant, we can gather as one Body of Jews and Gentiles, one in Messiah. The promise of the New Covenant, anticipated by the prophets (Jeremiah 31:31 -34), has been realized through the sacrifice of Messiah. As Messianic congregations, we apply all of the *Tanakh* by the authority and purpose of the New Covenant (2 Timothy 3:16).

Myth 5: "Legitimate Messianic congregations have Jewish majorities."
In some Messianic communities where Gentile believers make up the majority of the congregation, there can be a sense of lack of validation. This attitude is harmful because every Messianic congregation is called to share

Messiah with everyone in their community, Jew and Gentile alike. In light of the fact that most of the world's population is Gentile, an effective Messianic congregation should actually expect to welcome many Gentile believers into their fellowship. Your congregation should be reflective of the community surrounding it. If only 10% of your community is Jewish, you should expect Gentiles to make up 90% of your congregation if you are indeed bringing the Good News to everyone around you, not "throwing any back" based on their ethnicity. As they join the congregation, these Gentile believers must be discipled properly, so that they will learn to express their faith in a way that testifies to the greater Jewish community. The Good News, though "to the Jew first," is to be shared with all with ears to hear, and dictates that all who respond be accepted, discipled, and loved.

Myth 6: "Messianic Gentiles are Jewish wannabe's."

Certainly, God loves Jews and Gentiles equally (John 3:16), and does not want Gentiles to become Jews any more than He wants Jews to become Gentiles. In fact, God's plan for Gentiles to express their faith in Messiah proves that He is faithful to Israel (Romans 11:11). The existence of Gentile believers demonstrates that Yeshua is the true Messiah of Israel and therefore Savior of the world, for in Yeshua all the nations of the earth would be blessed (Genesis 12:3; Galatians 3:8). So Gentiles, by practicing their faith in a Jewish frame of reference, are not seeking to become Jews, but are testifying to the blessings they have found in the Messiah of Israel (Colossians 2:10; Ephesians 1:3).

Myth 7: "Messianic Congregations must be led by Messianic Jews."

Because of this myth, some congregations have overlooked qualified Gentile believers and "laid hands" on some not so qualified Jewish believers. Being a Gentile believer doesn't invalidate a person as an effective Messianic leader any more than being a Jewish believer validates a person as an effective Messianic leader. In all Messianic congregations, both Jewish and Gentile believers should be equally discipled in Messianic values so that, as they mature, they will naturally take their place in Messianic leadership, even stepping up as congregational leader of a Messianic congregation. The Messianic world needs Messianic Gentile leaders like Luke and Titus as well as Messianic Jewish leaders like Paul and Timothy to lead Messianic congregations and the Messianic movement for the glory of the God of Israel.

Notes:

PART 1

ESTABLISHING A HEALTHY CONGREGATION

CHAPTER 1

THE GATHERING STAGE

"Go therefore and make disciples of all the nations..." – Matthew 28:19

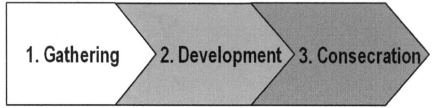

Figure 1.0

The birth of a new Messianic congregation can be likened to the birth of a new baby. Just as a baby must spend nine vital months in the womb, being woven together by the Lord as He prepares them for arrival into the world, so also for a congregation to be healthy at birth, there is much that must first take place!

Following the initial vision for a congregation, there are three essential stages that must be completed before the actual birth of the congregation: the Gathering Stage, the Core Group Development Stage, and the Consecration Stage. Each of these stages has three steps, and each are vitally important. As we touched on in our first Messianic myth, a group may call themselves a congregation simply because they have weekly fellowship around a Shabbat meal; however, there is much more to a congregation than this! As we work through these three stages, we will consider what truly makes a congregation a congregation from the perspective of the Word of God.

In Matthew 28, we see that Yeshua sent out His *talmidim* (disciples) to go make more *talmidim*. This mandate will be our focus during the Gathering Stage of congregation planting.

Many years ago, when conducting a training for a group of about thirty Messianic leaders, I asked them, "How many of you have ever discipled someone?" Only one person raised their hand. Discipleship is not a common practice in congregations today, but it is a biblical practice, and an essential one for us to implement in our congregations. However, before discussing these matters further, we must first consider the foundation that is necessary in order for discipleship to occur.

If you went to a prayer meeting for rain, what would you bring along with you? An umbrella of course, for you would want to be prepared for the answer to your prayers! Likewise, before you begin reaching out, you need to be prepared for people to respond to your outreach. I once spoke with a young man who wanted my counsel about his idea to start an outreach ministry for Jewish college students. "That's a great idea!" I told him. "Now what will you do with them once they come to faith?" This man was surprised by my question; he thought of himself as a person who could persevere in the ministry no matter the hardships he faced, but he hadn't thought about what he would do if someone actually came to faith! He was not prepared for success.

The importance of preparation cannot be overstated. It can take from 3-36 months or longer to move through the Gathering Stage, from vision to conception. Though many can be thrown off by this number, anxious to move forward faster, we must realize that maturity takes time. Just as you do not expect your child to be ready for a job by the time he is three years old, God's Word teaches us not to lay hands on people for service too quickly.

Paul says in 1 Timothy 3:6 that a Messianic leader is not to be a "novice." The Greek word used here literally means "neophyte," a word used to describe a young plant. In his use of this word, Paul was making reference to Leviticus 19 which teaches that the fruit of a newly planted tree was not to be eaten for its first three years of growth. The fourth year, the fruit was to be for God, and finally in the fifth year, it could be eaten. This is because the fruit needed to be mature before it could be partaken of. Likewise, in the planting of a congregation, we are not to be impatient. Time is required in order to build a mature congregation; one that will be set upon a firm foundation, able to weather storms which will test the integrity of its foundation.

Notes:

_____

_____

_____

_____

_____

_____

_____

_____

_____

_____

_____

_____

_____

_____

_____

_____

Notes:

Though we may want this stage to be checked off quickly so that we can move on to the next thing, we must be wary of holding to a cultural, rather than Scriptural perspective on these matters. You can only finish well if you begin well; half-built towers are never a good testimony! The Gathering Stage is the most difficult, yet most foundational stage of the process, well worth the investment you put into it.

The Gathering Stage, the time between vision and conception, consists of three steps:

✡ *The Preliminary Step:* This step of personal and community preparation is often overlooked, but it is foundational for everything that comes afterwards.

✡ *The Outreach Step:* This is the hardest step of the hardest stage, yet one that will yield fruit and determine the direction your congregation will take in the stages to come as you use every means to reach out in order to find those who will make up your core group.

✡ *The Discipleship Step:* This step will make an incalculable impact on the future health and growth of your congregation as you bring each person onto the same page with your values.

THE PRELIMINARY STEP

Are you personally prepared to plant a Messianic congregation?
Before a planter can bring others on board, he must first take an inventory of his own life. Here, we will touch on several foundational matters which must be taken into consideration as a person prepares to plant a congregation. As you read through this list, make an inventory of how these things are seen in your life. If you find you are weak in one or more of these areas, do not despair, but step back and prayerfully work through the matter, building a firm foundation in your own life as you prepare to move forward in ministry to others.

VITAL SPIRITUAL MATTERS FOR A PLANTER

PRAYER

The first matter to consider is the state of one's personal prayer life. This is of utmost importance for the planter, as well as for his team. Ultimately, a congregation is God's work, and we must depend on Him in prayer throughout the entire process, lest we find we "have not" because we "ask not."

The importance of prayer in our service is illustrated in Israel's first battle after coming out of Egypt (Exodus 17:8-16). Joshua may have physically led the Israeli army as they fought the Amalekites in this battle, yet their victory that day was found as Moses stood at the top of the mountain overlooking the battle with his arms outstretched to God. Just as prayer was key to Israel's victory, prayer is the key to our victory day-to-day. Though we may be gifted in many areas, apart from Him, we can do nothing (John 15:5).

A congregation planter must not only be in prayer himself, but also have others consistently praying for him. Throughout the long battle with Amalek, Moses' hands grew tired. He needed Aaron and Hur to come alongside him, supporting his hands as he fought in prayer for his people. A prayer team is greatly needed to assist, stand alongside, and undergird the work of planting as it moves forward. Beware of becoming so focused on what needs to be done that you forget to talk about it with the Lord.

ACCOUNTABILITY

Planters tend to be entrepreneurial pioneers; however, this does not diminish their essential need for accountability. As a planter, it is vital to seek out a godly mentor who truly cares about you enough to ask you straightforward questions such as, "Have you been praying lately?" "How is it going with you and your spouse?" "Are you taking a Shabbat each week?"...

Accountability may be available if you are part of a larger network or organization already involved in planting congregations. If, however, you do not have this resource, it is vital to seek out mentorship. It may be wise to find several mentors. Here are five qualities I suggest to look for in a mentor. He should be an individual with:

✡ Experience, able to provide sound counsel

Notes:

✡ Personal love and concern for you
✡ Objectivity
✡ Proven character
✡ Not controlling, but rather always seeking what is best for you and your situation

Notes:

_____

_____

_____

_____

_____

_____

_____

_____

_____

_____

_____

_____

_____

_____

_____

_____

_____

_____

_____

MARITAL UNITY

"You husbands in the same way, live with your wives in an understanding way, as with someone weaker, since she is a woman; and show her honor as a fellow heir of the grace of life, so that your prayers will not be hindered." – 1 Peter 3:7

Being single does not disqualify one from becoming a planter, but if you are married, the importance of unity between you and your spouse cannot be overstated. Here, Peter warns that if a husband is not treating his wife well, his prayers will go unanswered. This reminds us that no matter how important the work in the congregation, marriage must always come first. Indeed, the work of the congregation is an outworking of the ministry already taking place at home (1 Timothy 3:5).

It is essential that one's spouse be committed to the work alongside you, embracing it as her calling as well. If a planter's spouse is not prepared to assist in the congregation plant, it may not be God's timing to begin. However, as both support the ministry, the couple can face issues and difficulties in the work together. Her gifts will join his in contributing to the ministry of the congregation. Valuing and empowering one's spouse embodies the very values of the congregation.

One leader I knew waited three years before beginning to plant a congregation as he knew it was essential for his wife to be in full agreement with the ministry. On another occasion, I counseled a planter to remove a valued person from his core group because the person's spouse was against the family being a part of a Messianic congregation. These examples serve to show that the planter must demonstrate his unwavering commitment to families, and see his family as his primary calling, for a congregation is only as strong as the families which make it up. There is blessed power in "couple-power" (Genesis 1:28) when it comes to planting and leading a Messianic congregation.

CLEAR VISION

The planter must have a clear vision and conviction as to the biblical purpose of Messianic congregations. If a person does not know where they are going, it does not matter what route they take. Therefore, a planter must have a clear understanding of a Messianic congregation's mission (reason for existence), vision (where the congregation is going), and values (how to reach the vision). With these in focus, you will be able to move forward, acting on what will help you to reach your vision. (For more on mission, vision, and values, see page 84).

SOUND TEACHING

A healthy congregation is one that is firmly planted on the Word of God. Sound teaching is always focused on Yeshua, and whatever distracts us from Him is a *"doctrine of demons"* (1 Timothy 3:16-4:1). A planter must know God's Word and be able to discern truth from error, growing as he continually studies and applies the Word to his own life. Sound biblical teaching is the foundation of your work as a planter.

VALUABLE QUALITIES OF A PLANTER
(and his core group)

"… I have become all things to all men, so that I may by all means save some."
– 1 Corinthians 9:22

By the lengths he personally went to in order to communicate the Good News, Paul reminds us that we are not to be dominated by our personalities, but only by Yeshua, that we may be like Him in all ways, growing in becoming "all things to all men." Whether introverted or extroverted, careful or spontaneous, we must grow to live by God's Word rather than by what feels most natural or comfortable to us, laying down our own preferences, past, and personality for the sake of the Good News (See 1 Corinthians 9:19-23).

Keep this in mind as we consider this list of qualities that are valuable for Messianic leaders to have. Though this list of Scriptural traits may seem overwhelming, the truth is that no single person possesses all of these qualities perfectly (except Yeshua!). Though you may not be strong in all of these areas, you must believe that if God has called you to plant a congregation,

Notes:

He will provide all that is needed to see it to completion. As you build your core group, search for individuals who possess the qualities which you lack. Trust God in all these things, realizing that the task of planting a Messianic congregation takes more than one talented leader. The qualities of the core group as a whole will always surpass those of any one individual.

Notes:

FAITH-VISION

"Now faith is the assurance of things hoped for, the conviction of things not seen." - Hebrews 11:1

The first quality that is essential for a planter is faith. A person of faith sees what is not there (yet). They believe God for all things and will take risks for Him. To plant a Messianic congregation means to venture out "into the water" (Joshua 3:8).

In the very early stages of one of the congregations I planted, there was a division in the core group which threatened the very existence of our new congregation. In the midst of this trial, I was discipling a new believer, Rich. It was Friday evening and our Erev Shabbat service was to begin in a few minutes, but Rich and I were the only ones there. "Sam," he asked, "What will you do if no one comes back?" I replied, "Rich, we will start again, because I believe that the Lord wants a Messianic congregation here."
Though these matters weighed heavily on me, I believed the Lord wanted a Messianic congregation established in this town. Eventually, healing and unity was restored in the group, and we were able to move forward. Such challenges are typical, and men of faith are needed in order to meet them. A planter is not, however, to be imprudent. Faith may be bold, but is not rash or foolish. A planter sees what God wants to see accomplished and trusts the Lord to provide for how it will be accomplished.

FAITHFULNESS

"In this case, moreover, it is required of stewards that one be found trustworthy." - 1 Corinthians 4:2

Faithfulness speaks of the character of the individual, as well as the integrity of the person. A faithful person models the faith and is seen as an example of what it looks like to honor the Lord. A planter must keep the commitments he makes (Psalm 15:4). We are to be found faithful (1 Corinthians 4:2), and this is only possible as we abide in Messiah (John 15:5).

In listing the qualifications for elders, 1 Timothy 5 explains, *"For if a man does not know how to manage his own home, how will he manage the assembly of God?"* The value of faithfulness needs to be seen in the home first in order to then be reproduced in the congregation. I am thankful that the Lord does not call the qualified but rather qualifies those He calls, as quite often I have felt ill-prepared, both in experience and skill, for the challenges I have faced in ministry. However, early on I learned that my faithful reliance upon the Lord will provide the very fruit He desires. In my early days of ministry, it wasn't unusual for me to arrive home completely exhausted. Nevertheless, I knew my wife and kids needed a husband and dad who was present. I quickly learned that before I put my key in the door, I needed to pray and ask for His empowerment.

VISION-CASTER

Vision-casting is the ability to clearly communicate your vision for a Messianic congregation to others. A clear presentation of your vision provides focus, clarity and a sense of direction, so that others can join in and work towards the goal together. Vision casting helps build unity as each member of the group catches the vision and together takes ownership of it.

At times, difficult circumstances can distract us and diffuse our focus in moving forward. At times like this, the planter's responsibility is to keep the team mindful of the mission and vision God has called them to accomplish, and if needed, bring redirection so you can continue working towards the goal.

READY WITNESS

"For I am not ashamed of the Good News, for it is the power of God for salvation to everyone who believes, to the Jew first and also to the Gentile." – Romans 1:16

Not everyone is a gifted evangelist, but every believer has been given the responsibility to share the Good News with others; this is a crucial part of the great work to which God has called us. Even if you are not naturally

Notes:

_____

_____

_____

_____

_____

_____

_____

_____

_____

_____

_____

_____

_____

_____

_____

31

Notes:

_____

_____

_____

_____

_____

_____

_____

_____

_____

_____

_____

_____

_____

_____

_____

_____

_____

bold, all of us need to grow in being a ready witness, one who intentionally reaches out with the Good News, ready to share Yeshua 24/7. Proverbs 11:30 states, "_He who wins souls is wise._" We must learn how to better relate with those who do not yet know the Lord, considering ways to reach out to them, and asking God to give us a vision and hope for their lives to be fulfilled in Messiah.

Therefore, be ready and willing at all times to lovingly interact with others, as some witnessing opportunities are planned and others are unexpected. For instance, when I travel, I always assume the person sitting next to me is ordained to hear the Good News. A Messianic congregation cannot be planted without the Good News being shared. If you are not prepared to do this, then you are not prepared to plant a congregation.

SELF-STARTER

"_Poor is he who works with a negligent hand, but the hand of the diligent makes rich._" – Proverbs 10:4

Accountability is essential, yet a planter must not allow himself to become fully dependent on others. In many cases, a planter does not have a human boss to report to about his work, and so must answer to the Lord alone. Therefore, the planter needs to be able to be a "self-starter," allowing the Holy Spirit to motivate and encourage him to serve and accomplish his work faithfully. A healthy planter has an intrinsic motivation for service as he is driven by the Spirit's desire to accomplish the will of God. Relying on the Lord's guidance, he will take the initiative in leading his family, growing in the disciplines of prayer and studying the Word, and faithfully reaching out to others.

RESOURCEFULNESS

"_And large crowds gathered to Him, so He got into a boat and sat down, and the whole crowd was standing on the beach._" – Matthew 13:2

The planter and his team must be resourceful, ready and willing to improvise when things do not work out according to plan. Yeshua modeled this attribute for us, even being willing to use a boat as a pulpit when necessary. A resourceful planter knows how to utilize what is available, continually aware of existing opportunities in the community.

Though you can plan for the unexpected, it is also important to be able to "think on your feet." At one congregation I was planting, there was a day when the worship leader was unable to make it to the service. In order to redeem the situation, I found a hand drum and led the group in a few simple praise songs. Though a number of people volunteered to replace me on the spot, the service continued without interruption. In order for the work to continue smoothly, one must be ready to make use of whatever is available for the sake of the Good News .

REDEMPTIVENESS

"For while I was passing through and examining the objects of your worship, I also found an altar with this inscription, 'To an Unknown God.' Therefore what you worship in ignorance, this I proclaim to you." – Acts 17:23

A community is full of new opportunities for the Good News, and it is important for a planter and his team to seek out these open doors. As we see in the account of Paul and the Athenians, in better understanding the community around us, we will better be able to utilize its distinctiveness for the sake of the Good News. As Paul used his Roman citizenship for the Lord's purposes, so we also utilize all that is available to us for Yeshua's sake, responding with willingness and creativity as occasions arise, redeeming the time and the opportunities available to us. (Ephesians 5:16)

RESILIENCE

"Above all, keep fervent in your love for one another, because love covers a multitude of sins." – 1 Peter 4:8

A planter and his team need to be able to adapt to adversity, to continue to function in the midst of trials. As it has been said, there are many bumps and potholes along the highway to holiness. The planter must be prepared to deal with problems as they come up, being focused on God's calling, not easily giving in to discouragement. Though we are to be caring and gentle at all times, this does not mean we need to be fragile. Leaders must grow in having a "*forehead like a flint*" (Ezekiel 3:9), being willing to "take a hit," without becoming easily offended. As trials and frustrations arise, it is

Notes:

_____

_____

_____

_____

_____

_____

_____

_____

_____

_____

_____

_____

_____

_____

_____

_____

the responsibility of mature leaders to serve as shock-absorbers rather than shock-emitters.

GOAL-ORIENTATION

Notes:

"Brethren, I do not regard myself as having laid hold of it yet; but one thing I do: forgetting what lies behind and reaching forward to what lies ahead, I press on toward the goal for the prize of the upward call of God in Messiah Yeshua." – Philippians 3:13-14

Like Paul, we must be focused on the primary issues of the work of God, always working towards this *"one thing."* As we face minor trials, we need to learn to see these for what they are and never allow them to take our focus off the major issues of life. This goal-orientation keeps the vision we are aiming towards alive, and helps the team to remain dedicated and encouraged. Through ups and downs, we must be oriented towards the finish line of what God has called the team to accomplish.

MULTIPLIER

"So we, who are many, are one Body in Messiah, and individually members one of another." – Romans 12:5

As pioneers, many planters are accustomed to doing all the work themselves. However, a good planter understands that the congregation will only develop as others join him in taking ownership of Messiah's work. When a team shares the vision and values of the work, joining together in service, it builds cohesiveness in the Body. A planter moves forward in obedience to Messiah by motivating others to get involved, delegating responsibilities, and working to keep the work on track. He shares the work with his team, refusing to control all the information or authority himself, for he is looking to develop an empowered community.

FLEXIBILITY

"Come now, you who say, "Today or tomorrow we will go to such and such a city, and spend a year there and engage in business and make a profit." – James 4:13

34

Flexibility is vital in congregational work. Though we would prefer it if life were always smooth and predictable, this is rarely the case. This can be especially true in congregation planting as unforeseen obstacles arise. For instance, a person from your core group may inform you of their decision not to be involved in the congregation plant, or the building where you have been meeting may turn out to be unavailable. In spite of the challenges, you must continue to move forward, being willing to experiment with different approaches and strategies in order to accomplish the goal. Through this process, it is essential that you continually surrender all your plans into the hands of God (James 4:15). He will equip you for everything that comes as you continually seek His will, power, and calling.

Notes:

VISION OF A PLANTER

What will the congregation look like when we "grow up"?

"but speaking the truth in love, we are to grow up in all aspects into Him who is the head, Messiah" – Ephesians 4:15

A clear vision of what you are aiming for is essential as you set out to plant a Messianic congregation. Without this, you may be moving, but you will not know where you are going. As it says in Proverbs 29:18, *"Where there is no vision, the people are unruly (in rebellion)."* In casting vision, a Messianic leader must make certain that his vision lines up with God's Word. Just as the Written Torah envisions Yeshua, the Living Torah, our vision must be centered on Yeshua, for He is the One we want to grow up to be like! (Ephesians 4:15) Only by looking to Him can we run the race set before us with endurance.

People can't see Yeshua, but they can see us, His Body. As such, we are representing the will of the Head. When a congregation has a vision of Yeshua, they will live Him out *"to the Jew first and also to the Gentile"* (Romans 1:16). In our love for one another, we evidence the very character of God. Planting a congregation is not merely a work to be done, but the life of Yeshua to be lived out. God is working to conform us to the image of Messiah, to the fullness of the stature of the Son of God. Your congregation is called to be a living testimony in your community that Messiah is in your midst.

CONCEIVING VISION

When we surrender our life in service to God, He asks us to join Him in His

Notes:

work, entrusting to us His burden for the world. God is the One who gives vision, and also the One who can change it. We see in Acts 16 that though Paul desired to further the work of Messiah in Asia, the Holy Spirit prevented him from doing any further work there. Instead, He gave Paul a vision of a man from Macedonia, beseeching him to come and bring the Good News to his people. This vision shifted Paul's ministry focus, and opened a new door for ministry into Europe.

Today, God continues to search for people who will join Him in His work. He is the One who asks us to join Him in His vision to reach Israel and the nations for Messiah, planting and establishing Messianic congregations in order to testify of His faithfulness.

God places vision on the heart of an obedient servant as they seek Him through His Word, through persistent prayer, and through the counsel of godly leaders. At times, He also gives providential experiences which orient us to His calling in His Word. If you believe God has given you a vision, search His Word to test that it is truly of God, as a vision from the Lord cannot contradict the Word of God.

COMMUNICATING VISION

The work it will take to implement a vision is always greater than what one individual can accomplish on his or her own. Once you determine that your vision is truly of God, it is essential that you bring others on board as soon as possible. In congregation planting, there must be unifying vision in order to keep the team's focus on the work needing to be accomplished.

When it is time to communicate your vision to others, first objectify the vision; write it out for others to review, ensuring that it communicates clearly and biblically. In presenting the vision, carefully express the why, what, and how of what needs to be done. Effective communication is the beginning of a plan's accomplishment and the first step toward the vision's fulfillment.

We see this demonstrated in the life of Nehemiah, cupbearer to the king of Persia, and servant to the God of Israel. Though living in exile, Nehemiah was a man surrendered to God. As he sought the Lord, God entrusted him with a burden for His people, putting a vision on his heart to rebuild the broken walls of Jerusalem (Nehemiah 2:12).

In Nehemiah 2, we see the manner in which Nehemiah communicated his vision to those who would be a part of his team:

"Then I (Nehemiah) said to them, "You see the bad situation we are in, that Jerusalem is desolate and its gates burned by fire. Come, let us rebuild the wall of Jerusalem so that we will no longer be a reproach." I told them how the hand of my God had been favorable to me and also about the king's words which he had spoken to me. Then they said, "Let us arise and build." So they put their hands to the good work." - Nehemiah 2:17-18

IDENTIFY

First Nehemiah identified with the people: *"You see the bad situation* **we** *are in."* He made it clear that they were all in the situation together, that it was their shared problem.

PROBLEM

Nehemiah explained Jerusalem's need clearly, in order for everyone to be on the same page about the nature of the problem before he began to address it.

SOLUTION

Nehemiah clearly and simply communicated the action necessary to complete his vision. He presented this charge confidently, calling for others to join him in the solution.

REWARD

Nehemiah didn't ask his people to join in this endeavor without giving them motivation to participate. The completion of his vision would bring benefits for everyone involved; as they rebuilt the wall they would no longer be a reproach.

TIMING

Nehemiah chose the right timing in which to present his vision. Because of this, the moment was seized by everyone as they understood the need, the goal, and the plan of direction that God had revealed to Nehemiah. The people left ready to put the plan into action at Nehemiah's direction.

Notes:

_____

_____

_____

_____

_____

_____

_____

_____

_____

_____

_____

_____

_____

_____

_____

_____

HINDRANCES TO VISION

Though of vital importance, unifying vision can be difficult to achieve. Once, I was invited to assist in a new congregation plant which was barely off the ground but was already facing serious issues. When I arrived, I found the core group of five leaders in disarray because they could not determine which direction to proceed with God's work. In order to assess the situation, I met with each leader individually and asked them each to explain the vision they had for their congregation. As I did this, I received five very different answers! One told me he was passionate about teaching Hebraic roots, another said he wanted to focus on evangelism, yet another was focused on the congregation keeping Torah. Afterwards, we gathered together and I told them that in order for the congregation to survive, it was crucial that they agree on a unifying vision.

Because unifying vision is so essential for congregational health, let us briefly consider several major matters which often serve to hinder such a vision.

FEAR

"For God has not given us a spirit of fear, but of power and of love and of a sound mind." – 2 Timothy 1:7

One very common hindrance to unifying vision is fear. In pioneering a new work, fear creeps in easily as new challenges are uncovered. When we give in to fear, it makes the vision to which God has called us appear unreachable. However, in this fearful world, God calls us to be people of faith. Life is filled with difficulties, trials, and problems, but we must accept the truth that God is greater than any problem we will face. David could stand up to a Goliath, not because he minimized the problem, but because he knew the Lord, the only One bigger than the problem.

In the face of problems, learn to be wise rather than fearful, looking to the Lord as well as reaching out to others for help. Have courage to ask for the prayers of the believing community around you, embracing their support and treasuring their encouragement.

STEREOTYPING

"But the LORD said to Samuel, 'Do not look at his appearance or at the height

of his stature, because I have rejected him; for God sees not as man sees, for man looks at the outward appearance, but the LORD looks at the heart.'" – 1 Samuel 16:7

Beware of limiting the work of God by stereotyping others whom God has placed in your life. It can be tempting to reserve leadership positions for those with particular personality profiles, but this can hinder your congregation from moving forward in fulfillment of your vision. In Scripture we see that we must rely on God's view of individuals rather than on society's perceptions of them. According to the Scriptures, I am not who people say I am, and am not even who I say I am, but rather, I am who God says I am. Each person is a child of God, and if yielded to Him, is not limited by his or her circumstances or personality. In Messiah, each of us has all the needed resources to fulfill His will, and we are more than conquerors through Him who loves us (Romans 8:37). Get rid of stereotypes and trust the Lord to work through whomever He pleases, recognizing that His ways are higher than ours, and that His grace is sufficient for any person.

FATIGUE

"But he (Elijah) himself went a day's journey into the wilderness, and came and sat down under a juniper tree; and he requested for himself that he might die, and said, 'It is enough; now, O LORD, take my life, for I am not better than my fathers.'" – 1 Kings 19:4

A lack of passion resulting from fatigue can do much to hinder vision, undermining your ability to press to the mark of our higher calling. If you find yourself exhausted, look to the Lord for strength and ask Him to re-energize you by the Holy Spirit. To guard against exhaustion, it is important that the planter take care of himself, taking time for prayer and keeping a personal Shabbat in order to be renewed and refreshed in the Lord. Refuse to let fatigue rob you of your passion and erode your vision.

SHORT-TERM THINKING

"For which one of you, when he wants to build a tower, does not first sit down and calculate the cost to see if he has enough to complete it?" – Luke 14:28

Another subtle hindrance to vision is short-term thinking. Although we must care for one another, it is wrong to give in to every request we receive

Notes:

39

for immediate needs to be met. In obliging to every such appeal, the planter may miss out on more strategic aspects of the work of the congregation. In these scenarios, the planter must not give in to short-term thinking, and must learn to recognize the tasks which would best be delegated to others.

Notes:

UNQUALIFIED LEADERSHIP

"It is actually reported that there is immorality among you, and immorality of such a kind as does not exist even among the Gentiles, that someone has his father's wife." – 1 Corinthians 5:1

Unqualified leadership can do much to disrupt vision. If a leader is immature and not prepared for the task at hand, he should place himself under the mentorship of more mature leaders, in order that the whole team can understand and share in a unifying vision. Lack of qualified leadership will eventually limit congregational growth.

TRADITION

"… by this you have invalidated the Word of God for the sake of your tradition." – Matthew 15:6b

Jewish tradition is of great value, and Messianic congregations should utilize tradition as they communicate the truth. However, it must be emphasized that all tradition we use should serve to reflect the truth of Scripture, never to replace it. We need to be aware of the danger of becoming distracted from our vision on account of tradition. Yeshua is our vision and the center of everything we do, for He is the fulfillment of the Hebrew Scriptures (John 5:39). Allowing ourselves to become distracted from the centrality of Messiah, even by good ideas, will prove to be disastrous and keep us from serving the Lord. However, as we look unto Yeshua and remain faithful to His vision, we will bring Him glory and honor.

As we conclude this section, remember that a vision will only be fulfilled as we are dependent upon grace, through faith. God's grace always proves to be sufficient to accomplish the vision that He gives. The fulfillment of a vision from God is beyond our present victories, and, therefore, beyond our present wisdom. We need to realize that God is not dependent upon our strengths or limited by our weaknesses. As God encouraged Paul, *"My grace is sufficient for you, for My strength is made perfect in weakness"* (2 Corinthians 12:9).

VALUES OF A PLANTER

How will we reach our vision together?

"A new commandment I give to you, that you love one another, even as I have loved you, that you also love one another. By this all men will know that you are My disciples, if you have love for one another." – John 13:34-35

Notes:

Values are beliefs put into action; those things which are most important to you in the way you live and work as a community. By your values, you determine your priorities and move forward to reach your vision. As we touched on earlier in our discussion of Messianic myths, by our values we evaluate whether something is good or bad, right or wrong, and then either validate or invalidate accordingly.

Your congregation's unifying values will guide your actions and clarify your decisions, for values have to do with actual behaviors; it is not sufficient for a group to share in a set of mere concepts or ideas. Agreed upon and lived out values are necessary in order for a congregation to be healthy. So how do you determine what your values as a congregation should be? First, you must clarify what you believe.

KNOW WHAT YOU BELIEVE

"Can two walk together unless they be in agreement?" - Amos 3:3

Scripture assumes unity of values in order for there to be unity of fellowship with God and with one another (Amos 3:3, 1 Corinthians 5:1-13, 2 Corinthians 6:14-16). However, in what areas must people agree in order for them to walk together? If two people believe in Yeshua, isn't that enough?

When I bring couples through pre-marital counseling, I give them each a piece of paper and ask them to write out their ten most important beliefs. As they compare notes, the similarities or differences between their core beliefs become quickly apparent. For instance, if he believes that praying and reading Scripture together is an essential part of a marriage relationship, but she doesn't prioritize these things as important, the two are not really walking together.

41

Notes:

It is essential that you know what you believe, and that there is agreement among your team regarding these beliefs. If your congregation does not establish what its most important beliefs are, you are at risk of majoring in the minors. If this be the case, it is very likely that you will be minoring in the majors. A clear understanding of the difference between primary and secondary matters will help you as you work through and objectify your core beliefs.

PRIMARY & SECONDARY MATTERS

*"Woe to you, scribes and Pharisees, hypocrites! For you tithe mint and dill and cumin, and have neglected the **weightier provisions** of the law: justice and mercy and faithfulness; but these are the things you should have done without neglecting the others."* – Matthew 23:23

Aren't all beliefs, if based on Scripture, equally significant? Many are surprised to realize that Scripture makes a clear distinction between the primary, our most important beliefs that we must be in agreement on, and the secondary, those beliefs where there is freedom to differ.

Through His ministry, Yeshua clearly taught that there are great commandments and least of commandments (Matthew 5:19; 22:36-40). In Matthew 23:23, He rebuked the scribes and Pharisees for focusing on secondary matters that, though not unimportant, were hindering them from focusing on the weightier matters of the Torah. In 1 Corinthians 15:3, Paul states that the teaching he gave to the Corinthian believers was of first, not secondary, importance.

It is vital that we also understand the difference between primary and secondary matters, for if your congregation does not understand this, they will continually argue about secondary issues where they should instead be ready to give liberty. But how can we know the difference? Many times the distinction is clear. For example, if a person came to your congregation and wanted to be a part of your community, but did not have the same color kippah as most other people there, you would welcome that person anyway! However, if the person said, "I don't believe Yeshua is Lord," you would welcome them as a visitor, but not as a member of your community. We all make distinctions between primary and secondary matters every day. As a congregation, we have unity in the primary, liberty in the secondary, and charity in all matters.

Primary matters fall into three main categories: matters of salvation, matters of mission, and matters of community. We will briefly consider each of these areas.

MATTERS OF SALVATION

"He who believes in the Son has eternal life; but he who does not obey the Son will not see life, but the wrath of God abides on him." – John 3:36

Primary matters of salvation are those matters which biblically make us children of God. We hold these things in common with all other true believers in Yeshua:

Matters of salvation include such foundational beliefs as:

- ✡ The Divine Nature of Messiah
- ✡ The truth that Yeshua is Lord
- ✡ The Person and Power of the Holy Spirit
- ✡ The lost state of humanity
- ✡ The truth of salvation by grace through faith
- ✡ The Authority of the Bible
- ✡ The existence of the universal and local Body of Messiah
- ✡ The second coming of Messiah (The hope of Israel and the establishment of the Messianic Kingdom)

These biblical truths are what make up the Articles of Faith of a believing congregation.

Every person who confesses Yeshua as Lord, holding to these primary matters of salvation, is a child of God, and whether they be Messianic, Baptist, Nazarene, Pentecostal, Presbyterian, etc., will all spend eternity with one another.

These matters of salvation make us eternally effective as a faith community.

MATTERS OF COMMUNITY

"I wrote you in my letter not to associate with ... any so-called brother if he is an immoral person, or covetous, or an idolater, or a reviler, or a drunkard, or a swindler—not even to eat with such a one." – 1 Corinthians 5:1-13

Notes:

_____

_____

_____

_____

_____

_____

_____

_____

_____

_____

_____

_____

_____

_____

Notes:

Primary matters of community are those matters which impact the congregation's testimony, health, and unity.

These are the community's standards of personal godliness which should be laid out in the Constitution of your congregation. These include matters such as commitment to membership, regular attendance, active service, tithing, sharing one's faith, having an active prayer and devotional life, etc., as well as refraining from immodest attire, gossip, foul language, lying, disorderliness, or anything that would hinder the health and unity of the community.

As a leader, you are here to evaluate the effectiveness of your community and set the expectations. Some may be put off by the idea of expecting such standards of your congregation. Yet, if you do not expect them, they will not be present in your community. Loving and caring for one another in all these ways is what defines us as a community.

These matters of community make us internally effective as an actual community.

MATTERS OF MISSION

"But by their transgression salvation has come to the Gentiles, to make them (Israel) jealous." – Romans 11:11

Primary matters of mission are those matters which distinguish the calling of a Messianic congregation from other local believing congregations.

These include what others may consider to be secondary matters:

- ✡ The unchanged calling of the Jewish people (Israel)
- ✡ The calling of Gentiles to love Israel
- ✡ The equality of Jews and Gentiles in Messiah
- ✡ The priority of evangelism and discipleship
- ✡ The use of Torah
- ✡ The observance of Shabbat and the Feasts of Israel
- ✡ The use of Jewish traditions

Messianic Congregations are living proof that God is not finished with the Jewish people. As we've seen a distinctive not being addressed in the Body

44

of Messiah, we are stepping up as a testimony of God's unending faithfulness to Israel. We bring the Good News to the Jew first, but equally to the Gentile. Using the whole Word of God, we disciple both Jewish and Gentile believers to love Jewish people and serve as a witness to them. In light of our calling, we express our faith in Messiah in a Jewish frame of reference.

These matters of mission make us externally effective as a Messianic community.

SECONDARY MATTERS WITHIN A COMMUNITY

You may be wondering, "If all this is primary, then what is secondary?" Secondary matters are any matter that is not primary. All secondary matters are deemed morally neutral in accordance with one's own conscience, and are areas in which to give liberty, neither commending nor condemning.

Some believe that because we have this God-given liberty, we are free to do whatever we want. However, this is far from the case, for our love limits our liberty.

Scripture gives instruction regarding how to use our liberty in a loving way. In 1 Corinthians 7 and following, Paul addresses specific secondary matters that the congregation in Corinth had written to him about. The Corinthian believers were abusing their liberty, thinking that because they were free in the Lord, they could eat, dress, and do whatever they wanted to do. Paul wrote to correct these false patterns of thinking and laid out why our liberty in these areas must be limited by love...

...SO NOT TO STUMBLE THE WEAK BELIEVER

"... if food causes my brother to stumble, I will never eat meat again, so that I will not cause my brother to stumble." – I Corinthians 8:13

✡ *For the mature, liberty is to edify the least* ✡

In 1 Corinthians 8, Paul is addressing issues that had come up regarding food. Gentiles who had come to Messiah out of paganism had a weak conscience on these matters, and were easily stumbled when they saw believers eating food that had been sacrificed to idols. Paul emphasizes that although believers are free in this area, they should not use that liberty if it would

Notes:

45

Notes:

_____

_____

_____

_____

_____

_____

_____

_____

_____

_____

_____

_____

_____

_____

_____

cause a weaker believer to stumble. The real issue here is not the food, but caring about the brother.

This principle extends to other areas as well. For instance, if you invited a recovering alcoholic to your home, would you serve them wine? Many immature believers are tied to a cultural expression of faith, and may find it off putting to give up what they are accustomed to eating and drinking, or reconsidering ways they are accustomed to living; however, we must all grow to care more about loving people than enjoying pleasures.

... SO NOT TO HINDER THE GOOD NEWS

"... we endure all things so that we will cause no hindrance to the Good News of Messiah." – I Corinthians 9:12

✡ *For the mature, liberty is to evangelize the lost* ✡

Paul chose to use his rights, those things that were under his authority, not for his own purposes, but for God's purpose of furthering the Good News. If anything would be a hindrance to the Good News, he refused to do it. Those who are mature use their liberty to share Messiah with unbelievers, to get the Good News out. Our "rights" today, those things which are under our authority to use, include such things as our time, talent, and treasure. Those who are immature use these things for their own purposes, living for the occasions when they can "let their hair down." However, as believers, we never have a "day off" from God. This is a ridiculous thought, for our God is always with us! No, as we grow in maturity, we want to live more fully for Him, using our time, talent, and treasure to get the Good News out, seeing every situation as an occasion for the Good News, not the cause. Even on vacation, we should never "leave home without Him," but live for Him in whatever situation we are in.

... SO NOT TO DISHONOR THE LORD

"... Do you think you are stronger than God?" – 1 Corinthians 10:22

✡ *For the mature, liberty is to exalt the Lord!* ✡

God was not happy with Israel when they used their position as the chosen people as an opportunity for arrogance rather than for service. We must take heed, lest we allow an attitude of arrogance to lead us to dishonor the Lord. Even if there is no one around to stumble or witness to, we know that He will never leave us, and we use our liberty to honor Him. The mature use their liberty to exalt the Lord, taking time to honor and praise Him. Their aim is to do nothing that would dishonor the Lord, but in all things, to honor Him, whether other people are around or not.

In every situation, we are to use our liberty to edify the least, evangelize the lost, and exalt the Lord! Those who are mature do not use their liberty for their own preferences or comforts, but to fulfill their calling, demonstrating God's faithfulness to Israel and the nations, hastening the redemption of Israel, and blessing for the world! In light of this, when we think about our liberty, our question should not be, "How much can I get away with?" but "How best can I love?" We use our liberty for the Lord!

Even after being instructed in these matters, some people will still choose to be contentious, as they were in Corinth (1 Corinthians 11:16). To these people, Paul did not have anything further to say, because these matters were secondary, not primary. Some will always choose to remain immature, but refuse to argue with them about such things, as doing so will take your focus away from what is primary.

Secondary matters of liberty include such things as:

- ✡ A person's personal use of time, talent, and treasure
- ✡ A person's private spiritual walk
- ✡ A couple's marriage interaction and other close relationships
- ✡ A person's personal attire, cultural tastes, recreational choices and food preferences
- ✡ A person's economic status, material possessions, social standing, educational attainment, scholarly achievements, and political affiliations

The wise handling of these matters makes us effective as a discerning community.

Be careful, though, of addressing a secondary matter as unimportant simply because it is not primary. Secondary matters have value, because through them, we live out the primary matters. For example, honoring the Lord of the Shabbat is a primary matter. The day of the week on which we observe Shabbat is a secondary matter through which we live out this primary mat-

Notes:

_____

_____

_____

_____

_____

_____

_____

_____

_____

_____

_____

_____

_____

_____

_____

Notes:

_____

_____

_____

_____

_____

_____

_____

_____

_____

_____

_____

_____

_____

_____

_____

_____

_____

ter. It is wrong to focus on the secondary matter, the day of the week, over the primary matter of honoring the Lord. Though we live to honor Him every day, most Messianic congregations observe Shabbat on Saturday in order to live out another primary matter, our mission to communicate the Good News to the Jewish people. If a person is passionate about observing Shabbat on Saturday, but is not passionate about reaching Jewish people, their focus is in the wrong place.

This being said, we are not to judge others whose views on secondary matters differ from our own. At one congregation where I was leading, a visitor was upset that we did not have organ music in our services. In response, I kindly pointed him to a congregation down the street that had the type of music he valued. For this man, the secondary matter of instruments used during worship was primary. We are not to judge people who hold different views on these matters, but help direct them to a place where they would feel more comfortable. Likewise, we are not to judge another leader's flock. You are responsible before God for the way in which you lead your community and the values you uphold there. As Daniel modeled when he refused the king's food that was offered to him, "I don't care what you put in your mouth, but I care what you put in mine."

As a congregation understands the difference between primary and secondary matters, they will be able to develop unifying values around which true fellowship is built. In working through these matters, do not allow any issue to take your focus off Yeshua, for where two or three are gathered in His Name, He is in their midst (Matthew 18:20). Yeshua is with us in the primary, not the secondary. It is a leader's responsibility to understand these matters and to edify the flock accordingly on these things, helping them to understand as well, and teaching them that though we have been given liberty in secondary matters, our love will limit our liberty as we care for those around us.

CLARITY ON GOALS & DIRECTION

After establishing your primary beliefs, the next step in working through your values is to clarify your specific goals for the congregation. What will your services look like? Will you hold any classes as well? What activities will the community take part in? Developing clear goals will assist you in making decisions of what things to prioritize, and will help you to remain focused, regardless if others disagree or attempt to put pressure on you. For instance, if a person approaches you and asks, "I hear you're starting a Messianic congregation. Will you be teaching Israeli dance?" In light of the primary goals and direction of your congregation, you may respond to this by saying, "Yes we will, but not for a couple of years; right now we need to focus on more foundational issues." Hearing this may turn some people away. Even so, you must stand your ground on these matters, maintaining your focus on those things that need to be established first.

Your specific goals and direction of movement must all reflect the biblical mission and vision of your congregation. If this is not the case, no matter how faithfully you work to move forward, it will be to no avail. Sincerity is good, but a person can be sincerely wrong. Allow me to share an illustration: During a series of war games that were being held in Europe, an American captain sent out a group of privates telling them, "Go guard the bridge in the woods over there, until you are relieved." So the privates went and guarded the bridge...and guarded the bridge...and guarded the bridge, until eventually they were found. It was then that they found out they were guarding the wrong bridge. Faithfully. There are a lot of people who are faithfully guarding the wrong bridge. Their faithfulness is not in question, but they are not effective unless they are guarding the right bridge.

UNDERSTAND SPIRITUAL GIFTS & SKILLS FOR SERVICE

"As each one has received a special gift, employ it in serving one another as good stewards of the manifold grace of God. Whoever speaks, is to do so as one who is speaking the utterances of God; whoever serves is to do so as one who is serving by the strength which God supplies; so that in all things God may be glorified through Yeshua the Messiah, to whom belongs the glory and dominion forever and ever. Amen." - 1 Peter 4:10-11

Now, as you look at the goals you have developed, you need to ask, "Ok, now how will we get there together?" A congregation is born through the spiritual gifting and skills of an entire group of people.

In this beginning stage of congregation planting, pray for God to bring the right people who will work together with you in the planting process. As your team grows, recognize that the Holy Spirit has given each person unique gifts that are to be used for His purposes; for the building up of the Body and for the testimony of the Good News in the community. All believers are gifted to serve in some capacity, some thirty-fold, some sixty-fold,

Notes:

49

and some one hundred-fold. In the New Covenant we see different lists of gifts for different communities addressed. (Romans 12; 1 Corinthians 12; Ephesians 4).

Notes:

As each team member contributes towards the goal, it is the planter's responsibility to make sure that each person is developing and employing their gifts for the building up of the individual, the furtherance of the work of God and the advancement of the Good News.

HAVE STANDARDS OF STEWARDSHIP

"Therefore be careful how you walk, not as unwise men but as wise, making the most of your time, because the days are evil." – Ephesians 5:15-16

It takes a great deal of time, talent (gifting), and treasure (finances) to plant a congregation. A planter must take a stewardship responsibility over these things not only for himself, but also on behalf of those on his team so they may all work towards the vision in a healthy manner. In the garment industry, it has been said, "measure twice, cut once." Likewise, a leader must carefully plan in regard to these important areas:

TIME

Paul exhorts us in Ephesians to redeem the time we have been given in light of the days we are living in. Congregational leaders must model how to redeem the time, being careful to begin services and meetings on schedule and treasuring the time of those serving. Realize that you cannot do more than the time of your personnel permits. If you are trying to do more than you have the resources for, you may need to re-evaluate and discontinue some of your programs.

TALENT

In the same way, we are to utilize people's talents in a wise manner. It may be easy to put all the work on those who are willing, but this is always wrong. You must ensure that the work is evenly distributed, or people may end up resenting what they do. In order to avoid the burnout of those who serve diligently, there must be a plan in place for rotation, encouragement, and appreciation. Ensure that those who are ministering are also being ministered to and are thriving in their spiritual walk. Perhaps a good way to guard them from burnout is to encourage them to give a "tithe" of their time in volunteering for the congregation. Giving two to four hours per week is a sufficient amount of time for volunteers to contribute. Wisdom in this area will keep volunteers healthy and resilient as well. Make sure that you go out of your way to show appreciation for each person whom the Lord has raised up to serve in your community.

TREASURE

We must also be careful in how we use our funds (2 Corinthians 8:20). In the work of God, we need to make sure that we are above reproach in all things so that there will be no taint on our testimony of Messiah. Sadly, in some congregations, precaution in this area is overlooked. For instance, if the congregational leader is the only one who knows the state of the finances, this speaks of deeper trouble. Delegating financial responsibility to a Board of Trustees will allow the congregational leader to focus on ministry to people. We must properly administrate the finances that God has entrusted to us.

Potential members of your congregation may ask to see your budget. This is a reasonable request. A budget is simply a schedule detailing how you will use your money. It is essential that you take time to carefully schedule how your funds will be utilized as you carry out strategic goals in accomplishing God's work in your congregation.

BE TOTALLY SUBMITTED TO YESHUA

By far, the most important value for a leader to have and for a core group to share is their total submission to Yeshua. Are you and your team dominated by Yeshua's Lordship (Philippians 1:21; 1 Corinthians 11:1)? Everything you do as a planter is all about Him. It is our privilege and our aim to live for Him; absolutely nothing else comes close to the importance of this. If a woman were to ask her fiancé, "What is your most important value?" and he answered, "I don't know; I guess football," then she had better reconsider her decision to marry this man. If Yeshua is not our most important value, we are in deep trouble. He is the reason behind everything we do; every aspect of our lives is for His exaltation and glory!

Notes:

_____

_____

_____

_____

_____

_____

_____

_____

_____

_____

_____

_____

_____

_____

_____

The values you are building for your community are values that you will uphold every day, not just when you meet together on Shabbat. There is only one value system in Scripture, and we need to live as godly people wherever we are. If you are not submitted to Yeshua's leadership 24/7, you will be the blind leading the blind, most likely right into a ditch. No one wants to be the congregational leader of "B'nai Ditch!"

Notes:

_____

_____

_____

_____

_____

_____

_____

_____

_____

_____

_____

_____

_____

_____

PRACTICAL MATTERS IN PLANTING

As you prepare to move on to the Outreach Step, there are several practical matters which must first be taken into consideration. Time spent determining and planning for these matters will provide clarity and guidance as you move forward.

DEVELOPMENT OF MATERIALS & DOCUMENTS

An important practical matter to consider at this stage is the preparation of materials and documents which will be needed in order for your congregation to function in a healthy manner.

DOCUMENTS THAT EXPLAIN YOUR MISSION, VISION, & VALUES

As you spend time working through your mission, vision and values during this Preliminary Step, it is of utmost importance that you write things down, objectifying what you believe. You will be able to make changes later, but it is important to get it all down on paper as a basic foundation to work from as you move forward. As you objectify these vital matters, do not share them with others until there is full agreement concerning them between you and your spouse.

As you compile, rewrite and revise these things, they will form the basis for your congregation's Articles of Faith, Constitution, Values Statement, and Mission Statement. These articles will clearly outline those matters which are primary and those which are secondary in your gatherings.

✡ Your Articles of Faith will include the primary teachings (or doctrines), which will distinguish your congregation in light of its faith.

✡ Your Constitution will state your congregation's values, by-laws and policies. The congregation is not to be run by the power of the planter's personality, but rather by even-handed, fair-minded policies, which all can understand and abide with.

✡ Your Values Statement will explain your congregation's core values, outlining how you plan to move toward your vision.

✡ Your Mission Statement will explain why your congregation exists, and will help the core group better understand their purpose in being a part of it.

The final draft of these documents must be user-friendly and familiar to the members of your congregation. This way, members will not be thrown off by the opinions of visitors who may express different views than those held by the congregation. An understanding and implementation of the Articles of Faith, Constitution, Values Statement, and Mission Statement will bring your members to the same page, in order to move forward in the same calling. And, when a visitor asks, "So what do you people really believe?" you will be able to hand them a document detailing the answer.

Once your congregation is established, these documents you have developed will only have a value as they are acted upon. So, review these things frequently in order to ensure that they continue to be relevant for your community. Your mission, vision, and values must be intrinsic to the day-to-day life of your community, aiding you as you minister in the lives of real people, not just words on pieces of paper which sit on your shelf. These documents must reflect values that are actually important in your community, and be used in communicating these values to all involved.

(See samples of these documents in Appendices 6-7)

MATERIALS THAT PRESENT THE GOOD NEWS TO THE JEW FIRST

You need to be prepared with material to give to unbelievers who will visit your congregation. It is also vital that you find or design Messianic Good News literature for use in congregational outreach. Be ready for action!

MATERIALS THAT PROVIDE BASIC MESSIANIC DISCIPLESHIP

You will also need basic discipleship materials readily available for use as people come to the Lord through your ministry, or come into your congre-

Notes:

Notes:

_____

_____

_____

_____

_____

_____

_____

_____

_____

_____

_____

_____

_____

_____

_____

_____

gation having never been discipled. Remaining prepared for this demonstrates that discipleship in the Word is a value in your congregation. It is worthwhile to write your own discipleship material in light of the specific values of your congregation. Word of Messiah also has Messianic discipleship materials available if you are not yet able to write your own. (See page 264).

YEARLY PLANNING AROUND THE BIBLICAL CALENDAR

In light of its mission to bring the Good News to the Jew first, a Messianic congregation will make the most of opportunities to identify with, and reach out to, the Jewish community. A wise leader will take advantage of the occasions God has provided throughout the year for this purpose, and so will plan their congregational calendar around the *mo'adim* (God's appointed times, the Feasts of Israel).

The *mo'adim* outline God's redemptive calendar. As Messianic congregations, we have the great responsibility and privilege of observing each of these feasts with Yeshua at their center, for they all "*testify about Him*" (John 5:39). With Yeshua as the foundation, a congregation must then decide how they will celebrate the feasts. There is much freedom in this matter as the New Covenant gives little information concerning the first century believers' celebration. It is clear, though, that observance of the mo'adim was something that all the early believers had in common. Though the Corinthian congregation was predominantly Gentile, Paul wrote to them in light of their understanding of Passover, clearly teaching them to continue to "*keep the feast*" (1 Corinthians 5:8).

For many congregations, being able to celebrate on the exact day of the feast is not always easy. Facilities that are available for a Shabbat morning service may not be available for a midweek evening festival service. To accommodate this issue, a congregation can hold a special observance or teaching on Shabbat during the week of the festival, or host a "Preparing for Passover, Shavuot, or Yom Kippur..." service. It is not necessary for a congregation to observe the biblical feasts on their precise dates. Holding rigidly to this expectation may communicate to others that these celebrations are more about externals than about testifying of Messiah (Colossians 3:16-17).

Since a spiritually healthy Messianic congregation understands evangelism, the special services for the feasts should be organized as outreaches as well as community worship. This provides an opportunity for the congregation to invite relatives, neighbors, co-workers, and friends to hear the Good News proclaimed through these biblical celebrations which are such an intrinsic part of Jewish life.

Even if you are very familiar with the *mo'adim*, take time to study their background and purpose in light of your calling as a Messianic leader, and work through how you will celebrate each Feast in order to best communicate Messiah.

SPRINGTIME & SUMMER FEASTS

The feast of *Pesach*, or Passover, is the first feast of the year, reminding us that our lives begin at redemption. Just as the blood of the Passover lambs brought redemption in Egypt, the blood of Yeshua, the Lamb of God, brings redemption from sin. This feast provides an opportunity to speak of how sin is removed through faith in Yeshua as we instruct our community in the traditional practice of removing leaven from our homes. We maintain a consistent testimony as we ensure there is no leaven at the *oneg* (food and fellowship time after service) during Passover week. Another way to utilize Passover as an outreach opportunity is to organize a Passover Seder, providing a high profile outreach to the larger community around you.

Be mindful at this time that all who join your celebration may not share the same past experiences. Some believers, for example, may never have celebrated Passover, whereas others may have grown up celebrating it every year, but never in light of its fulfillment in Messiah. As you plan your Passover celebration, you may need to find or compile various materials, such as a Passover *Haggadah* if you plan to hold a Seder meal.

Immediately following Passover and the Feast of Unleavened Bread is *Reishit*, or the Feast of First Fruits.

This feast is a God-given opportunity to speak about the resurrection of Messiah, our *"firstfruits from among the dead"* (1 Corinthians 15:20). A traditional observance at this time is the counting of the Omer, stemming from the command in Leviticus 23 to count fifty days before the feast of Shavuot begins. (Leviticus 23:16) This time lends itself to opportunities such as leading your congregation in fifty days of prayer, Bible reading, or witnessing.

Notes:

Notes:

The final spring feast, *Shavuot*, or Pentecost, is called, "The Season of the Giving of the Law," as it is a time when we remember the giving of the Torah at Mount Sinai. This feast was fulfilled when *Ruach HaKodesh* (the Holy Spirit,) was given (Acts 2:1). Consequently, observance of Shavuot lends itself to teaching about the work of the Spirit, and our unity in the Body of Messiah. At *Shavuot*, dairy is traditionally served at the oneg following the service.

AUTUMN & WINTER FEASTS

The Fall Feasts are perhaps best known by the traditions that clothe them. For example, the feast presented in the Bible as *Zikhron Teruah* (a reminder by blowing of trumpets, Leviticus 23:24) is certainly better known as Rosh HaShanah. The biblical feast of *Zikhron Teruah*, or the Feast of Trumpets, can be used to teach on the last shofar, which Paul speaks of in 1 Corinthians 15:51-52. Focusing on this aspect of the feast exhorts all to be ready for our blessed hope (Titus 2:13). And although Rosh HaShanah is not found in the Bible, its traditions can be utilized for the purpose of the Good News. Rosh HaShanah is traditionally called *Yom HaDin*, or Judgment Day. The traditional Jewish understanding of this day provides an opportunity to teach the truth that our names can be written in the Book of Life, not only for the coming year, but also for eternity.

The observance of *Yom Kippur* provides us an opportunity for worship and witness as we gather for a solemn assembly and fast day (Act 27:9). As Messianic believers, God's Word tells us that we are to mourn with those who mourn, even with the greater Jewish community, who fast on this day without recognizing the atonement which Yeshua provides. For testimony purposes, the congregation should be informed not to bring food or drinks into the service on this day. It should also be understood that small children and those who are frail should not fast, and medications should continue to be taken. At *Yom Kippur* services, it is appropriate to teach on the necessity of blood atonement, and the fact that repentance and fasting are customary expressions of faith in that atonement.

The final feast of God's redemptive program, *Sukkot*, or the Feast of Booths, is a time of rejoicing and fun for the families of the community. If space is available, building a *sukkah* (booth) and decorating it together can be a wonderful community project. For the first seven days of *Sukkot*, worship services should be celebratory. Since lulavs and etrogs are essential elements of the celebration, but may not be available for each individual to have one, Scripture permits the use of other branches for this feast (Nehemiah 8:15). *Sukkot* testifies of God's provision and protection of His people as it points to Yeshua (John 1:14; Romans 8:1; Colossians 2:9-10; Revelation 7:9-17).

There are many more occasions in the Jewish calendar, in addition to the mo'adim of Leviticus 23, which present opportunities to testify of God's glory and grace. *Simchat Torah*, which means 'Rejoicing in the Torah,' though a traditional addition to the calendar, is a great reminder that God's Word is not only authoritative, but also a cause for real celebration. The drama and joy of *Purim* (see Esther 9:26), as well as the solemnity of *Yom HaShoah* (Holocaust Remembrance Day) are poignant reminders that despite the Hamans and Hitlers of our day, God's promises keep His people and all who will trust in the Lord.

Hanukkah (see John 10:22) is a yearly reminder that God can only be glorified in a cleansed temple, and as such we are bought with a price. Families in your congregation may be encouraged to celebrate these additional holidays in their homes as well as in the community.

As you plan your year around God's great theme of redemption, your congregation will be continually oriented around Messiah Yeshua, the One to whom all the Feasts are pointing. The yearly celebration of God's Feasts serves as a demonstration of His unending promises to the Jew first, but not to the Jew only (Romans 1:16).

STRUCTURE OF A MESSIANIC SERVICE

When people think of a Messianic congregation, the first things that come to mind may be a specific day of the week or a particular model of worship service. In the Messianic world, however, worship models and styles vary greatly, depending on the planter's convictions and the community of which the congregation is a part. Based on these factors, a planter will decide the model which is most appropriate for his congregation. Here, we will consider three different models of worship common in the Messianic movement. As you read through these, consider the needs of the community in which you serve, and what would be most effective in reaching them.

Notes:

Notes:

TRADITIONAL RELIGIOUS MODEL

A traditional religious model follows a normative Jewish format. Shabbat services in Messianic congregations reflecting this traditional order may open with customary prayers followed by the *Shema* and its blessings, continue on with the *Amidah*, and then climax with a Torah service followed by the message and a closing prayer. Some who follow this model keep to Orthodox tradition, separating men and women during the service and refraining from instruments in worship. Others are more Reformed, not requiring men to wear a *kippah* (skullcap; Yiddish: *yarmulke*) or *tallit* (prayer shawl), and using instruments during the service.

CONTEMPORARY MESSIANIC MODEL

In a contemporary Messianic model, Shabbat services contain some of the traditional liturgy, such as the *Shema* and *Birkat HaKohanim* (the Aaronic blessing), as well as contemporary Messianic worship music. Within the service, emphasis is placed on the message from the Scriptures. This model is often effective in speaking to communities where the majority of Jewish people are not religiously-oriented.

MESSIANIC SUNDAY MODEL

A Messianic Sunday model might seem a bit unusual, however there are some large and well-known congregations that use this approach (i.e, Beth Israel Congregation in Wayne, NJ). In their worship and jargon, these services communicate the Good News with a Messianic orientation. They may have Friday Bible studies as well as Sunday morning services and will likely observe the Jewish Festivals.

How does one determine the style that is best for his congregation? Though the planter may have various personal convictions, he must consider what will most clearly and effectively communicate the Good News to the community he desires to reach. As Messiah's love compels us, we will be stretched beyond the limits of our own comfort zone. We see this reflected in Paul's methodology:

"For though I am free from all men, I have made myself a slave to all, so that I may win more. To the Jews I became as a Jew, so that I might win Jews; to those who are under Torah, as under Torah though not being myself under To-

rah, so that I might win those who are under Torah; to those who are without Torah, as without Torah, though not being without the Torah of God but under the Torah of Messiah, so that I might win those who are without Torah."
- 1 Corinthians 9:19-21

Paul's flexible *halakhah* (method of practice) for the sake of the Good News may have led to various models of service which differed as he moved from more observant to more secularized communities.

The planter must understand the culture of the community in which he will plant. It is common knowledge that no two Jewish communities are perfectly alike. As it has been said, "three Jews, five opinions." Your congregation will need to adjust to the surrounding greater Jewish community in order to effectively communicate the Good News and not be a stumbling block in any way. For example, if you are ministering in an Ultra-Orthodox neighborhood, you would need to adapt to the standards of dress held by the community in order to communicate effectively and not appear as lawless in their eyes.

On the other hand, if you are ministering in a secular community, it is of great importance that your congregation not appear more Jewish than the Jewish community that you are in. For example, if a secular Jewish person sees a person wearing a *kippah* on the street, they will probably avoid them, thinking they have nothing in common with that individual. Also, many Jewish believers who come from a more secularized background may not feel comfortable in a liturgical setting, and may be more drawn to a church where they are seen as the "smartest person in the room" rather than stay at a congregation where they feel like the "dumb Jew in the group." Be wise on these matters. Know the community you are in and keep a low threshold of expectation for visitors so that people will not feel awkward.

If you grew up in a religious community, but are now ministering in a secular one, you will need to adapt to the culture for the sake of the Good News. If you have certain convictions, and therefore wish to do certain things in your congregation, you will need to appreciate that this may have a down side. By no means would you want to water down your values in order to attract more people to your congregation. However, it is vital to be sure you know what your values are and certain that they are truly of biblical value. In light of the importance of the message we bring, a planter needs to step outside his own paradigm and be aware that his community may be put off by his own ideas of success.

Notes:

Better understanding of your community will bring about more effective communication. In both appearance and speech, you need to be able to communicate with the people you are ministering to.

A Sephardic Jewish community may or may not speak Spanish, an Ashkenazi community may or may not speak Yiddish. In general, it is of great importance to know the area and neighborhood in which you are ministering, and so prepare accordingly. As you identify your specific meeting location, you will also need to consider matters such as parking, handicap accessibility, and other such practical issues in order to minister most effectively to the community you desire to reach.

It is important to realize, though, that although you may find a convenient, centralized meeting location, the majority of Messianic congregations are commuter, rather than community congregations, due to the fact that there are not yet Messianic congregations in every town. This means that the majority of your members will have to travel, sometimes long distances, to get to your services. In such congregations, the ministry generally has to be "stacked" on Shabbat, since people might not be able to meet as often during the work week. However, as community develops in proximity to the congregation, there may be opportunities to develop more activities throughout the week, such as training classes in Scripture and Messianic life, as well as children's classes and activities.

PLANTING METHODOLOGY

There is more than one way to plant a Messianic congregation. The particular strategy you choose to move forward with will depend on prayerful consideration, organization, and the resources currently available to you.

PIONEERING

The most common method of congregation planting is called "Pioneering." In this method, a planter begins making contacts through evangelism in a particular area in order to gather a core group necessary for the planting of a new congregation. This method is usually necessary in areas where there are no other Messianic congregation partners who can assist the planter. An example of a congregation planted using this method is Hope of Israel Congregation in Charlotte, North Carolina.

BRANCHING

Another planting approach is called "Branching." In this method, a core group "hives off" from a parent congregation, while staying in the same general vicinity. This is not a disgruntled group splitting off from a struggling congregation, but a strategic move to begin a new work with the blessing of the parent congregation. The value in branching is that it provides an already established core group with developed values and relationships. Also, the new congregation has a built-in support system from the parent congregation nearby. As the core group already shares the same values and practices, less time will be needed for core group development. An example of a congregation planted using this method is Shoresh David Messianic Synagogue in Lakeland, Florida.

COLONIZING

"Colonizing" happens when members of an established congregation form a new core group and intentionally move from the parent congregation to plant a new congregation in a completely different area. This method provides an already developed core group, but does not provide the support system of a nearby parent congregation. Therefore, the people involved must know each other well and be on the same page throughout the planting process. The trust and unity they have in Yeshua will be the basis for their new community.

SEEDING

The "Seeding" method occurs when, because of a job or other circumstance, key leaders of an established congregation relocate to a new area and develop a core group there, leading to the formation of a new congregation. This can also happen if a few families move together to a new area.

ADOPTING

Another approach is "Adoption." This happens when a Messianic core group or fellowship approaches an established congregation for help with resources, and the established congregation decides to embrace and sponsor the fledgling group. Certain denominations utilize this method of planting. For example, the Southern Baptist Messianic Fellowship (SBMF) is involved in this type of approach as part of the North American Mission Board (NAMB).

Notes:

PARTNERING

"Partnering" is what happens when several smaller groups cooperatively to begin a new congregation. A historic example of this approach happened in the 1960's when the Jerusalem Assembly, which began as four separate Bible studies, combined to form one congregation.

REVITALIZING

When a congregation is not doing well or is on its last legs, a new work may really mean "Revitalization," or the re-starting of an old work. This may be done through new leadership or by trying a different approach in the community. Revitalizing is difficult; as is often said, it is easier to give birth to babies than to raise the dead. It is, however, one approach that God can use.

TRANSPLANTING

"Transplanting" is the inverse of revitalizing. Here, a congregation and its membership relocate to start one, or possibly several, new congregations. In the past, this was sometimes seen in the phenomenon known as "white flight." As a community changes its ethnic demographics, some congregations may want to move on in order to reach more people with the Good News.

CATALYZING

"Catalyzing" happens when a dynamic, vision-casting Messianic leader sparks the start of many new congregations as he casts the vision for them in many different communities. This is sometimes considered "apostolic," but in reality catalyzing is a part of what many missionaries do.

This concludes our section on the Preliminary Step of the Gathering Stage. Though some may be put off by the amount of preparation involved in this step, a long runway is necessary in order for a plane to be able to take off and be able to fly for a long distance.

Notes:

THE OUTREACH STEP

"But you will receive power when the Holy Spirit has come upon you, and you will be My witnesses in Jerusalem, in all Judea and Samaria, and even to the ends of the earth." - Acts 1:8

We move now to the Outreach Step, the second step of the Gathering Stage. At this point, a planter steps out in faith and begins to reach out in order to gather 10-15 Jewish and Gentile believing 'family units,' (families, couples, or individuals), who will later become the members of his core group, sharing in the vision and values of the new congregation. The best way to find these people is to lovingly reach out and begin sharing the Good News with everyone you come in contact with, praying for God to give the increase.

As Messianic believers, we are called to share our faith and to make disciples. Reaching out with the Good News is a normal way of life for all followers of Messiah, as the Scriptures teach that the redeemed will share their faith with others (Psalm 107:2). Ultimately, only the Father can draw people to Yeshua through the Spirit (John 6:44); however, our faithfulness is seen in how we handle this stewardship which God has entrusted to us. We obey the Lord's command and are enabled by the Holy Spirit to share our faith (Acts 1:8).

As we reach out, we must be people of confidence, who are *"not ashamed of the Good News"* (Romans 1:16). We must also be people of integrity; being careful not to mislead anyone, neither tarnishing His Name, nor withholding from anyone the only means of salvation. Finally, we must be people of love, praying for the love of Messiah to constrain our hearts so that we can boldly share the only message which can save those who are lost, Jew and Gentile alike.

In these beginning stages of your congregation, outreach must be at the very forefront of your focus, as you must reach out in order to gather enough people to begin a congregation. You will be able to say that contact-making is *"This one thing I do"* (Philippians 3:13), because at this stage, it will be all you do. However, as you reach your goal in finding these people, this is not the end of your outreach, for your future congregation will only be healthy as you continue to share the Good News. To neglect this essential element opens the door for your community to become self-absorbed, ingrown, and dysfunctional.

Notes:

63

_____

_____

_____

_____

_____

_____

_____

_____

_____

_____

_____

_____

_____

_____

_____

_____

_____

Outreach, therefore, must be factored into the DNA of the congregation right from the beginning. As you lead people to faith, you must disciple them in this essential value, helping them understand that to testify of Yeshua is our God-given purpose this side of heaven. To attempt to introduce this later when your group is already established can prove to be difficult as people may be hesitant to jump on board, viewing outreach as a side issue or merely the responsibility of the leadership. Therefore, as your congregation grows, continually ensure that outreach is kept at the heart of your congregation.

As we consider the Outreach Step, and following this, the Discipleship Step, we will look at the foundational aspects of each, and how they relate to the Gathering Stage. In Part 2 of this book, we will expound on the ministries of contact making and disciple making and the ongoing role they will play as we study the essential responsibilities and systems of a healthy congregation.

MAKING CONTACTS

The goal of the Outreach Step is to intentionally meet potential contacts; people whom you can follow-up on. As we share the Good News, we must ensure that we collect people's contact information in order to continue in ministry to them, following-up with them by email, phone, or visit. If evangelism were the only goal of the Outreach Step, we could announce that Yeshua is Lord to everyone we meet, and accomplish our purpose in having done so. However, our goal as Messianic planters and leaders is to make disciples. We are here to make *talmidim*, not merely to get the Word out. Those who respond to our outreach must be recorded so that we can follow-up with them, continue to share the Good News with them, and disciple those who come to faith!

ACTIVITIES TO MAKE CONTACTS

As you embark on this step, you need to start somewhere, experimenting with many different ideas and putting many fishing lines out into the water. Do not be inhibited in this, as bad ideas are better than no ideas at all; trust the Lord and do not be afraid of failure. As you step out and get moving, you will quickly learn what works well and what does not. It is important that we grow to think outside the box, learning to be creative, and seeking helpful ideas from other leaders. Reach out and make contacts in any way that is legal, ethical and consistent with your values.

To start you out, here are a few tried and true ideas:

- ✡ Hand out Jewish-oriented Good News pamphlets to crowds of people in your community
- ✡ Put ads in local papers about upcoming events you are hosting
- ✡ Give away Bibles, or calendars, etc. with your congregation's contact information on them
- ✡ Make friends with those who have Jewish friends
- ✡ Put up posters, flyers, bulletin board info, etc. in supermarkets, drugstores, or public places
- ✡ Utilize the yellow pages to find those with Jewish names in your area
- ✡ Go door to door, leave door hangers
- ✡ Conduct surveys or questionnaires door-to-door, at malls, in parks, etc.
- ✡ Host a campus book table at a local college
- ✡ Carry out service projects in local neighborhoods
- ✡ Go to businessmen's / women's Bible studies and make yourself available
- ✡ Organize a pro-Israel campaign
- ✡ Hold Jewish holiday outreaches in the community (not at your meeting place)
- ✡ Host a podcast, radio, or TV show!

Notes:

One method of contact-making is to utilize the tangible needs of the community in order to make people curious about your fellowship. For example, perhaps you could gear an outreach toward inter-faith couples in your community who would like to know how to get on the same page with one another. Community outreach communicates the message that, "We're here." It may take a while, but pray and wait for God to give the increase. In the meantime, if nothing else, you are putting a good name on your future congregation in the community.

Unfortunately, this model of contact-making is not as popular among congregations today as it was in decades past. Today, many groups find themselves dependent on people coming to them from other places. Their growth and health can become tied to people who have left their church or other congregations to come to them. This is not healthy and can prove to be very harmful. We need to be reaching out rather than waiting on people to become dissatisfied in their places of worship and eventually come to us.

EVENTS TO MEET CONTACTS

Special events such as holidays and life occasions are a perfect time to make new contacts. Holidays are a dual blessing, as they are a wonderful time for worship and also for witness. Utilize such events to provide natural opportunities for people to come "try out" the congregation. Experiment with all different kinds of events, and do not be afraid to try new things.

As visitors come, do not expect too much from them at first. They may be interested, but are not yet ready to commit to a congregation. Simply love them, ask how you can pray for them, and invite them to come back. For each person you meet, you will need to evaluate where they are spiritually in order to determine how to best follow-up with them. Your congregation's relationship with each person will look different depending on whether they are an unbeliever, an unaffiliated believer, or a committed member of another believing congregation.

FOLLOW-UP WITH CONTACTS

WITH UNBELIEVERS

Our goal with an unbeliever is to share Yeshua with them and lead them to the Lord.

WITH UNAFFILIATED BELIEVERS

Our goal for unaffiliated believers, those who are not part of a believing congregation, is to bring them into Messianic discipleship.

WITH COMMITTED MEMBERS OF BELIEVING CONGREGATIONS

Our goal for those who are already committed members of a believing congregation is to help them to understand that although we may do things differently than other believing congregations, we also love the Lord and are born-again believers. Assess if the person is willing to become a "friend of the congregation," and join you in praying for the work, and then encourage them to grow and bloom where they are planted. As much as it may be tempting, do not try to recruit these people for your congregation. We make *talmidim*; we do not steal sheep. Even if the person is Jewish, let the Lord lead them in how Jewish they should be. Do not try to manipulate or

Notes:

dissuade them. Be wise in these matters and mindful of the fact that as you sow, this also will you reap (Galatians 6:7).

If the person feels that the Lord has led them to be part of your congregation, tell them to share this with their pastor or rabbi in order to receive his blessing to transfer to your congregation. Be wary, however, of people who wish to join your congregation simply because they are disgruntled with their current congregation. If they are disgruntled there, they may eventually become just as disgruntled with you as well.

MEETING LOCAL LEADERS

Introducing yourself to other leaders in your local area is another very important part of outreach, as others may assume that you are a cult until they understand who you really are. If you do not introduce yourself to other leaders, your silence will come across as arrogance and they may assume the worst about you. Do not allow other people to define you by your lack of communication. Also, do not be arrogant and keep to yourself, thinking that you are the only group who knows what you are doing.

LOCAL EVANGELICAL PASTORS

Let them know that you are a genuine believer

When you are meeting with Gentile pastors of evangelical churches, you must first let them know that you are also a born-again believer (John 3:3), as they may be confused about this by the fact that your congregation operates differently than theirs. When talking with them, clearly explain to them that you love and follow "Jesus Christ." Just as we use Messianic terminology in order to effectively communicate with those whom we are reaching, we must use terminology that Gentile believers will understand as we speak with them, becoming all things to all men for the purpose of the Good News. When meeting with pastors, you must clearly communicate to them that you are a brother who loves the Lord and is passionate about the things of God.

Make friends if possible; if not, give them your contact information

Notes:

67

Notes:

_____

_____

_____

_____

_____

_____

_____

_____

_____

_____

_____

_____

_____

_____

_____

_____

After you establish the fact that you are also a believer, you can then explain to them a little about what you are doing and who you are, your vision and values. Let them know that you can help them follow-up on their unsaved Jewish contacts, and seek their prayer support for your ministry. If they still view you as suspicious, give them your contact information and tell them to call you right away if they hear people speaking negatively about your group. If this happens, you will be able to provide explanation concerning the matter in question and clear up any misinformation people may have as to the reasons why you express your faith differently than them. Be careful to communicate well so as not to make enemies of people with whom you will spend eternity.

Leaders and churches who respond positively to you and your ministry may be interested in sharing space with a Messianic congregation. Many local churches have been quite willing to allow a Messianic congregation to utilize their facilities on Saturday mornings. This type of agreement can provide a mutual blessing for both the church and the Messianic congregation.

(For more about a Messianic congregation's relationship with the greater Body of Messiah, see Appendix 5).

OTHER LOCAL MESSIANIC LEADERS

Make friends if possible; if not, give them your contact information

Reach out to other Messianic leaders, and try to make friends, acknowledging their ministry, and the fact that you are working for the same cause. If they are resistant to this, give them your contact information and ask them to give you a call if they hear people speaking negatively about you.

OTHER COMMUNITY LEADERS (NON-MESSIANIC RABBIS...)

Make friends if possible; if not, give them your contact information

For other community leaders, such as non-Messianic rabbis in your area, reach out through personal contact, extending friendship. Again, if this is not possible, give them your contact information and ask them to give you a call if they hear people speaking negatively about you.

THE DISCIPLESHIP STEP

"If anyone wishes to come after Me, he must deny himself, and take up his cross daily, and follow Me." – Luke 9:23

We now come to the Discipleship Step. Once you have gathered your group of 10-15 committed family units, you must make sure that each individual is properly discipled in the basic values of the beginning congregation which were established during the Preliminary Step. The process by which a person is trained in these values is called *talmidut*, or discipleship.

WHAT IS DISCIPLESHIP?

The word "discipleship" comes from the Hebrew word *hanakh*, which means to "make narrow, dedicate, or train." This is where we get the word for *Hanukkah*, the Feast of Dedication. Even as the Hebrew Scriptures teach us to be "dedicated ones," discipled servants and sons (Genesis 14:14, Proverbs 22:6), so our Messiah expects all believers to be involved in discipleship and nurtured in His Word (Matthew 28:19-20).

What is the difference between teaching and discipleship? Teaching is instruction, through which you present an expectation. Discipleship, then, is application, through which you inspect to make sure the person is following through on the expectation. This is because people do not do what you expect, but what you inspect. Through discipleship, we do not simply teach people about their walk with Messiah, we walk with them in how to actually live it out. Discipleship transforms a believer into a mature follower of the Lord who has a firm grasp of their identity in Messiah, prays daily, knows the Scriptures, values fellowship, and shares their faith with others. A disciple must learn these things and then incorporate them into their life in order to actually grow into them. This process is life long, and grounded believers continue to grow into the fullness of the stature of Messiah (Ephesians 4:13-16; Romans 8:29). Our entire life is about growing into His likeness, and formal discipleship is just the beginning. Because discipleship is of eternal value, you never outgrow it, but rather, grow into it.

Discipleship is a form of coaching, a *"training in righteousness"* (2 Timothy 3:16). Just as in sports, training in these foundational matters of faith is vitally important because practice is the only way these things will become

Notes:

_____

_____

_____

_____

_____

_____

_____

_____

_____

_____

_____

_____

_____

_____

69

Notes:

_____

_____

_____

_____

_____

_____

_____

_____

_____

_____

_____

_____

_____

_____

_____

_____

_____

_____

habits in a person's life. Day-to-day, when the pressure is on and we feel frustrated, tired, or upset, we will resort to our flesh unless we have developed godly habits that teach us to pray rather than to react. These things must be built intentionally, and will only develop into habits as a person matures. Discipleship is an exercise program through which we are trained in righteousness.

This type of dedication is the normal way of life for a believer. However, Yeshua taught that the children of darkness are wiser than the children of light (Luke 16:8). Although the principles by which they live are unredeemed, they take them seriously and follow-through on them (not wasting time because "time is money"). Many believers, though, take a more casual approach to prayer and spending time with God in His Word, thinking, "I'll get to it when I get to it," or, "I won't pray unless I really need to." This type of attitude is abnormal and dysfunctional, never okay for a believer to have. God gives time, talent, and treasure for us to redeem; we are to use them for His glory.

✡ *God expects evangelism to lead to discipleship*
just as He expects pregnancy to lead to parenting ✡

When you lead a person to faith, it is essential that you now disciple them! It would be crazy for a parent to think that their work is done once their child is born. So also with discipleship; we must feed our own children. To assist in this, have your own discipleship material ready (see pages 138-147 for guidance in subjects to cover during discipleship), or find Messianic discipleship material that your congregation can use (see page 264). It is crucial that you have a framework for this important process, not making it up as you go along with each person.

However, in order to properly disciple others, you must first make sure that you have been properly discipled yourself, for you cannot give what you do not have. For assistance and support in any of these matters, please contact us at Word of Messiah. Discipleship is a multiplication process. Once a planter has been discipled, he can then disciple his wife. Next, each of you can disciple one other person. Now you will have four people who have been discipled and are equipped to disciple four more. As you work through this process, eventually you can draw these individuals together to meet for prayer, discipleship oriented study, or training in different areas of outreach such as home leadership, discipleship, and evangelism.

WHY DO WE MAKE DISCIPLES?

Many congregations do not have any structure at all for discipleship. Why make it such a priority in our community?

TO OBEY YESHUA'S COMMAND

"And Yeshua came up and spoke to them, saying, 'All authority has been given to Me in heaven and on earth. Go therefore and make disciples of all the nations, immersing them in the name of the Father and the Son and the Holy Spirit, teaching them to observe all that I commanded you; and lo, I am with you always, even to the end of the age.'" – Matthew 28:18-20

We make disciples at the command of our Messiah. Yeshua's statement in this portion to *"make disciples"* is a *mitzvah* (a command) which we are to implement.

WE ARE CONVINCED OF MESSIAH'S LORDSHIP

"All authority has been given to Me in heaven and on earth" - Matthew 28:18

Yeshua's command to make talmidim is based on His authority, for all authority has been given to Him in heaven and on earth. As *Ben Elohim* (the Son of God), Messiah's authority was intrinsic. Through the incarnation, He emptied Himself of all prerogatives, and was highly exalted as He gave His life to bear the sin of many (Isaiah 53:11). Now, as our risen King, He has all authority as Lord of all (Psalm 2:7-8, Isaiah 9:6).

WE ARE COMMITTED TO MESSIAH'S DISCIPLESHIP

"Go therefore and make disciples of all the nations, immersing them in the name of the Father and the Son and the Holy Spirit, teaching them to observe all that I commanded you" - Matthew 28:19

To the degree we are convinced of Messiah's Lordship, to that degree we are committed to His discipleship, and no more. The result of discipleship is a dedicated life, as one moves from being a mere believer to a true follower of Yeshua, a doer of the Word (Jacob 1:22). In Yeshua's command to make *talmidim*, we see four discipleship life commitments:

Notes:

✡ Discipleship is a purpose-oriented life: "*go therefore*"
As you go, wherever you go, you have an underlying purpose: you go to make disciples! Whether you are next door, at work, shopping, or on vacation, you have a commission from the Lord: to be Messiah's messenger, sharing the Good News and making disciples.

✡ Discipleship is an other-oriented life: "*make disciples of all nations*"
Our service for the Lord is entirely others-focused. As we disciple people, we edify and serve them in their walk with the Lord. We are to reach out and make disciples of people from all nations, not showing favoritism or prejudice for any one group of people.

✡ Discipleship is a Messiah-oriented life: "*immersing them*"
Through immersion, we identify with Yeshua, united with Him in His death as we die to sin (Romans 6:5), and are raised to live for Him. Through our lives, we represent Him, modeling His life to those we are serving.

✡ Discipleship is a Scripture-oriented life: "*observe all*"
The goal of teaching is obedience. As we make disciples, we teach them to obey the commandments of God, for these are the convictions of the saints. Through discipleship, we learn to live out of obedience to God's Word rather than out of natural inclination. Messianic testimonies come from living out of conviction, not crisis.

WE ARE COMPLETED IN MESSIAH'S FELLOWSHIP

"*I am with you always, even to the end of the age.*" - Matthew 28:20

The Resource for Discipleship is found in Messiah's personal fellowship: He is Immanuel, God with us! The resurrection was intended to fulfill God's greatest desire. He created man for relationship with Himself, and Messiah came to restore what sin had destroyed. We are never without the Resource to do all that God has called us to do; the only way we can make disciples is through Messiah. Yeshua's fellowship is also perpetual; He will never leave us nor forsake us. Completed in His fellowship, we have the love of God poured into our hearts by the *Ruach* given to us.

TO EMPOWER OTHER BELIEVERS TO HONOR YESHUA

When a person prays and makes a decision for Messiah, it is merely a starting point. Discipleship reveals what the person actually prayed about.

Notes:

Through discipleship, we teach a person what it means to live as a believer: walking with the Lord as they pray, study God's Word, share their faith, etc. Do not assume that people are already doing these things, as these are spiritual and not natural disciplines which are not easily implemented until they are taught.

✡ *We must move from Decisions to Disciples* ✡

Discipleship is about growing to become more like Messiah as we follow Him. We do not want mere believers to become members of our core group and later, our congregations; we want our membership to be made up of disciples. It is possible to be a believer who is alive in Messiah, yet dysfunctional, and not growing as God intended for them to grow. Likewise with a congregation. If there were a congregation on every street corner in town, it would not make much of a difference if each of them were dysfunctional. A dysfunctional individual or congregation cannot help themselves, let alone anyone else. Effective discipleship is needed for a person to become mature and functional, ready to serve in the Body of Messiah. Through discipleship, we mature to be like Yeshua and follow in His ways, walking in the dust of our rabbi.

✡ *Faith in Yeshua makes you a child of God;*
Discipleship is God's way for you to mature as His child. ✡

As people grow in their relationship with the Lord through discipleship, they are ready to move from milk to "*solid food*" (Hebrews 5:14). Through reading and understanding His Word more and more, they gain insight in how to live faithfully for Him, honoring Him, and seeing the difference He makes in their life.

✡ *Just as there is no salvation without faith in Yeshua,*
So there is no spiritual growth without discipleship. ✡

Believers are not growing unless they are properly grounded and rooted in the faith. If they do not have an actual prayer life and are not consistently in the Word, they are malnourished and unplugged. Though their knowledge of the externals may be impressive, be wise and very careful about this important matter. Do not make assumptions unless you know for sure that a person has been discipled. If you neglect to do this, you will end up with people in your congregation serving and teaching who do not share your values.

Notes:

_____

_____

_____

_____

_____

_____

_____

_____

_____

_____

_____

_____

_____

TO HAVE A FUNCTIONAL, UNIFIED COMMUNITY

It is essential that from the very beginning, your core group has a firm grasp of what your congregation is all about. When a group of people is not unified, leading them can be like attempting to herd a group of cats! The same discipleship for all members of the community brings a unity of vision and values. This type of true unity is vitally important for congregational health. Unity comes as people actually walk together in agreement (Amos 3:3); when they have shared values. Just because a couple has the same last name, it does not mean that they have unity. Likewise, simply because a group of people are part of the same community, it does not mean they have unity. Unity is not found in common personality traits or hobbies, but in sharing the most important things of life together. People will naturally move towards division unless they are taught unity through discipleship in common values.

Lack of discipleship is often the tragic cause for congregational disunity & immaturity. If you are not discipling people in your community's vision and values, beware! There are always more rams in the flock than shepherds, and without unifying values, those who are strong-willed will end up taking over and enforcing their values on others. People are imperfect, and personalities will always clash, but through discipleship in unifying values, they will be held accountable to the fact that the primary value of love must dictate how disagreements are dealt with in the congregation.

TO PROTECT THE FLOCK FROM MERELY "FITTING IN"

We must protect our flocks from the self-deception of "fitting in." This is especially important in light of the fact that there will be wolves who will enter your community in pursuit of the undiscipled, those who are ungrounded, who are straying from the flock. These undiscipled believers may appear to fit in, knowing when to stand up and when to sit down, how to hold their Bibles the right way, etc, but do not know why they are doing these things. Do not be fooled, for people like this have simply been acculturated, not truly discipled, and will be undermined as quickly as they are recruited. If they have not been discipled, they do not understand the values behind your behavior and may continually compare your group with other congregations, asking why your community does things so differently than others do.

Notes:

Once, I was involved in a congregation where a group of people wanted to put a cross up in our building to be like other groups around us. To address the issue, we called a meeting, allowed these people to make their case, and then brought out our constitution containing our values. We showed them that the reason we could not put up a cross is because we were a Messianic congregation which held to a Jewish expression of faith in order to be a testimony to the Jew first in our community. I explained that though we "bear the cross," we do not "wear it," and showed them that this is what they had signed on to. As people in your congregation are discipled in your values, but find they do not agree with them, they are free to find a different community which holds to the values they agree with.

WHO DO WE DISCIPLE?

✡ New believers

New believers must be rooted and grounded in their newfound faith, being taught right away that we pray not just when things go wrong, but because we are in a relationship with the living God. We read His Bible because it feeds our soul, etc. These foundational concepts must be clearly communicated and modeled to a new believer.

✡ Undiscipled believers

Undiscipled believers are those who are unaffiliated with any congregation, and may be roaming from one group to another, looking for new nuggets of truth. The undiscipled believer is the dysfunctional member of the Body of Messiah, and these people must be developed through discipleship in order to become spiritually functional. Undiscipled believers should by no means be placed in positions of service or leadership until they have been properly discipled. Beware of depending on transfer-growth, assuming that people who join your community from other congregations have already been discipled. Time spent in discipleship with these people is valuable, for through it they will grow to become rooted and grounded in their faith, developing into a functional member of your community.

✡ Mature believers

Mature believers joining your community must also be discipled in your values as a congregation so that they will be able to disciple others in these values as well. You must have a normalized system of disciple-making so

Notes:

_____

_____

_____

_____

_____

_____

_____

_____

_____

_____

_____

_____

_____

_____

_____

_____

that your community as a whole shares the same values and are able to make disciples of others. A healthy congregation is focused on making contacts who in time become lifelong disciples of Yeshua.

(For more information on addressing the specific needs of different groups of people through discipleship, see pages 138-147)

WHO DO WE NOT DISCIPLE?

✡ Unbelievers

Some people are so surprised to find an interested unbeliever that they do not know what to do with them, and may try to disciple them without first leading them to faith. Every person must confess personal faith in Yeshua before they can become His disciple. Do not put the cart before the horse.

✡ Affiliated believers

If a member or committed attendee from another congregation approaches you asking to be discipled, they need to be sent "home." This is because a person going through discipleship in your community will be trained in the values of your community, and this may perhaps put them in conflict with those of their own. If the person tells you that they do not have discipleship at their home congregation, tell them to talk with their pastor or rabbi and insist that the leadership begin to disciple people. Members of other congregations should be welcome to visit or to be a friend of your congregation, but if you agree to disciple them, it will appear to others that you are sheep stealing.

WHEN DO WE MAKE DISCIPLES?

✡ New believers: Immediately

Do not wait for a new believer to show interest before starting discipleship with them. Begin meeting with them right away, in order to establish and encourage them in their new faith, building the foundation for a lifetime of growth.

Notes:

_____

_____

_____

_____

_____

_____

_____

_____

_____

_____

_____

_____

_____

_____

_____

_____

_____

✡ Undiscipled believers: Upon commitment

When you try to disciple a person who is not willing to commit to the community's values, you will waste your time teaching someone who does not care. Make certain the undiscipled believer has a commitment to the community before beginning discipleship with them.

✡ Mature believers: Upon ownership of the calling

Many mature believers are mature not because they went through a standardized discipleship program, but because they have grown as they have been under the teaching of the Word over the years. Regardless of maturity, a person cannot make disciples simply on the basis of wonderful sermons they have heard. They must be equipped with a method for making disciples. Going through discipleship themselves will prepare them with what they need in order to disciple others. Do not start discipleship with them, however, until they take ownership of the calling for themselves.

THE BASIC VALUES FOR TALMIDUT

As you prepare to make disciples, here is a list of basic values to consider. In discipleship, we value…

✡ … a "whole Bible" approach

"All Scripture is inspired by God and profitable for teaching, for reproof, for correction, for training in righteousness …" – 2 Timothy 3:16

✡ … a literal interpretation of Scripture

*"Now these things, brethren, I have figuratively applied to myself and Apollos for your sakes, so that in us you may learn **not to go beyond what is written**, so that no one of you will become arrogant in behalf of one against the other."* – 1 Corinthians 4:6

✡ … a New Covenant orientation

"'Behold, days are coming,' declares the Lord, 'when I will make a new covenant with the house of Israel and with the house of Judah…I will put My Torah within them and on their heart I will write it; and I will be their God, and they shall be My people …'" - Jeremiah 31:31-34

Notes:

_____

_____

_____

_____

_____

_____

_____

_____

_____

_____

_____

_____

_____

_____

_____

77

✡ . . . application of Scripture as essential

"If you know these things, blessed are you if you do them." - John 13:17

✡ . . . a home-oriented approach as vital

Notes:

"if a man does not know how to manage his own household, how will he take care of the assembly of God?" - 1 Timothy 3:5

STRUCTURE OF DISCIPLESHIP MEETINGS

CONSISTENT PRINCIPLES FOR MEETINGS

A person is discipled not only through the content of the material, but also through the structure of the discipleship meetings themselves. As you are discipling a person, it is very important that you meet with them in a consistent, orderly fashion. You must set the standard for what will be expected of them, modeling consistency in all things, for maturity is seen in consistency.

Make sure you tell the person up front what will be expected of them as you walk with them through discipleship. Let them know that they will need to consistently apply the material they are learning through discipleship, arrive at the discipleship meetings on time, and do their homework. If the person is not ready to commit to these parameters, do not begin to disciple them until they are.

CONSISTENT APPLICATIONS

As you work through the discipleship material, always discuss applications specific to the person's life, then follow-up with them each week to ensure they are putting these things into practice. For example, if you are teaching them about prayer, let them know that at your next meeting you will ask them how often they have been praying. These things are a joyous part of our relationship with God, but must start out as disciplines so that they can grow into habits. Be careful not to put unreasonable expectations on the person, as some may feel that if they cannot pray for an hour at a time, they might as well not pray at all! Help them to set reachable goals for themselves, starting out by setting aside five minutes per day for prayer. Encourage them as they meet these goals!

CONSISTENT APPOINTMENTS

Growth in maturity is also seen through punctuality at consistent appointments. Teach the person to treat others with respect in this area, redeeming the time and not wasting it. As a discipler, make sure you model this by always arriving on time for discipleship meetings. Let the person know that just as it is important that they get to work on time, they also need to arrive at their discipleship meetings on time.

Notes:

Establish the value of this by agreeing to let each other know right away if either of you find you have to miss an appointment for any reason. If this happens, find a new time to meet and stick to it! Never stand anyone up once an appointment has been made.

CONSISTENT ACCOUNTABILITY

"and let us consider how to stimulate one another to love and good deeds, not forsaking our own assembling together, as is the habit of some, but encouraging one another; and all the more as you see the day drawing near." – Hebrews 10:24-25

Hold the person accountable for doing their homework and applying the material they are learning. You must do this consistently, and let them know that if they do not do their homework, you will not have a meeting that week. If they come to a meeting without their homework done, tell them to come back once it is complete. By doing this, you are modeling the truth that we must give our best for the Lord, our utmost for His highest. Sadly, many people have pitifully low standards and expectations when it comes to the things of God, yet He deserves our very best! Through discipleship, train people to orient their lives around the Lord, and grow in His priorities.

Treat the person you are discipling like an adult and hold them to their commitments; if you do not do this, you are simply re-enforcing and justifying their problems. Love people too much to let them get away with things.

One major reason why people do not hold disciples to a high standard or do not make disciples at all is because they were not properly discipled themselves. They may feel wrong expecting of others what was not expected of them, so they keep expectations to a minimum. Realize, however, that if you start the bar out low, it will only get lower. Remember that no one is perfect and that we all press on to the mark together. I tell those whom I take through discipleship, "Now you're able to correct me because we live by the same standards." Teach them to do this privately and in love, but open the door to help each other to grow, as iron sharpening iron.

Notes:

CONTINUAL PRACTICE IN MEETINGS

As far as the actual structure of discipleship meetings is concerned, here I will share the framework I use to train those under my stewardship, as it has proven to work very well over the years.

I recommend meeting one hour per week for discipleship, going through the steps listed below during each session. Although your discipleship meetings may only last an hour, you can love the person you are discipling all week long. Let them know that you are always there for them when things come up during the week. When they reach out to you, take time for them, praying with them and loving them. We are 24/7 people, and we share life with those we are serving.

START WITH PRAYER

In discipleship, just as in every other area of life, we are fully dependent on the Lord. Always begin your meetings with prayer. At this point, do not get into talking about your week and sharing prayer requests. Take time for this at the end, for if you start it now, you will never be able to move on to anything else.

GO OVER THE HOMEWORK

Next, go over the homework from the previous session, listening as they recite their memory verses for the week. Also, take this time to ask them about how they have been applying the material you have gone over together so far.

GO OVER THE CHAPTER & SUBJECT

As you go over the subject matter for the week, remember not to move faster than your sheep, going slow enough for the person actually to become a disciple. You should not move on until you are sure that the person has grasped the material and is able to put it into practice. At times you may need to stay on one subject or chapter for several weeks, reviewing it and making sure the disciple understands it well. This is love; we need to care about the person's growth, no matter how long it takes.

SHARE PERSONAL ISSUES FOR PRAISE & PRAYER

After all this, now you can ask them what they would like prayer for, and listen if they would like to share more about what is going on in their life. Praise God for the blessings together, and bring the requests to the Lord.

END WITH PRAYER

For some, this framework may seem to be too formal. Many are not used to this type of structure when it comes to discipleship. It is true that there are many different routes to the same destination, and the end result is what is most important. The purpose of discipleship is to produce strong disciples who are mature in the Lord. Wisdom is known by her children. However, as you consider the method of discipleship you will use in your community, make sure that the process you choose is re-producible, so that others will be able to follow it as well, for we are making disciples who can then make disciples. Your community needs to know that disciple making is a priority not just for the leadership to be involved in, but for each one of them to pursue.

Also, make sure your method of discipleship is intentional. Remember that discipleship is more than just friendship. We see in Scripture that God's kind of friendship is different than what we might expect. He says in John 15:14, *"You are my friends if you do what I command you."* This is not the kind of friend we are used to, yet this describes what a true friend is. God is not a friend who winks when we make mistakes, one who downplays our bad choices. When God gives us a commandment, it is not because He wants to boss us around. His *mitzvot* are His priorities for our souls; His will for us. So, when He commands us to do something, we need to embrace it as the best thing for our lives. When we are walking in His will, we are walking with Him.

(For more on the system of disciple-making within the structure of an established congregation, including its impact on families, homes, and congregational life see page 129).

Notes:

CHAPTER 2

THE CORE GROUP DEVELOPMENT STAGE

"For You formed my inward parts; You wove me in my mother's womb. I will give thanks to You, for I am fearfully and wonderfully made; wonderful are Your works, and my soul knows it very well." – Psalm 139:13-14

Throughout the Gathering Stage, you identified the priorities of your future congregation and brought each individual onto the same page with these values as you formed your core group. Now, through the Core Group Development Stage, you will bring the group onto the same page with each other, guiding them as they begin to express these priorities through the working systems of a formed community. Whatever is in the DNA of this initial group, and what is normally done by them at this point is what will later characterize the congregation as a whole.

At this point, though you are not yet a congregation, you have come to the point of conception, and will now move into a near-birth experience as your core group grows and develops. The length of this stage will depend upon how the group has already begun to form during the Gathering Stage, and can take between 3-18 months, or longer if needed.

In the Good News accounts, we see how Yeshua chose and then discipled those who would become the leaders of the first Messianic congregation. Later, through the first five chapters of Acts, we see a type of core group development in this new community. During the Core Group Development Stage, our focus will shift, but we must not neglect outreach or discipleship, continuing to engage in these things, as they will become intrinsic to the ministry of your congregation.

82

To understand the importance of this stage, and the necessity of the time spent on it, let us again consider the process through which God brings each of us between our conception and our birth. Psalm 139 explains how the Lord knits each person together in the womb, preparing us to be able to live functionally apart from our mother when it comes time to be born. At birth, all the necessary systems need to be in place and able to work together in order for us to survive. Children who are born prematurely may not have all these systems fully developed, and as a result, may experience difficulties throughout their life. Premature birthing of a Messianic congregation can likewise lead to dysfunctionality. Though it may be tempting to rush into birth, the Core Group Development Stage is critical in order to get these 10-15 family units prepared!

The Core Group Development Stage, the time between conception and birth, consists of three steps:

- ✡ *The Instruction Step:* In this step, we look to develop unity of vision and values as a group, bringing everyone on to the same page in regards to their core beliefs and shared commitment to the Messianic calling. Through this step, greater unity and trust will be developed in the community.

- ✡ *The Integration Step:* Next, we will grow in unity of priorities and structure, looking at a number of tools for leaders to utilize in order to address issues which arise in the Body. Through this step, the core group will understand what it means to be a functioning part of a community.

- ✡ *The Application Step:* Lastly, we will consider what it means to have unity of service, as each member of the core group must apply what they have been learning, committing to serve in order for the Body to be functional.

THE INSTRUCTION STEP

When the Lord brought Miriam and I to serve in Charlotte, North Carolina, we actively engaged in evangelism and saw many come to faith through our monthly outreaches. We averaged several hundred visitors at these meetings, and began to pray about planting a congregation. However, as we began to form a core group and work on building unifying values, we found our numbers were reduced to about ten families. This core group spent the

Notes:

next several months meeting together, where we worked through not only a unifying vision, but also unifying values as a group. Though our group was not growing in numbers during this time, we knew that this was a crucial time period which, in the long run, would serve as a foundation for future stability and healthy growth.

Notes:

_____

_____

_____

_____

_____

_____

_____

_____

_____

_____

_____

_____

_____

_____

_____

_____

_____

_____

DISCUSSIONS ON UNIFYING VISION & VALUES

Up to this point, you have spent multiple hours objectifying the mission, vision, and values of your community, as well as working through them one-on-one in discipleship with each person in your group. Now, you will lead and instruct your core group as a whole in all these matters. Through this, you will work to grow a community of shared values, carefully discussing each of these matters together. It is essential that you do this as a group, for you will have a very limited congregation if the only person with whom each member has a relationship is the leadership. During this time, you will facilitate discussion...

✡   ... Identifying the Messianic Mission of the congregation

At this point, you will go over the matters as to why you, as a Messianic congregation, exist. (For more on mission, see page 14).

It is incredibly important for each member of the community to have a deep understanding of this matter, so that they will be able to explain it to others, beginning with their own children. When children ask, "Why does our congregation have to be so different from others?" or, "Can we go somewhere else that has better music?" parents in the community must be ready with an answer from God's Word.

✡ ... Clarifying the Messianic Vision of the congregation

You also must be ready to discuss the vision God has given you for the congregation, a vision of Yeshua, and how you as a community will grow together into Him as members of His Body. (For more on vision, see page 35). You may consider holding classes to present different aspects of your vision to the core group as these will be the people who will be working together to make the vision a reality.

✡ ... Unifying the Messianic Values of the congregation

The core group must own the values of the congregation. It is crucial that they understand why these values are important and how you plan to accomplish them together. It is vitally important to discuss this for as long as it takes for them to truly grasp it. At this point of the process, group members have been known to drop out as they realize that the group is actually serious about living out the values which you have been discussing through discipleship. It is crucial that these values are understood not just in theory, but in practice, and held to by each member of the core group. (For more on values, see page 41).

Take time to discuss each of the strategic areas for unity of values which we covered earlier: Unity in what you believe concerning primary and secondary matters, unity of goals and direction, agreement on spiritual gifts and service, recognized standards of stewardship, and submission to Yeshua in a Yeshua-oriented life. When you are on the same page in all these things, you will have a healthy community, committed to the same values, united against threats, working towards a common goal together.

EQUIPPING THE CORE GROUP AS CHANGE AGENTS

Through the Instruction Step, you continue to pour into your core group, for they will soon be pouring into others through discipleship. Therefore, they must be strong disciples themselves, continually on their game, ready to address questions posed by visitors, and willing to share the heavy lifting in order to keep the community running smoothly. As you go through this step, you continue to equip your core group for this calling by...

✡ ...Testing their assumptions by asking questions

This is how you will discover what each person actually believes about your mission, vision, and values. To make sure they really understand and are on board with the values of the community, ask specific evaluatory questions such as: "What do we mean when we say that Yeshua is Lord?" Though this may seem to be very basic, do not naively believe that each person in your group is on the same page without testing this assumption.

Beware of being fooled, like a parent who desires to believe all his children are saved, and so does not ask too many questions. Just as in marriage the

Notes:

time to ask questions is before you say "I do," this is the time to ask questions of your core group, before you bring them into a committed role in your community. Be careful of getting too busy to attend to this basic, essential matter. If you assume that people are in agreement without overtly making sure of it, you are inviting weakness and division.

Notes:

✡ Continuing to develop the core group as disciples

Your role as a discipler is not finished once you gather the group together for discussion. Discipleship will carry on as you continue to help these people grow, training them in the wholesome values that will reflect the community of which they are a part.

✡ Explaining the differences between primary and secondary matters

As you work with your core group, and later lead in the congregation, you will hear more than your share of questions concerning primary and secondary matters. Though this may become tiresome, be thankful that people in your community are coming to you with these matters rather than going to others who would not point them to the Word. Questions are to be welcomed because through our answers, we get to share our values. So, you must be prepared to address many such questions from those who are in your stewardship.

For those who are not a part of your stewardship, you must not attempt to instruct, but rather pray for them, for you are not everybody's teacher. In my stewardship, I am a teacher to those who accept my teaching. We must be careful of thinking that we are here to correct the wrong thinking of those outside of our community.

THE INTEGRATION STEP

In the Integration Step, the mission, vision and values of the congregation will now be fleshed out as you discuss what a healthy, functioning congregation actually looks like.

THE ESSENTIAL SYSTEMS OF A CONGREGATION

What foundational systems must be in place in order for a congregation to be healthy? As we study God's Word, we see the essential systems of a healthy congregation are relative to the essential responsibilities of the elders in a healthy congregation. These fall into three major categories:

- ✡ The Ministry of Prayer/Worship: We are a people who pray
- ✡ The Ministry of the Word (Evangelism & Edification): We are a people who follow the Word
- ✡ The Ministry of Overseer (Eldership): We are a people who handle our responsibilities decently and in order

We will cover each of these ministries in much more detail in Part 2 of this book. Make sure that you take time to go through this section in preparation for the Integration Step, as it is crucial that the core group understands and incorporates these essential systems into their lives. As they live them out in their homes, they will be able to grow into leadership in the community as well.

REFLECTING OUR RELATIONSHIP TO YESHUA

In going over the details of healthy congregational structure, be sure to emphasize the fact that everything we do within these systems is based upon our relationship with Yeshua, and must serve to reflect Him.

During the Integration Step, we take time to make sure each participant understands how a healthy congregation is to function under the Lordship of Yeshua so that they will be ready to step up in service during the Application Step.

THE APPLICATION STEP

As the core group takes ownership of the vision God has given you for the congregation, as well as the priorities in its structure, they are ready to step up and participate in the work. Their contributions will make your congregation a living example of the body of Messiah, not just an audience for one person's teaching and preaching. The Application Step is essential, for people do not learn as they hear, they learn as they do!

Notes:

_____

_____

_____

_____

_____

_____

_____

_____

_____

_____

_____

_____

_____

_____

_____

CORE GROUP DISTINCTIONS

Notes:

_____

_____

_____

_____

_____

_____

_____

_____

_____

_____

_____

_____

_____

_____

_____

_____

_____

In your discussions with your core group, you will find that people will have different levels of ownership of the vision, some being willing to make a higher level of commitment to the work than others. People in your core group will generally fall into two categories: those who will be partners and those who will be participants as you move forward.

PARTNERS

Your partners will be those who share equal acceptance of the vision and are fully committed to the work along with you. If you are married, your first partner in ministry should be your wife. Depending on her gifts and abilities, she can be involved in the work in a variety of capacities. However, if she has responsibilities of family or work which preclude heavy involvement, it is the couple-power that matters most. The two of you must be on the same page, working towards the same vision by way of the same values. Regardless of her level of involvement or gifting, it is important for a planter to value and cherish his spouse as a partner in service.

Other partners are those families or individuals who share the vision you have for the congregation and are fully committed to the work. They are the ones on whom you can count to be right there with you sharing the burden of the work, laboring in prayer with you, mourning with you through difficulty. These are the people who will support you though the victories and trials of planting a congregation. A partner may actually stay up at night as often as the planter does, doing all they can to make sure the work of God moves forward. In light of their level of commitment, the planter can comfortably share his challenges and concerns in the planting process with his partners.

A partner's commitment is to be appreciated and the sacrifices they make viewed as a gift for the Lord. Partners are a precious gift not be taken for granted; thank the Lord if you have them. I pray that out of your 10-15 family units, there will be one other strong couple or family who will become ministry partners with you, sharing the burden of the work.

Once the congregation is established, the responsibilities of the planter and his partners may transition smoothly to those of elders in the congregation.

Until then, the partners can be seen as elders-in-training as you grow together in the ministries of prayer, the Word, and overseer responsibilities.

PARTICIPANTS

Notes:

Participants are those who are willing to serve on your team in some way, but are not able to give the same level of time and commitment as a partner. The majority of the members of your core group will be participants.

Here are some characteristics that will be valuable to look for in your core group participants:

✡ **Capable**: Each participant will bring different skills, abilities, and experience to the group. Different participants may be gifted in teaching, music, finances, children's ministry, service, etc. The planter must recognize these gifts and utilize them carefully, as the person is willing, to further the work.

✡ **Available**: Participants must be available to give of some of their time and talents to assist in the work. Though a cliché, it is still true that the greatest ability is availability. When there is a need, participants can step up and make themselves available for service.

✡ **Responsible**: Participants must be able to be counted on, proving themselves trustworthy in all their tasks. In any area of service, the novelty may quickly wear off, but these people need to be able to follow-through with their commitments in order to complete their service (1 Corinthians 4:2). This level of trust is necessary in every area of responsibility.

✡ **Responsive**: The planter and his partners may be leading in the vision of what needs to get done, but the participants are to be responsive and manageable in carrying out the work. They must be able to flex with the leadership and be ready to adjust to new plans.

✡ **Enthusiastic**: Participants need to have a right attitude before the Lord, knowing how to "*cast their cares on Him*" (1 Peter 5:7), and joyfully serve others.

✡ **Teachable**: As followers of Messiah, participants should be willing to learn new skills in service. Though they may have previously served in a specific capacity as members elsewhere, they need to be willing to learn new things. The Core Group Development Stage is meant to get everyone on the same page regarding these distinctions and similarities of vision and values.

Notes:

As you work with your core group, it is important that you discern between those who are your partners and those who are your participants, and give due respect to the commitment levels of each group. If the difference between these roles is not taken into consideration, it can lead to confusion and disappointment, as partners may feel underappreciated, and participants overwhelmed or frustrated.

DELEGATION OF RESPONSIBILITIES

Once there is unity of values among your core group (accomplished through the Instruction Step), and an understanding of the systems of a congregation (accomplished through the Integration Step), there now needs to be delegation of tasks relative to those systems. This provides opportunity for both partners and participants to apply what they have been discussing.

As you become familiar with the essential responsibilities of a congregation concerning the ministry of prayer, the ministry of the Word, and the ministry of overseer, you will develop a good grasp of the tasks which need to be accomplished in order to keep the congregation functional and healthy. Out of this understanding, you will be able to delegate responsibilities, entrusting tasks to those who are willing to serve in light of what needs to be done.

Membership develops as leadership delegates. If, as a leader, you are not delegating, you are hindering your group from developing. It is only as people apply the teaching they are receiving through service that they will grow. While a planter may be willing and able to lead in many various capacities, the goal of a Messianic congregation is for the members to eventually be the leaders in the ministry. As much as they may be able to do so, the planter and his spouse should not attempt to do everything themselves. (For specific guidelines on how to delegate, see page 183)

TEAM ROLES

What are the tasks that will need to be delegated during the Application Step? There are numerous responsibilities which factor in to the functioning of a healthy congregation, and many leaders are needed to fill these important roles. Some of these leaders will become *z'keinim* (elders) and *shamashim* (deacons) in your community.

Notes:

Elders are known by different titles in different communities. An "elder", or *z'kein*, means one who gives wise counsel. A "shepherd" or *roeh*, means one who feeds and cares. An "overseer", or *pakeed*, means one who manages. We see all three terms used synonymously in Scripture for the leadership responsibility (Acts 20:28, Titus 1:5-7, 1 Peter 5:1-5). The term "deacon" or *shamash*, meaning "servant," is used to describe those who serve alongside the elders, leading in various ministries and capacities (see 1 Timothy 3:8-13). These terms, like the words "apostle" or "prophet," are all used to define a responsibility. The only person among the believers in the New Covenant for whom the term "rabbi" is used is Yeshua.

Considering the list of roles below, you may wonder where you are going to find all of these volunteers, however, as your congregation is established, you will need to look no further than your core group members. The members of your core group, whether they be partners or participants, are being developed so that they can be involved in the activities of the congregation.

As you work through the process of developing your core group, you will need to wear multiple hats for a time until more are ready to fill these team roles that will be needed as your fellowship grows. You can only do as much as you have personnel for, so at first you will need to focus only on the ministries most necessary for the congregation to be able to exist. For example, you may not have enough volunteers to put together an *oneg* after the service every week. This is ok; you will be able to work up to these things step by step, growing into this list of roles:

PRIMARY VISION CASTER / CONGREGATIONAL LEADER

The primary vision caster is usually the planter of the congregation; the one who provides leadership and direction, and who will probably also give the major teaching each week from the bema. This leader will be the one casting the vision for the group as they move forward.

Notes:

PRAYER / WORSHIP LEADER (CANTOR)

The prayer and worship leader is a person who is able to plan, recruit, and train others in worship and prayer. This person will oversee others serving in this area of ministry, such as the worship team, the dance team, and prayer teams. The worship leader will need to adapt to the needs of the community, whether the format of prayer and worship be more liturgical or informal. Once more, all people involved in the worship ministry should certainly take ownership of the congregation's vision and values before being placed up front.

CHILDREN & YOUTH MINISTRY LEADER(S)

It is of utmost importance to have a person committed to faithfully minister to the children and youth of the congregation, even if there are only a couple of children who attend. A congregation is simply a community of families joined together, and families are much more likely to feel at home in your congregation if they know there is a safe place for their children. As the congregation grows, there may be a need for a second leader to coordinate a separate ministry for the youth.

The children are the future of the congregation, and we must effectively pass the baton on to them if we do not want our congregation to end with us. We train our children up to become disciples of Messiah, and this does not happen automatically. A children's ministry exists to serve the parents, the children's primary disciplers, reinforcing what is already being taught in the homes. In light of all this, the children's ministry leader must not only have a love for kids, but also be able to plan, lead, recruit, and train others in the ministry.

BIBLE TEACHERS

As your congregation grows, teachers will be needed in various settings, such as Shabbat school classes for adults, youth, and children, home *chavurot*, sisterhood and brotherhood gatherings, etc. This can add up to quite a bit of teaching, and it is not preferable for the planter to be the only one able to teach. As you select teachers, it is vitally important to ensure that all are in full agreement with the vision and values of the congregation, and able to explain them to others.

RECRUITERS / EVANGELISTS

Recruiters and evangelists are networkers; people who can reach out into the community individually or as head of a team, sharing the Good News and inviting people to meetings and services. These individuals must be friendly and able to interact effectively with people, growing in the Lord and motivated by His love as they reach out to others.

LEADERS IN SHEPHERDING, CAREGIVING, FOLLOW-UP

This role is for people who are relational, motivated to intentionally care for those around them. A shepherd reaches out to those who may be in need, hurting, or wounded. This is essential, for a congregation must care for the weakest, even as Messiah demonstrated through His priorities as He ministered on earth. Strong leaders are needed to reach out and care for the least among us.

TREASURER & TRUSTEES

To fill these roles, you must find people who are trustworthy and above reproach, able to handle the business and administrative needs of the congregation. Members of this team will need to be in charge of official documents as well, such as tax forms and other matters required by the government. As you delegate these matters carefully, you will grow as wise stewards over what has been entrusted to you. Those who step up for this role may eventually be needed to assist in designing systems of accountability within the congregation.

GREETERS

The ministry of a greeter is of great importance as these people will convey the first impression a visitor receives upon entering your door. Greeters need to be friendly, approachable, possessing good people skills, and able to address questions visitors may have, either by answering or directing them to the right person. One leader will need to step up to organize those involved on the greeting team.

FACILITIES TEAM

The behind-the-scenes ministry of the facilities team is vital in the upkeep of a healthy congregation. This team takes care of set up and tear down for

Notes:

_____

_____

_____

_____

_____

_____

_____

_____

_____

_____

_____

_____

_____

_____

_____

_____

_____

services and events, as well as security for the congregation. The people on the facilities team must be willing to give of their time, arriving early before a service, and staying late afterwards in order to make sure everything is secure and ready for the next meeting. Again, one person will need to be the point person in charge of this team.

Notes:

TECH TEAM

Another important ministry is that of the "tech team," those who will run the A/V equipment at your meetings, as well as those responsible for the design of your materials (such as bulletins and visitor packets), your internet presence (website, social media), and logo. These areas are an increasingly important part of a congregation's identity. For these roles, look for people with an eye for practicality and good design (training in these skills as well would be helpful).

ONEG

Oneg is a time of extended fellowship after the service where food is provided. If a congregation does not offer an *oneg*, most people will not stay around long to *shmooze* after the service. The ministry of *oneg* provides an atmosphere for visitors to get to know the congregation better in a relaxed setting as contacts are being made. Normally, food such as bagels and cream cheese is sufficient, but at special services, other traditional dishes are appropriate to offer. The person coordinating the *oneg* needs to be organized and able to plan ahead, anticipating the needs of the visitors and members during various times of the year.

As you appoint different people to these leadership roles in your congregation, you need to make certain that they are all committed believers who have been discipled in your community and are all evaluating by the same paradigm and value system, regardless of the size of the ministry. They each must know what makes their particular ministry functional so that it can contribute to the functionality of the entire congregation. It is essential to ensure that all ministries of the congregation remain functional and healthy as one dysfunctional ministry will easily throw everything out of joint.

ADDITIONAL CONSIDERATIONS

In moving through the Core Group Development Stage, a core group should not call themselves a congregation until they are adequately prepared to handle the responsibilities as such. Up until this time, they may refer to themselves as a "fellowship," "*chavurah*," "*minyan*," or "Bible study." Though it may be tempting to identify yourselves as a congregation before this time, do not rush into this too quickly as certain systems must be in place before a congregation is ready to be born.

For instance, before the end of the Application Step, you will need to develop a budget detailing your probable expenses over time. Work on a draft of a three-year budget in which you prioritize the essentials for your congregation: rent, utilities, materials, etc. As you work through this, trust God to give the increase as He wills (Jacob 4:13-15). Remember that this document will be subject to change, but it is essential that you have a solid framework from which to begin. Also, before monies can be collected for the ministry, you must apply to be recognized as a non-profit entity (a 501-C3 in the United States). This is very important in order to be able to provide tax-deductible receipts to those who will give tithes and offerings. As you set up a bank account and work through these systems, you will need to appoint a treasurer to oversee these areas for your group.

If you have not done so already, also take time to create a draft of the calendar you will be implementing for your congregation. At the core of your annual calendar should be the various appointed feasts and other celebrations which characterize the Jewish year (See page 54). Be mindful that these special times will become crucial elements in the testimony of your congregation.

Through the Core Group Development Stage, you have been hard at work. First you have brought your core group of 10-15 family units to a unity of values through the Instruction Step. Following this, you developed a unity of priorities through the Integration Step. Finally, you have wrought a unity of service as tasks were understood and delegated through the Application Step.

As your core group is developed at the completion of these stages, you are now ready for the exciting step you have been waiting for: the consecration and birth of your new congregation! Be very careful to note, however, that

Notes:

_____

_____

_____

_____

_____

_____

_____

_____

_____

_____

_____

_____

_____

_____

_____

_____

_____

_____

_____

_____

_____

_____

_____

_____

_____

_____

_____

_____

_____

_____

_____

_____

_____

this consecration can only take place once you have fully completed all the previous steps, and the core group is adequately handling their basic responsibilities. Beware that you do not become impatient and try to begin your congregation too quickly with too few people. At this point you have a critical mass issue, as it takes a certain number of people just to keep a congregation running in a healthy manner. If you begin your congregation with too few people, you may become overwhelmed by the expectations of those who expect you to be doing the full work of an established congregation.

When I was asked on one occasion to provide counsel for a congregation that was struggling, I met with the leadership and quickly realized the problem. This group had birthed their congregation without having a solid mission and vision statement! Because the core group was getting impatient, they decided to go ahead with the birth of the congregation without these vital elements in place. Though it seemed like a good idea at the time, it led to great dysfunction as they struggled from a lack of firm foundation.

In order for a congregation to be healthy, its birth cannot be rushed. The importance of taking things one stage and step at a time cannot be overstated. Be very cautious of getting ahead of yourself, or allowing yourself to be pressured into doing things for which you are not yet ready.

CHAPTER 3

THE CONSECRATION STAGE

———————————◇———————————

"When they had appointed elders for them in every congregation, having prayed with fasting, they commended them to the Lord in whom they had believed." – Acts 14:23

Times of consecration are holy occasions which we take in order to set ourselves apart, personally before the Lord, and also publicly before others. When a couple declares their marriage vows to one other, it is a time of consecration. Through their wedding ceremony, they communicate to others how their marriage is going to work, what they believe in, and what they will prioritize in their life together.

The Consecration Stage is the official birth of your congregation. This is the moment you have been waiting for; for your core group, it is a milestone, a victory. *Mazel Tov*! Like a wedding, your consecration service will be a public testimony of your values: who you are, what you believe, and how you are going to live.

The length of this stage will vary depending on how long it will take to organize everything properly and carry out the consecration service wisely, potentially 1-3 months.

The Consecration Stage, the time between near birth and birth, consists of three steps:

✡ ***The Group Consecration:*** At this point, the core group will dedicate themselves to God as His congregation.

✡ *The Leaders' Consecration:* Then, the leaders will dedicate themselves to God as His servants.

✡ *The Public Consecration:* Finally, the congregation will dedicate itself to God through a public ceremony.

Notes:

THE GROUP CONSECRATION

At this point, the group will set themselves apart to the Lord as His congregation, recognizing that a Messianic congregation is a holy community.

During this time, the core group will affirm the truth that they are called to be a light in the darkness, and establish themselves to live this out as a community. It is vitally important that the core group truly view themselves in this way because this is how God sees them. We need to have a high view of our holy calling before God, as God Himself does, and press on to the high mark of it.

As a group, this is when you will vote yourselves in as the founding members of the congregation (Romans 11:16). You will also vote in your Constitution, your Articles of Faith, and your Mission and Values statements. Through this process, you are recognizing that these are the tools you will utilize in your congregation to do the work God has called you to.

THE LEADERS' CONSECRATION

The leaders also will take this time to consecrate themselves as servants of a holy God in this congregation of holy people. This is a very important time to recognize your leaders for stepping up as servants in the congregation. We call our leaders servant-leaders because we see them as people who are called to serve as they lead in the community.

This great calling and responsibility is not to be taken lightly. We see in Scripture that the closer to the Holy of Holies the *kohanim* (the priests) served, the more circumspectly they had to walk. From this we understand that to whom much is given, much is required. We give due appreciation to those who step up to serve in the congregation.

THE PUBLIC CONSECRATION

Now comes the time when the congregation as a whole will dedicate themselves to God in a public consecration service.

This service is a wonderful opportunity to testify of God's faithfulness to your community, and a joy to plan together. During the consecration service, you get to explain who you are as a community, and the reason why you are planting a Messianic congregation. This is a time to clearly explain to all who are present that you are not Messianic simply because you like Jewish things, but in order to testify of Messiah. You exist to proclaim God's faithfulness to Israel and the nations as you lift up His Name.

For this public service, make it a point to invite those people who have supported and prayed for you, including local pastors in the area who have been an encouragement to you. This is a wonderful opportunity to invite people from your local community to rejoice with you and to hear Good News!

As you plan the details of the consecration service, think about the best time for which to hold it. *Shavuot* (Pentecost), the anniversary of the birth of the Body of Messiah, is always an appropriate time for a consecration service, though other times of year can be very meaningful as well. If the space is available, plan to hold the service at the location where you will be meeting regularly so that guests will know where to come back to. Delegate each task involved in carrying out the service, making preparations for a nice *oneg* afterwards, in order to welcome and make contacts with your visitors.

This consecration service is your "kick-off," serving to demonstrate to the community what your group is all about, and letting people know that from here on out, this is what you will be doing every week as a Messianic congregation.

Notes:

_____

_____

_____

_____

_____

_____

_____

_____

_____

_____

_____

_____

_____

_____

PART 2

ESSENTIAL SYSTEMS
OF A HEALTHY
CONGREGATION

CHAPTER 4

MEASURING HEALTH

So far, we have taken a broad look at the process by which a healthy Messianic congregation is planted. Now, we will take a step deeper, expanding on the essential responsibilities and systems of a healthy congregation which we touched on during the Integration Step of the Core Group Development Stage. In order to be able to fully explain these systems to your core group during the Integration Step, you must have a firm grasp of these matters. Through your study and presentation of these essential matters, your core group will begin to see how a congregation is to properly function according to God's Word, what ministries are to be prioritized, and how leadership will therefore be able to evaluate functionality. These are the building blocks through which a unified Messianic community is grown.

This material is to be used in the establishment of new congregations, but also as an evaluation tool for those already established. Just as a doctor has a paradigm of health by which he measures his patients, we have a biblical paradigm by which we measure our congregations. And, just like a patient, when we do not measure up, we do not need to see it as a personal failure leading to guilt, but rather use the paradigm as a guide in order to better grow in health. As you evaluate your congregation in each of these areas, first pinpoint the areas that are already healthy, and appreciate all that you are doing right!

Before we address the three essential responsibilities of a healthy congregation, let us consider several other factors which contribute to congregational health.

3-SELF THROUGH THE SPIRIT

A healthy Messianic congregation has a "3-Self" (Through the Spirit) structure. This means it is:

Notes:

✡ Self-Supported

A healthy congregation realizes that depending on outside sources for support brings weakness and lack of ownership. An example of this principle is seen in raising children: If you are supporting your children financially, you as a parent determine what school they go to, what foods they eat, what clothes they buy, etc. The child will only be able to make these decisions on their own when they reach the point of being able to support themselves. Likewise, when others are paying for the operation of your congregation, they will have a say in what is done with the funds they provide.

✡ Self-Propagating

A healthy congregation also takes responsibility for their own growth. They do not depend on others to do the tasks of outreach and evangelism for them. Although God may use people from outside the congregation to build up His body, you must have a plan to move forward in these areas and not depend on others for the propagation of the message.

✡ Self-Governed

Finally, a healthy congregation must ensure that there are no outside groups making decisions for them. The congregation should be led by its own leadership who are led of the Spirit. These people are accountable to God and each other to make decisions which are reflective of the Word of God.

THE "WIFE" OF YESHUA

We can also define a healthy congregation by its functionality, as the "WIFE" of Yeshua, serving as a:

✡ **W**orship Center

"My house will be called a house of prayer for all the peoples." – Isaiah 56:7

If nothing else, God would have us to be a praying and worshipping community. Through our prayer and worship together, we are preparing for our life before the throne in heaven. As we worship with "all peoples," it seems that God does not want us to be any pickier than He is!

✡ Instruction Center

"For the commandment is a lamp and the teaching is light; and reproofs for discipline are the way of life." – Proverbs 6:23

Admittedly, this is a bit of a "chicken and egg" situation. Prayer is certainly of utmost importance in a congregation, but there cannot be proper worship without proper biblical instruction. False teaching leads to false worship, and so proper biblical discipleship is required for proper biblical worship. Indeed, there is no worship or spiritual growth apart from God's Word.

✡ Fellowship Center

"A new commandment I give to you, that you love one another, even as I have loved you, that you also love one another. By this all men will know that you are My disciples, if you have love for one another." - John 13:34-35

As hard as it is for the carnal mind to understand, God is love. In other words, God is relational, and we cannot be godly (like God) if we do not love one another. This love is our most effective testimony, even as David wrote, *"Behold how good and pleasant it is for brothers to dwell together in unity"* (Psalm 133:1).

✡ Evangelistic Center

"But you, be sober in all things, endure hardship, do the work of an evangelist, fulfill your ministry." - 2 Timothy 4:5

Though in heaven there will not be anyone to whom we can witness, here on earth, this is our commission from the Lord (Mark 16:15). We are called to be witnesses of Yeshua to the community around us as well as to people around the world. Every Messianic congregation should not only have established programs for outreach, but also encourage and train its members to share Messiah even *"to the Jew first and also to the Gentile"* (Romans 1:16). Right from the beginning, encourage those in your congregation to "each one, reach one."

THE ICEBERG PRINCIPLE

There is much more to a healthy, functioning congregation than meets the eye. A congregation does not become effective simply because it has solid teaching or powerful worship. Effectiveness is tied to faithfulness, and this goes far deeper than the externals.

Just as the largest part of an iceberg lies beneath the water, unseen, so there is always more going on below the surface than meets the eye. Indeed, most of the functioning of a healthy congregation takes place "below the water line." What you see above the surface is only possible because of the remaining seven-eighths below. As you are faithful in the areas which people cannot see, you will serve to present an effective testimony which will be seen by all.

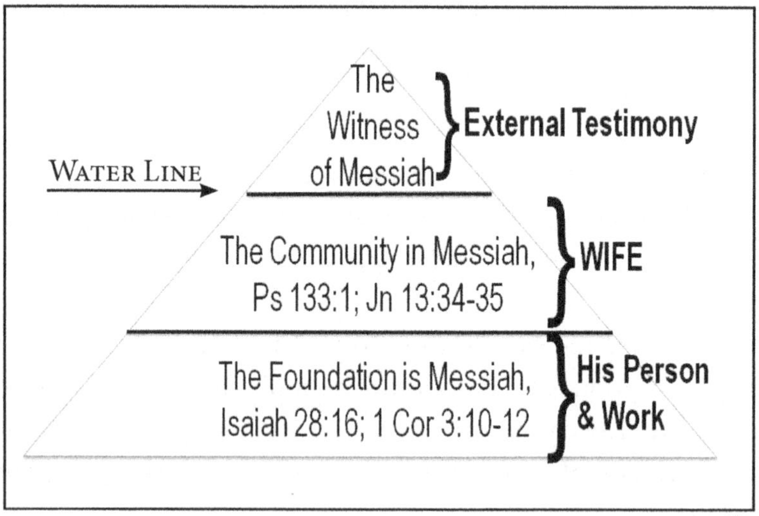

The
Witness } External Testimony
WATER LINE →   of Messiah

The Community in Messiah, } WIFE
Ps 133:1; Jn 13:34-35

The Foundation is Messiah, } His Person
Isaiah 28:16; 1 Cor 3:10-12   & Work

Figure 4.0

The foundation of our congregational "iceberg" must be Messiah, for no other foundation can be laid apart from Him (1 Corinthians 3:11, Isaiah 28:16). In Him we have redemption, forgiveness, and salvation; every spiritual blessing is only found in Him (See Ephesians 1). He is our everything, and He must be foundational in all we do in ministry.

Built upon this foundation is what we just looked at: the Community of Messiah, the "WIFE." In order for your community to be a community, there must be more to the ministry of your congregation than simply what happens on Saturday mornings. All of this behind-the-scenes work contributes to your community's witness of Messiah, the part of your community that others can see. If the externals are all that there is to your community, you have a big problem. Without the rest of the iceberg present below the water line, you are just an ice cube, floating around without any substance.

We build a firm foundation below the water line so that we can have a legitimate external testimony of Messiah above the water line. All that we do externally is for the purpose of our witness; for the sake of others. This is true in every area of life. When a young man or woman tells you, "I can wear whatever I want to," this is just not true. We dress to honor the Lord, not to distract other men or women. We need to teach others to be wise in these matters of public testimony. Just as you put a bumper sticker on your car in order to communicate a message to others, all that you do outwardly communicates something to others about your God.

THE ESSENTIAL SYSTEMS OF A CONGREGATION

We are now ready to delve into the essential responsibilities and systems of a healthy Messianic congregation: the ministry of Prayer / Worship, the Ministry of the Word, and the Ministry of Overseer.

These three areas are taught as normative throughout Scripture, both for the people of Israel (Exodus 18:19-22) and for congregational life (Acts 6:1-7). On pages 172 - 181, we will take an in-depth look at these passages in light of their application for us today.

THE RESPONSIBILITY OF WORSHIP

Ministry of Prayer

Prayer and worship provide the spiritual support of the community. The first lesson Israel learned after coming out of Egypt was that God was their Provider, for He brought forth water for them in the desert, even from a rock. Following this, they learned that He was also their Protector. As we covered earlier, He protected Israel during their first battle with the Amalakites, fighting for them as Aaron and Hur helped keep Moses' hands lifted in prayer. Through these experiences, Israel learned that the most important thing a person or nation can do is pray. It is not about the size of your army or congregation, or even your level of maturity, it is about your prayer life. It is God alone Who gives the increase, Who protects you, and Who brings the victory.

Notes:

THE RESPONSIBILITY OF TEACHING

Ministry of the Word

The ministry of the Word provides the spiritual maturing in the congregation, for solid food is for the mature (Hebrews 5:14). The Word of God is what matures us; therefore, we must prioritize a nutritious diet of the Word. Once, when asked what he was teaching to his congregation, a leader responded, "I only have two sermons, but 84 titles." Be careful of this. You need to make sure you are feeding your flock properly, not just clothing the same teaching in different packaging. We must faithfully administer the full counsel of God. (See Appendix 1 for more information on the process of preparation and presentation in teaching God's Word.)

THE RESPONSIBILITY OF MANAGING

Ministry of Overseer

The overseer ministry is what develops the spiritual fellowship for the congregation. For successful gatherings of prayer, worship, and fellowship, there must be people working behind the scenes, letting others know what is going on and when to arrive. The congregational leader must delegate this ministry to those who are gifted accordingly so that he can be free to focus on praying for his flock and administering the Word to them (Acts 6:2-3).

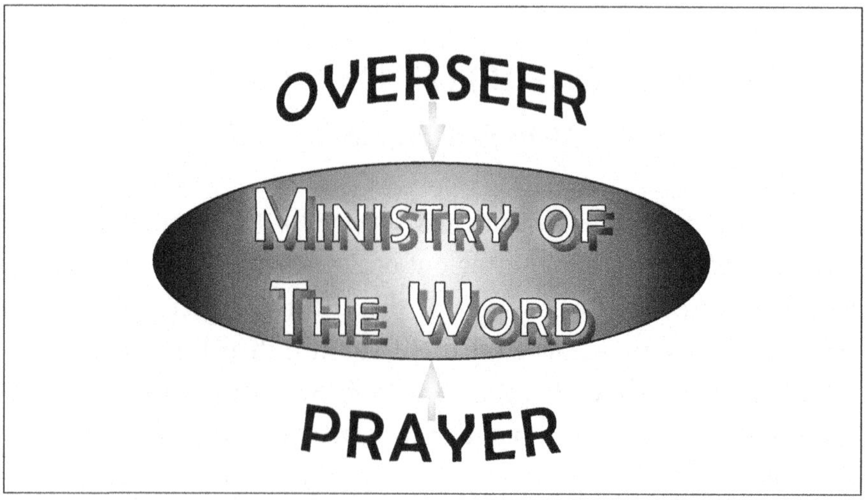

Notes:

Figure 4.1

THE REDEMPTIVE WORK OF MESSIAH

You might be wondering why the three areas of prayer, the Word, and overseer keep coming up in so many places throughout the Bible. This is because they all point to Yeshua! We see prophesied throughout the *Tanakh* that there are three areas of work which Messiah would perform. These He continues to perform in order to redeem those He loves.

MESSIAH'S WORK AS HIGH PRIEST

Ministry of Prayer

"The Lord has sworn and will not change His mind, 'You are a priest forever according to the order of Melchizedek.'" – Psalm 110:4

Messiah ever lives to make intercession for us (Hebrews 7:25). If it was not for this, there would be no way we could come to the Father, into the very presence of God. Messiah took His own blood before the Father and, as our *Kohen Gadol* (High Priest) sprinkled it accordingly so that we could be atoned. We need Him every day in order to have a relationship with God.

MESSIAH'S WORK AS PROPHET

Ministry of the Word

"The Lord your God will raise up for you a prophet like me from among you, from your countrymen, you shall listen to Him" – Deuteronomy 18:15

Messiah is the Living Word, the fulfillment of all Torah. He was not simply a prophet like Moses, but the One whom Moses was prophesying about! What Yeshua said in John 5:39 is also stated in the *Talmud* in Berachot 32b, *"All the prophets spoke only for the days of Messiah."* We see in Scripture as well as in Jewish thought that this is normative; all of Scripture is about Messiah, the greatest Prophet, indeed our Living Torah, the Living Word made flesh.

Notes:

_____

_____

_____

_____

_____

_____

_____

_____

_____

_____

_____

_____

_____

_____

MESSIAH'S WORK AS KING

Ministry of Overseer

"For a child will be born to us, a son will be given to us; and the government will rest on His shoulders; and His name will be called Wonderful Counselor, Mighty God, Eternal Father, Prince of Peace. There will be no end to the increase of His government or of peace, on the throne of David and over his kingdom, to establish it and to uphold it with justice and righteousness from then on and forevermore. The zeal of the LORD of hosts will accomplish this."
– Isaiah 9:6-7

Messiah is the King of Kings, the greater Son of David. He oversees our activities by His absolute authority, reigning with justice over our hearts and lives. He is the King who leads us in victory; all authority in heaven and on earth has been given unto Him (Matthew 28:18). Yeshua is God's redemptive ruler who oversees the fellowship of His people (Colossians 3:15).

THE RESPONSIBILITY OF THE LEADERSHIP

"As He is, so are we in the world" - 1 John 4:17

As we consider Messiah's work as Priest, Prophet, and King, and how He took these roles upon Himself in order to secure our redemption, we give Him praise, honor, and glory. As His representatives in this world, these three roles must now become our responsibilities. The ministries of prayer, the Word, and overseer are intrinsic to the congregation as they are first the responsibility of the leadership. All ministries in the congregation, even those not under the direct stewardship of the elders, should fall under one of these three categories. If a ministry does not represent Messiah, there is no reason to continue with it. Do not allow anything to take up ground in your congregation that will not serve to bear fruit. Messiah is the Head and we are the Body, and as we are yielded to the Head, we function as:

THE PRIEST WHO REQUESTS

Each week as we speak the *Birkat HaKohanim* (the Aaronic benediction) over our congregation, we are reminded of our priestly role and remember that this is just a picture of what Yeshua is doing forever, placing His Name upon us. In the godly role we have been given in our congregations, we undergird everything in prayer. When we are walking with the Lord and continually praying, we are His representatives. An active intercessory ministry is vital to the health of both a congregational leader and his congregation.

THE PROPHET WHO REVEALS

You represent Yeshua's work as prophet in your congregation as you lead in the ministry of the Word. In teaching the Word, you are His mouthpiece. In Scripture, we see that the work of the prophets was not only foretelling, but rather mostly forth-telling, exhorting people to take heed and obey God's Word. Indeed, *"the testimony of Yeshua is the Spirit of prophecy"* (Revelation 19:10). As you faithfully study and teach God's Word in your congregation, you serve as God's mouthpiece to edify and exhort the Body.

THE KING WHO RULES

In our ministry as overseer, we represent Yeshua's rulership. We take responsibility for our role as elders in the congregation as we address issues, delegate service, and provide organization and schedules to ensure that the flock is well taken care of.

Some may wonder how a person can be an effective leader if they do not use their authority to "crack the whip," so to speak. To address this, let us consider the first Scriptural mention of the word, "rule." In Genesis 1, we were told to "be fruitful," "multiply," "subdue," and "rule" (Genesis 1:26-28). Yet at this point, there was nothing to correct, judge, or restrain since sin had not yet entered into the world. What then was God's intention when He commanded man to rule? We find the answer in the way God Himself modeled ruling. As God created the world, He said over and over again, *"tov"* (good), and when He created humanity, He proclaimed, *"tov ma'od!"* (very good!) Following His example, we affirm, build up, and thank people for their service. We are here as servant leaders to encourage people in a redeemed community. This is what our leadership is about. As we serve as leader in our congregations, we make sure that people are healthy and growing, not being dominated. His model becomes our mission through our service as His reps.

A CONGREGATIONAL PARADIGM

Notes:

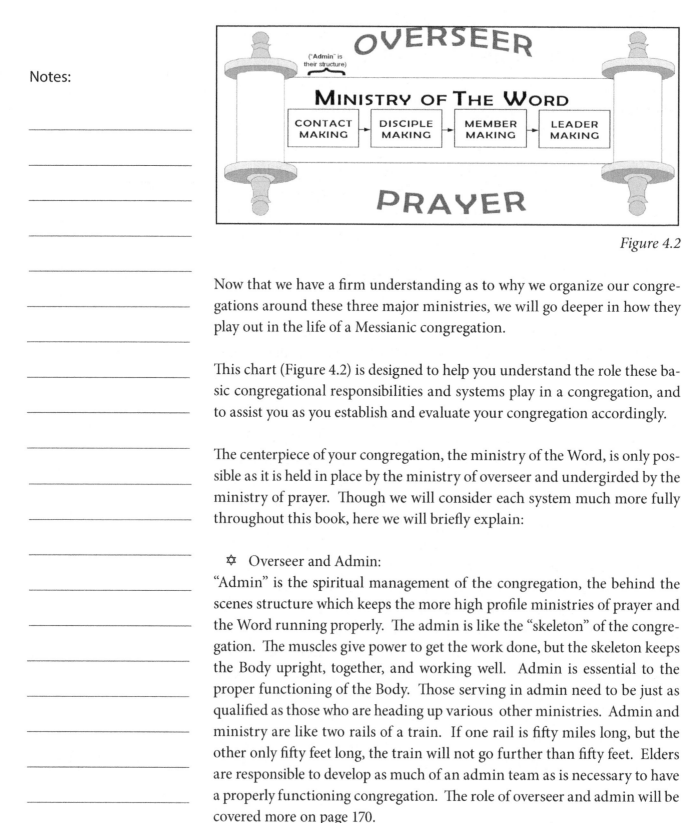

Figure 4.2

Now that we have a firm understanding as to why we organize our congregations around these three major ministries, we will go deeper in how they play out in the life of a Messianic congregation.

This chart (Figure 4.2) is designed to help you understand the role these basic congregational responsibilities and systems play in a congregation, and to assist you as you establish and evaluate your congregation accordingly.

The centerpiece of your congregation, the ministry of the Word, is only possible as it is held in place by the ministry of overseer and undergirded by the ministry of prayer. Though we will consider each system much more fully throughout this book, here we will briefly explain:

✡ Overseer and Admin:

"Admin" is the spiritual management of the congregation, the behind the scenes structure which keeps the more high profile ministries of prayer and the Word running properly. The admin is like the "skeleton" of the congregation. The muscles give power to get the work done, but the skeleton keeps the Body upright, together, and working well. Admin is essential to the proper functioning of the Body. Those serving in admin need to be just as qualified as those who are heading up various other ministries. Admin and ministry are like two rails of a train. If one rail is fifty miles long, but the other only fifty feet long, the train will not go further than fifty feet. Elders are responsible to develop as much of an admin team as is necessary to have a properly functioning congregation. The role of overseer and admin will be covered more on page 170.

The ministry of the Word encompasses several different areas, progressing naturally step by step:

✡ Contact Making:
The ministry of the Word starts with "Contact Making." Remember, we not only want to share the Good News, but make contacts with people, making sure we collect their information for follow-up. This is crucial, because it is through our contacts that we make disciples. Contact making is for the purpose of disciple making, not merely recruiting people to fill empty seats. Contact making will be covered more on page 125.

✡ Disciple Making:
In order to have a healthy community, we must have healthy people who are discipled in the faith. As contacts are made and people come to faith, they must now be discipled. If you fail to do this, a congregation full of undiscipled people will eventually undermine your community. Disciple making will be covered more on page 129.

✡ Member Making:
As they are discipled, people then move into membership in a congregation. Each person who is committed to your community needs to be brought to the same page regarding the mission, vision, and values of your congregation. As members, each must be shown equal love and care. Member making builds up your congregation; however, it is not an end in itself, for it is also the means by which leadership is developed. Member making will be covered more on page 148.

✡ Leader Making:
You do not get leaders from other places, you develop them. Leadership comes out of a membership that is properly discipled. In one of the congregations that I have planted, one-third of the people in the community are in leadership roles. Many are surprised to learn that all of these leaders have come from within the congregation. This paradigm of leadership development begins in your family as you train your children to be future leaders of a new home. Leader making will be covered more on page 156.

✡ Prayer:
Success in ministry is found not in working harder, but in praying more! An organized system to ensure that prayer is happening in your community is of utmost importance. The ministry of prayer will be covered more on page 115.

Notes:

This paradigm of a congregation's essential systems and responsibilities will only be effective as we are:

TOTALLY DEPENDENT ON YESHUA

Notes:

_____

_____

_____

_____

_____

_____

_____

_____

_____

_____

_____

_____

_____

_____

_____

_____

_____

_____

"Speaking the truth in love, we are to grow up in all aspects into Him who is the Head, the Messiah" - Ephesians 4:15

We have no foundation other than Yeshua. We must abide and depend upon Him in everything. Never let people forget that this is the most important thing for their families, their souls, and their community.

TOTALLY INTER-DEPENDENT WITH EACH OTHER

"from whom the whole body, being fitted and held together by what every joint supplies, when each part is working properly, causes the growth of the Body for the building itself up in love." - Ephesians 4:16

✡ We need each other
Each time a person joins our congregation, we must recognize that this is of the Lord. Many times we do not know our specific needs, but with each new contact, disciple, member, and leader, the Lord gives us someone precious who fulfills a need that we have. Each person has something unique that they contribute to the Body. We are designed to be totally inter-dependent with each other, not holy hermits, only to emerge once a week on Shabbat.

✡ We need discipleship
Ephesians 4:16 reveals that the Body is held together when each part is working properly. We make sure of this through proper discipleship. Only through discipleship can a person learn how to be a functional member of the Body of Messiah.

✡ We need to love
We exist in order to love and be loved. Growth in love is vitally important to the functioning of a healthy congregation.

CHAPTER 5

THE MINISTRY OF PRAYER

———◇———

The ministry of prayer/worship is the most important responsibility that we have because it undergirds everything else that takes place in the congregation. In *olam haba* (the world to come), there will be no more need to evangelize or disciple; however, prayer will continue to be the focus of our lives. Our prayer life on earth prepares us for our prayer life in heaven. We consider prayer and worship together because, whether we are singing or speaking, we bring our praise and supplications to the Lord in order to bless and bring honor to Him.

We prioritize training in prayer, knowing that this spiritual discipline does not come naturally. Instruction in prayer must be a part of basic congregational *talmidut*. Discipleship in prayer should never be assumed, even if a person has been a believer for many years. Many whom I have discipled have confided that though they had come to personal faith in Yeshua years before, they still did not have a fervent prayer life and did not feel comfortable praying out loud. These men were not expected to serve in any capacity in their previous congregations, and so were able to fit in just by showing up for worship services. Our congregations must not allow this to happen, but must be places for people to grow as praying disciples.

Through discipleship in prayer, we train the people in our congregations to:

- ✡ Cast their cares upon Him, 1 Peter 5:7
- ✡ Confess their sins to Him, 1 John 1:9
- ✡ Count on *Ruach HaKodesh*, Romans 8:26-27
- ✡ Consider the love, grace and glory of Yeshua.

PRAYER IN OUR BATTLES

"So it came about when Moses held his hand up, that Israel prevailed, and when he let his hand down, Amalek prevailed." – Exodus 17:11

Notes:

Our spiritual battles will not be resolved by strong personalities, but rather by prayer. As we saw earlier, this is how we won our first battle after leaving Egypt (Exodus 17), and this is also how we can be victorious over infighting in a congregation. Prayer was and is the essential issue for victory; for Israel, for our homes, and for our congregations. Prayer is our God-given way to respond to the problems and circumstances of life, and we saw early on that victories would only be possible through prayer.

After the victory over Amalek, Moses instructed that these events be written down as a memorial to be given to Joshua. Why Joshua? Perhaps Joshua, as a military leader and action-oriented man, would need to be reminded to pray rather than to fight in his own strength. In the book of Joshua we read of only two defeats, both resulting from prayerlessness. In Chapter 7, Joshua resorted to prayer only after a humbling defeat, and in Chapter 9, he did not pray before negotiating with an enemy. Lack of prayer can lead to defeat in any congregation, but victory will come as leaders model the necessity of prayer.

Once I was asked to assist a congregation that was continually struggling with division among their members. When I asked the congregational leader about his prayer life, I was taken aback as he told me that he does not like to pray. He spends hours of time each week studying the Word, but neglects to talk to God. This must not be so among us. Prayer is absolutely essential and must be at the center of all that we do. We must keep our eyes focused on Him, depending on Him through prayer, and never giving up or becoming discouraged.

PRAYER IN OUR FELLOWSHIP

"They were continually devoting themselves to the apostles' teaching and to fellowship, to the breaking of bread and to prayer." – Acts 2:42

God's desire for our congregations is that they be a *beit tefilah* (house of prayer) for all peoples (Isaiah 56:7). True fellowship occurs as people come together around the primary matters of prayer and worship. This builds unity in our communities, and opens the door for others to join with us.

PRAYER IN OUR SERVICES

"First of all, then, I urge that entreaties and prayers, petitions and thanksgivings, be made on behalf of all men." – 1 Timothy 2:1

Paul instructed Timothy as overseer of the congregation in Ephesus that prayer is of first importance in congregational life. All prayer, however, must flow out of a basis of sound biblical teaching (1 Timothy 1). This must be the basis of our prayer and worship ministry, otherwise people will not know about the One to whom they are praying. A person can be praying sincerely, but may not be praying as God desires. We know how to pray because Scripture teaches us how to pray. When Yeshua spoke to the Samaritan woman at the well (John 4), He emphasized this. As a result of their lack of sound teaching, the Samaritans' worship was wrong even though it was sincere (John 4:22-23). It is very possible to be sincere, yet wrong. We must guard against this by keeping strong biblical teaching at the heart of our prayer and worship ministry.

THE ELDERS IN PRAYER

As Yeshua ever lives to make intercession for us, so the elders of a congregation represent Him in their various prayer minstries, serving here on earth, and preparing to serve Yeshua in heaven.

THE ELDERS ON EARTH ARE PRAYING

"Therefore I want the men in every place to pray, lifting up holy hands, without wrath and dissension." – 1 Timothy 2:8

Elder-led prayer is biblically normative (Exodus 17:11, Jacob 5:14, Hebrews 13:17). Paul instructed Timothy that men were to be the ones lifting their hands in prayer, setting the pattern that men are the ones God has called to normally lead in prayer. This is true in the home as well. If men are not leading in prayer at home, how can they be expected to lead in prayer in the congregation (1 Timothy 3:5)? Not only do the elders lead in public prayer as a community, they also need to be praying for the community. Who knows

Notes:

what battles our "Joshua's" are fighting at home, at school and at work?

THE ELDERS IN HEAVEN ARE PRAYING

"the twenty-four elders will fall down before Him who sits on the throne, and will worship Him who lives forever and ever ..." – Revelation 4:10

Notes:

In the Biblical picture of heaven, the elders are forever falling down on their face before God, leading in prayer and worship (Revelation 4:10, 5:8, 14; 7:11; 11:16; 19:4). Whether in the home or in the congregation, prayer prepares us for heavenly service like nothing else can.

QUALIFIED LEADERS FOR PRAYER & WORSHIP

"Casting all your anxiety on Him, because He cares for you." – 1 Peter 5:7

Those leading a prayer team must first be people of prayer themselves. Those on our worship teams must be prayer leaders, that is, men and women with a strong prayer life. Having musical skills and a good voice has value, but is no substitute for prayer. An individual's prayer and worship life helps foster his or her healthy relationship with the Lord, and so all team members must desire deeper levels of prayer and worship. This is a matter both of personal growth and integrity before the Lord.

Those praying for others need to be able to cast their own cares on the Lord before they share in bearing the burdens of others. Prayer leaders should continually intercede for others and make themselves available to minister to those with prayer needs after the service. As you choose the people who will serve in this capacity, it is important to take into account the fact that visitors will likely consider anyone who serves from the front to be a leader capable of answering their questions. It may be tempting in the beginning stages of your congregation to allow any willing person to step up and lead in public prayer, but we must remember that this person will be expected to represent the congregation; therefore we should not lay hands on anyone too hastily (1 Timothy 5:22). Over time, more leaders can be trained and entrusted to represent the values which accompany their responsibility.

LITURGY & INTENTIONALITY

All prayer and worship must be from the heart

"… this people draw near with their words and honor Me with their lip service, but they remove their hearts far from Me, and their reverence for Me consists of tradition learned by rote" – Isaiah 29:13

Notes:

In order to be pleasing to God, prayer and worship must always be from the heart and not from rote tradition (John 4:22-23). Praying with intention (*kavanah*) is also a value in traditional Judaism. However, many will chant liturgical Hebrew prayers by rote memory without thinking about or understanding their meaning. There is certainly a value in using Hebrew prayers in your services, especially if your congregation is in a religious Jewish community. A problem arises, however, when no translation is provided for these prayers (or worship songs). It is also just as problematic when an evangelical worship service is designed to give a "worship experience" to the people participating. Caution must be taken in these areas because we give our *avodah* (worship) to honor *HaShem* ("the Name," a traditional way of refeering to God), not to fulfill a duty or to get something out of it for ourselves.

We must ensure that everyone can understand and participate in our services, without favoritism toward anyone. Paul emphasized this as he wrote to the Corinthian believers who were more desirous for public spiritual gifts than they were for the edification of others (1 Corinthians 14:13-17). All public prayer and worship must be presented or translated into the language of the community, conducted for the edification of all, so that all may participate with *kavanah*.

PRAYER IN YESHUA'S NAME

"Speaking to one another in psalms and hymns and spiritual songs, singing and making melody with your heart to the Lord; always give thanks for everything to God the Father in the Name of our Lord Yeshua the Messiah." - Ephesians 5:19-20

All prayer and worship is to be conducted in Yeshua's Name, and done for His honor. The congregation must have an understanding that this is what it means to pray *b'Shem Yeshua* (in the name of Yeshua), for if Yeshua is not honored, there is no true worship. All Messianic congregations must be Yeshua-oriented in their prayer and worship. As our Intercessor (Hebrews 7:25), Yeshua taught us that He is the only way to the Father (John 14:6).

ORDER & EDIFICATION

"But all things must be done properly and in an orderly manner." – 1 Corinthians 14:40

In 1 Corinthians 12-14, Paul gives much instruction about public worship. These chapters particularly focus on the congregational management of the gifts of prophecy and tongues. Since everything must be done in an *"orderly manner,"* if a person wishes to share something with the congregation, they must first bring it to the leadership who will decide if it would be profitable to share or better kept private. Through this teaching, we see that what is said privately, in one's own prayer closet, is for one's own edification, but that what is said in the congregation must be for the edification of all. Scripture gives us much instruction on the difference between private and public prayer:

Private Prayer	Public Prayer
Understandable to God (Romans 8:26)	Understandable to others (1 Corinthians 14:16-17)
As long as you want (Luke 6:12)	Succinct (Matthew 6:7-8)
Always and Constantly (1 Thessalonians 5:17)	Prioritized and Regular (1 Timothy 2:1)
Freely and openly (1 Peter 5:7)	Of sound mind and sensibly (2 Corinthians 5:13)
For one's own edification (1 Corinthians 14:2, 28)	For everyone's edification (1 Corinthians 14:16-17)

MUSIC IN WORSHIP

"Praise Him with trumpet sound; praise Him with harp and lyre. Praise Him with timbrel and dancing; praise Him with stringed instruments and pipe … Let everything that has breath praise the Lord!" – Psalm 150:3-6

The Messianic community has produced a great amount of worship music, especially in its pioneer days. When this music was first coming out, it was seen as cutting edge, even as Messianic ministry was seen as new in contrast to the normal Gentile cultural expression of worship in the greater Body of Messiah.

Times have changed, and this early music marked by its use of the minor key does not always have the same impact it once did. New Messianic worship songs are being produced and each community is finding its own unique expression of worship. In order to best reach their communities, congregations should experiment with different types of music as long as they hold to the same scriptural values and remain decidedly Messianic in accordance with our calling. Ultimately, it is the worship of *HaShem* that matters, not the musicians or musical style used. We must always seek to play music which focuses attention on Him so people in our congregations can readily worship.

As you plan your worship service, there are other matters to consider as well. For instance, if your congregation has a full liturgy and Torah service, as well as a full instrumental worship set, this may be difficult for some of your families and older congregants to sit through. If you desire to have an especially long worship service, you could set aside special evenings for this purpose rather than having it be your normal Shabbat routine. It is important that the leadership team discuss necessary time constraints beforehand rather than allow the worship leader to extend the worship time as long as he or she sees fit. Restraint is needed for worship leaders as well as for teachers as you seek to edify your flock without wearing them out.

DEVELOPING IN PRAYER & WORSHIP

"Pray without ceasing" – 1 Thessalonians 5:17

In the early stages of your congregation, your worship services will be limited by the personnel and training you have available. Despite your limitations, setting public prayer as a priority from the very beginning will reinforce the essential value of prayer to your core group. Every gathering should begin and end with prayer, and prayer continually presented as central to the life of the congregation. This is an intentional lifestyle choice which is vital to the growth of the maturing believer and growing congregation.

Notes:

121

THE SYSTEM FOR PRAYER

Notes:

_____

_____

_____

_____

_____

_____

_____

_____

_____

_____

_____

_____

_____

_____

_____

_____

_____

It is of great benefit to develop a prayer team who can meet together regularly in order to lift up the community, as well as pray for specific requests from members and visitors.

PRAYER NEEDS COLLECTED: PROPERLY

In light of the sensitive nature of prayer needs, the person to receive or collect prayer requests should be a trusted member of the congregation. Only those who share in the values of the congregation can share in the problems and their solutions through prayer.

PRAYER NEEDS DISTRIBUTED: LIMITEDLY

The prayer requests can then be passed along to the prayer team of members committed to this task. A prayer team must value discretion, keeping all prayer requests strictly confidential. One must not talk to anyone, not even a spouse, about what they learn in prayer about another person's personal issues. If prayer needs are publicized by email, etc., care must be taken that they not be passed along to anyone outside of the congregation. This may seem obvious, but people need to be informed of this policy and the policy enforced. If a person is inclined to gossip, they should not be permitted to be a part of the prayer team.

PRAYER NEEDS PRAYED: DISCREETLY

Prayer requests for a third party who has not requested public prayer should not be voiced within the congregation. No matter how good the intentions are, problems can arise when spouses or friends use public prayer for those they are concerned for. This situation often leads to more embarrassment than help.

Prayer and worship is the priority of a Messianic congregation; it is our joy to honor our Messiah in this way, and to lead others in praise of His Name. Prayer and worship undergirds the ministry of the Word as it brings us into communion with God through Yeshua, our High Priest and Intercessor. The necessity of prayer in all aspects of congregational life cannot be overstated. Many times, the failure to pray is the reason for failure. God says that we have not because we ask not (Jacob 4:2). In light of this, let us "draw near with confidence to the throne of grace, so that we may receive mercy and find grace to help in time of need." – Hebrews 4:16

Notes:

_____

_____

_____

_____

_____

_____

_____

_____

_____

_____

_____

_____

_____

_____

_____

_____

CHAPTER 6

THE MINISTRY OF THE WORD

The ministry of the Word has two dimensions of service: inward and outward. Within the Body of Messiah, God's Word provides edification, and outside the Body, that same Word ministers through evangelization. The Word testifies of Yeshua, and *"the testimony of Yeshua is the spirit of prophecy"* (Revelation 19:10). We proclaim the Living Word according to the written Word, and proclaim the written Word to exalt the Living Word.

There is no spiritual growth apart from God's Word. 1 Peter teaches us to *"desire the pure milk of the Word, so that by it you may grow in respect to your salvation"* (1 Peter 2:2). As the Word is taught, it must be applied, for without consistent application of the Word there can be no spiritual discernment (Hebrews 5:14). This is why His Word is the lamp for our feet and a light for our paths and life (Psalm 119:105, Proverbs 6:23).

The ministry of the Word consists of four different steps: contact making, disciple making, member making, and leader making. Each of these steps flows naturally into the next, as people are developed through the ministry of the Word. Though we covered aspects of some of these steps earlier through the Outreach and Discipleship Steps of the Gathering Stage, we will now consider the continued role outreach and discipleship will play in an established congregation, and how they will lead naturally into membership and then leadership.

Each step will grow to become a system in itself within the congregation, and each must remain a continual focus in order for a congregation to grow and develop.

CONTACT MAKING SYSTEM

Finding them, Filing them, & Following up on them

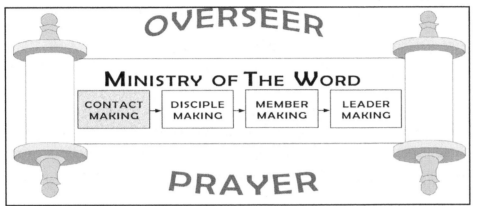

Figure 6.0

Notes:

As we discussed earlier, contact making must be established as part of the DNA of a congregation; it must be understood as the rule, not the exception. The very calling of Israel is to be a witness, a light to the nations; this comes out of living for the Lord (Isaiah 43, 44). Outreach is vital for the health of your community as well as for your own soul. Members must be taught that as Messianic believers, we *are* witnesses, and therefore this is what we do. A firm grasp of this concept will help those who struggle with fear when it comes to witnessing. Sharing Messiah's love with neighbors and friends and inviting them to services are ordinary day-to-day activities for a believer. To help equip new members of our communities to embrace this as a normal part of life, it is helpful to include practical experience in outreach and evangelism as part of the membership process.

As leaders, we model the values that we want others to have. If we want those in our community to be witnessing, we must be doing this first. You may not have the gift of evangelism, but take opportunities as the Lord opens them up before you, praying for your neighbors, and reaching out to people wherever you are, at work, shops, and restaurants. Use these seed planting interactions as illustrations in your sermons so that your congregation will pick up on the fact that this is an important value in your community, a normal part of your everyday lives. Our job is simply to plant seeds of the Good News in people's lives, to pray for those people, and to persevere in reaching out by His grace and love. Encourage your congregation that God is the One who brings people to Himself, causing the seeds we have planted to grow.

FINDING CONTACTS

OUTSIDE OF MEETINGS

Notes:

External outreach needs to be creative & courageous

Getting the message out to the community can happen in various ways. As instruments of love, we need to be continually reaching out to people, going out to look for them, getting the salt out of the salt shaker. This should become a normative part of your congregation. (For ideas of activities to reach those outside of your community, see page 65).

AT VARIOUS MEETINGS

Internal outreach needs to be compassionate & caring

We are all created in the image of God to love and be loved; everyone is longing for this. People may visit your congregation or different *chavurot* for various reasons, perhaps for a holiday or event, or perhaps because they are simply curious about your community. All people, however, need love, and are designed to love and be loved in a healthy community. This love is what draws people to the Lord. The greatest thing you can do for your visitors is to simply love them. Indeed, the "sizzle sells the steak."

Encourage members of your congregation to invite visitors to your services, and do all you can to bring people in, as word of mouth is the best advertising for your congregation. Through holiday outreach services and special events, provide opportunities for members to invite their friends and family into the community. All members need to be trained in how to be welcoming and loving to visitors, but those in certain roles will need extra preparation.

The greeters at the door are the first people whom visitors will meet. They are a congregation's frontline evangelists. In light of this unique responsibility, it is vital that this important role be filled by people of prayer. Greeters need to be trained, both when they initially begin and also on an annual basis. They will also need to wear nametags and be equipped with information packets for new visitors and bulletins for everyone, to be handed out at the door.

Those serving in the *oneg* ministry must also be trained in how to interact with visitors, being available to talk with them and being intentional in providing a positive experience for new visitors. It speaks volumes to a visitor when people from the congregation notice them and take time to talk with them after the service, even for just a couple of minutes.

FILING CONTACTS

It is essential that you collect and file the contact information of each person who shows interest in your congregation, whether through your external or internal outreach. Find a mechanism of collecting names, email addresses, addresses, and phone numbers from visitors who wish to share them, perhaps through visitor information cards distributed by the greeters at the beginning of the service. Make sure to provide an opportunity for people to give their contact information, but respect those who do not wish to provide it.

As you collect contact information, you will need to develop a system for organizing and filing it, whether through a computerized database or file folder system. Figure out what works best for your congregation and then delegate this responsibility to a dedicated and organized member of your community to ensure that the information does not get lost. This is a vital part of your outreach ministry, and an opportunity for service for those with administrative gifts.

FOLLOWING UP ON CONTACTS

No matter how you choose to file the contacts, you must have a system in place to follow-up with each one of them. This is vitally important; never fail to follow-up. Follow-up can be carried out in the form of a simple phone call, email, or card, with the purpose of maintaining a relationship with the person. You must be careful not to impose yourself on them, but to let them know that you remember and care about them. In your interaction with these individuals, invite them back to your services, and let them know about other events going on in your community (*chavurahs*, Bible studies, special services, etc.)

Each person who fills out a visitor information card is indicating that they wish to have someone from the congregation contact them. Often when

Notes:

Notes:

I ask a second or third-time visitor the reason why they came back, they tell me that it was because someone talked to them after the service or that someone contacted them within a couple of weeks. After a person visits the congregation, you have a two-week window in order to follow-up with them. You must have an effective follow-up system in place and "strike while the iron is hot."

People will need to be delegated for this task of follow-up. Men should follow up with single male visitors, and women with women. As you choose those who will serve in this way, make sure you give appropriate teaching and instruction before you expect anything of them. Then, make sure to follow-up with these servants as well! Ask them about how the follow-up is going and what specific conversations they have had with people, setting aside time to encourage them in their ministry.

VISITING A CONTACT

At times, you may want to pay a visit to a contact. Approach this situation with prayer, and be mindful of your conduct, attitude, and appearance, as this will provide your first testimony to the person. Before you go, set an agenda for your visit, having a basic sense of what you will say while you are there. At your visit, focus on relationship building, caring about who they are as a person.

As your conversation moves to spiritual topics, gauge the person's spiritual interest. If they change the subject, do not force the issue, but pray and wait for more opportunities. If the contact is not yet a believer, but shows interest in spiritual matters, share the Good News with them, and then ask them follow-up questions such as, "Can you think of one reason why you would not accept Yeshua?" If they are ready to commit their life to Him, lead them in a simple prayer of faith focused on Yeshua, confessing their sins to the Lord, and asking Him to cleanse their sins through the atonement of Messiah. When a contact prays to receive the Lord, welcome them into the family! Then give them an opportunity to confess their faith in Yeshua, perhaps to your spouse or another member of your community who will love and affirm them in their new life.

A congregation must continue to reach out in all these ways in order to stay healthy and grow. Keep in mind that a healthy congregation grows at a rate of about 5% per year. If you are not growing at this rate, take a look at your contact making system and assess what needs to be addressed. Have planning meetings with your leadership and talk through these things, evaluating your methods of outreach and contact making. This is a process that calls for continual assessment. It is a leader's job to keep on top of these things in order to keep the congregation moving forward.

DISCIPLE MAKING SYSTEM

Notes:

Figure 6.1

As contacts are made and people led to the Lord, many congregations welcome these new believers into membership immediately and move on. Another crucial step, however, is needed. As we saw in the Gathering Stage, all believers must be discipled, and the local congregation is the means through which this discipleship takes place. It is never appropriate for a group to focus on "birthing children" without having any intention of raising them. We make contacts in order to make disciples, and discipleship must not stop after your core group is trained and your congregation is born.

As stated earlier, another great problem arises when a congregation depends on transfer-growth, accepting people coming from other communities directly into membership, without requiring that they be discipled in the values of the community. This is dangerous indeed, for your ministry will be greatly hindered and disunity will ensue if your people do not understand or hold to your values. You must ensure that each and every potential member is properly discipled, rooted and grounded in their faith and ready to move into the commitment of membership.

Though Yeshua's directive for discipleship is clear (Matthew 28:19-20), *talmidut* is not prioritized as a ministry in many congregations. This unfortunate oversight can lead to many problems:

THE GAP BETWEEN BELIEFS & BEHAVIORS

Notes:

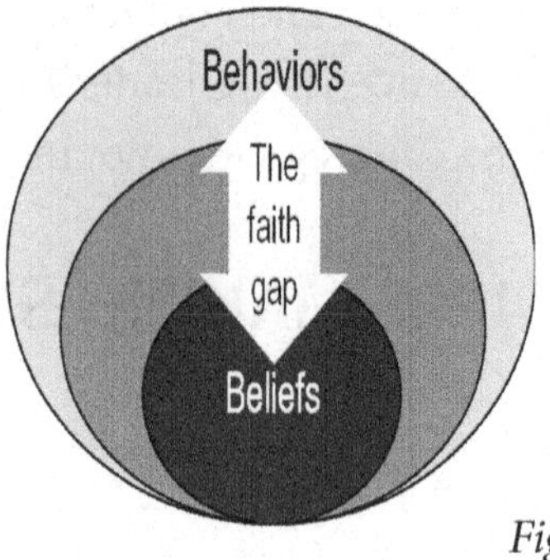

Figure 6.2

I have had leaders come up to me and express their frustration on these matters, saying, "I've given more sermons on prayer than I can count. Why is my congregation not praying?" Or, "I've taught them to be honest. Why are they such liars? This is disheartening indeed. Many times there is a large gap between the beliefs people hold and the behaviors in which they engage. Discipleship is the bridge to close this gap. As they are discipled, people move from merely holding to a bunch of beliefs to actually acting on them.

Vince Lombardi, former coach of the Green Bay Packers, would begin each season with his new players in the same manner. As the men gathered around for their first pre-season meeting, he would hold a football in front of him and begin: "Gentlemen, this is a football." Though it may have seemed to be "beneath" the level of his players, Lombardi was emphasizing that the secret to victory is not found in the most complex tactics, but in a firm grasp of the most basic techniques.

✡ *Consistent execution of the basics develops the required excellence for the team's sustained victory.* ✡

We mature into, rather than grow out of the basics, praying today to become great prayer warriors tomorrow.

People in many congregations today are over-educated and under-disciplined. These people have a great need to actually develop a prayer life, not just receive more information about prayer. This is what discipleship is for, for in discipleship, people are not just taught about prayer, but actually begin to pray. Everyone needs to have someone who can say to them, "Tell me about your prayer life; how has it been going this week?" A discipler is there to enforce these things so disciples can grow in incorporating them into their life. We are under Adonai's discipline, following Him, and it is only as His disciple that we can make disciples. When we hold those we are discipling to a higher standard, it is because they are under His discipline, not ours. We are just brothers and sisters helping each other in our walk with Him.

Many times people hold to certain beliefs, but they do not value them. For example, they may recite the *Shema* (Deuteronomy 6:4) and the *V'ahavta* (Deuteronomy 6:5-9) at Shabbat services and truly believe that the Lord is One, but then throughout the week they do not value this truth by living it out, loving Him with all their heart and teaching His Word to their children. Discipleship is what makes this happen. Telling your preschooler about brushing their teeth is irrelevant to them unless you take them by the hand and walk them to the sink, put the toothbrush in their mouth and begin to brush their baby teeth. People "discipled" in the art of tooth brushing grow up to be socially-acceptable adults. This is also true in spiritual matters. We must teach our spiritual children, not to mention our natural children, how to live and grow as a believer; understanding their identity in Messiah, praying, reading their Bible, fellowshipping with other believers, and sharing Him with others.

✡ *Discipleship in key values is the key to unity in the community* ✡

This is who we are: we pray, we are a people of the Word, we fellowship with one another, and we share Messiah with others. We honor the Lord in all our ways!

In planting a new congregation, remember that it is far easier to give birth to a baby than to raise the dead. If you do not put a discipleship system in place from the very beginning, it will be much harder to begin one down the road. Older congregations who wish to implement a discipleship system for the first time need to go about the process carefully. In such a scenario, begin by bringing the vision to the elders of the congregation, and then disciple them so that they can disciple their families. As the elders are on board, it is now time to bring in the community. In order for all to be on the same page, a congregational meeting is necessary to explain the value of discipleship from Scripture and give instruction concerning specific matters of implementation for the community.

Notes:

131

THE PEOPLE FOR TALMIDUT

The diversity of discipleship

Notes:

"You yourselves know ... How I kept back nothing that was profitable, but proclaimed it to you, and taught you publicly and from house to house." – Acts 20:20

In this passage, Paul was speaking to those he had discipled, who were now leaders of the congregation at Ephesus. His words here help to explain the various spheres in which discipleship must take place within a congregation.

Paul states first that he *"taught publicly."* A strong *bema* ministry in the congregation is vital, because proper discipleship includes public teaching. When individuals desire personal counseling, I encourage them to come to services regularly (Hebrews 10:25). In this way, they can hear the values of the congregation expressed in a bigger picture through weekly expository messages.

However, Paul also taught *"from house to house."* As Paul traveled to different homes, he encouraged personal application of the principles that had been taught publicly. As he visited people, Paul was not merely being sociable, but was seeking to build up individual lives and families. In addition to public teaching, there must also be personal discipleship of individuals in a congregation.

Here, we consider three areas of discipleship which stem from this passage:

I.   Primary *talmidut*: The family
II. Public *talmidut*: The congregation
III. Personal *talmidut*: Individually

PRIMARY TALMIDUT

The home front of the spiritual war

"If a man does not know how to management his own home how will he care for the assembly of God?" - 1 Timothy 3:5

Discipleship begins in the home. If you want your congregation to be committed to discipleship, you must first be a disciple of the Lord yourself, and committed to discipling your family in His ways. Indeed, anything you wish to see happening in the congregation, you must implement first in your own heart and home, renouncing within yourself before denouncing in others. In order to have the right to speak to issues in your community, these things must first be taken care of in your own home. Want more prayer in your community? You had better be praying at home!

Over and over again, God's Word emphasizes the importance of the home life. Proverbs 22:6 tells us to "*train up a child in the way he should go.*" Ephesians 6:4 exhorts fathers to bring their children up "*in the discipline and instruction of the Lord.*" The *V'ahavta* (Deuteronomy 6:5-9) is all about home life. You can teach God's words "*diligently to your children*" whether you are sitting down for dinner, on a walk outside, or getting everyone tucked in for bed. Through good days and bad days, you can teach them to trust in God's grace as they watch you depend on Him every day.

If you still have children living at home but this is not the way you have been raising them, it is not too late to start! After discussing all these things with your spouse, gather your children together and ask their forgiveness for how you have not made God's Word a priority in your family. Explain to them the importance of discipleship from Scripture and explain to them how things will change. Then, stick to it, depending on God's grace as you move forward in obedience! If your children are already grown, it is never too late to apologize to them for the things you did not do, and move forward in discipling others, pouring into your grandchildren and your spiritual children.

MESSIANIC IDENTITY IN YESHUA

As you live for the Lord as a leader at home and in the congregation, it is essential that you understand your own Messianic identity. You must be able to explain from Scripture to those entering your community what it means to be a Messianic Jew or Messianic Gentile. (For more information on this, see my book *Messianic Wisdom*). They need to see that this is the life we live, not just things we say and do on Shabbat morning. If you uphold the community's values during the service but live another way at home, your children will see the inconsistency and will drive a truck right through it. Whether at home or in the congregation, you must grow in consistently living out your Messianic identity. Remember, maturity is consistency!

Notes:

133

MESSIANIC MARRIAGE ISSUES

Notes:

As you understand your Messianic identity and how this plays out in your own life, you must bring this into your marriage, so that the two of you can be on the same page with God and with each other. This is why pre-marital counseling is so important. If a couple would only spend as much time on marriage preparation as they do on wedding preparation, many heartaches would be averted. The wedding ceremony should serve as a testimony of the values of the new home, how they as a couple will live for the Lord. Though important, this ceremony lasts for only thirty minutes or an hour, and then real life begins. Couples must be prepared for this.

When counseling couples, do not agree to perform the wedding too quickly. I do not agree to officiate at a wedding until after the end of pre-marital counseling when I am sure this couple is ready to be married. Through proper instruction, set the expectation for strong homes in your community. Following the wedding, you can inspect these expectations, by following up with the couple and asking how they are doing. You may consider meeting with each couple you marry on a monthly basis throughout their first year of marriage.

MESSIANIC TESTIMONY AT HOME

How is your home life a testimony to Messiah, living out your Messianic identity? A Messianic home is oriented around the *mo'adim*, God's appointed times. If you or your spouse do not come from a Jewish home, extra care must be taken in these matters, as you prepare to respond to questions from family members who may not understand things such as why you do not put up a Christmas tree. It is very important to love your family, but you must be wise concerning your Messianic calling and identity, otherwise you may be tempted to give in to pressure, disobeying God's command to "*leave and cleave*" (Genesis 2:24) as you begin your new family before Him.

If one of the child's parents is Jewish, Scripture permits us to hold a *Brit Milah* (circumcision ceremony) for our sons. Others may choose to have a baby dedication service. Through these ceremonies, it is really the parents who are dedicating themselves to raise the child to the glory of Yeshua, committing to teach God's Word at home and to pray over them every day. This is the first Messianic testimony in the child's life, proclaiming the orientation their life will take.

Placing a *mezuzah* on your doorpost serves as a testimony to the community (Deuteronomy 6:9). It says that those living in the house are living for the Lord. This is to be taken seriously, just as putting a bumper sticker that says "Yeshua," on your car means you need to represent Him well by not speeding. Fathers are to train up their children in God's ways (Proverbs 22:6), teaching them daily from His Word, and keeping it at the center of their lives.

In order for your congregation to be a place of discipleship, each home in your community needs to implement His Word in their homes. They will learn how to do this through proper instruction and consistent follow-up. Help and encourage the families in your community, coming alongside them in their commitment to live for the Lord.

PUBLIC TALMIDUT
The congregation

"Until I come, give attention to the public reading of Scripture, to exhortation and teaching." – 1 Timothy 4:13

THE CONGREGATIONAL SERVICE

Every ministry we have in the congregation must be seen in light of disciple-making, having one set of values from womb to tomb. We prioritize this because we desire for every child, youth, and adult to come to personal faith in Yeshua and grow to become great men and women of God.

In Acts 20:20, Paul stated that he both proclaimed to the Ephesians as well as taught them. Both teaching and preaching are needed in order to complete and mature the believer. (See also 1 Timothy 5:17)

In this verse, to *"proclaim"* means to reveal, announce, or openly divulge the truth (See also 1 John 1:5, Deuteronomy 5:5, Psalm 92:15). This underlies the importance of having a strong message at regular Shabbat services (2 Timothy 4:2). The word *"teach"* carries a different sense, *"to instruct in order to be carried out."* We see this as a theme carried throughout the Word (Deuteronomy 4:14, Matthew 28:20, 2 Timothy 2:2).

Notes:

Notes:

Paul stated that as he taught, he kept back nothing that was profitable. "*Profitable*" means that which is appropriate (Proverbs 19:10). This does not mean what is merely permitted, but what is actually good for the believer (1 Corinthians 6:12; 10:23; 12:7). Teachers are not to "tickle the ears" of their listeners with new spiritual fads (Acts 17:21), but help each believer to grow in the grace of God.

"*... solemnly testifying to both Jews and Greeks of repentance toward God and faith in our Lord Yeshua the Messiah.*" – Acts 20:21

In Acts 20:21, Paul continues on to say that he solemnly testified. "*Testifying*" means to "warn" as seen in Luke 16:28. Although humor can be a helpful way to communicate a point, the message itself is profoundly serious. Whenever one teaches from the Word of God, the message is never unimportant. Biblical issues are both vital and eternal.

Paul testified to both "Jews and Greeks." The unique unity that Jewish and Gentile believers have in Messiah means that no one may be excluded. Messianic leaders are to preach and teach with all people in mind, not showing partiality to anyone, but testifying to all of the unique unity found in the fulfillment of God's promise to Abraham (Genesis 12:3).

As Paul testified of "repentance" and "faith," he exhorted people to turn from their sin and trust in the Lord. In pointing the congregation to Messiah, the focus of the Scriptures, one must teach from the whole counsel of God. As the Word is presented through direct, expository teaching, the congregation will grow in their understanding of God's plan of redemption for Israel and the nations, and be challenged to respond and follow Him in it!

Through our public teaching, we build our community values. As you teach from the *bema*, you are forever re-iterating these values, serving as a reminder to your members and proclaiming to your visitors, "This is who we are; this is what we believe." Though you may not actually list these values systematically through your messages, you can cover them in whatever Scripture portion you happen to be sharing. Through your teaching ministry, you are building these values into the community, growing them to become community-wide values.

In order for all to be edified, it is essential that all parts of your service are able to be understood by all. Paul taught in 1 Corinthians 14 that all prayers and teaching in the congregation must be interpreted so that visitors will be able to understand and be edified. In light of this, make sure to fully explain any Hebrew or Greek words you may use in your message.

As you prepare your messages, keep in mind that you cannot make applications for every person in your congregation from the *bema*. Keep your applications general, and teach people to talk through the messages together and make their own applications at home. (For more information about sermon preparation and presentation, see Appendix 1)

THE CHAVUROT

Through *chavurot*, or small group Bible studies, people are able to meet in smaller groups outside of the regular congregational meetings in order to have interactive fellowship in prayer and the Word together. This provides an opportunity to get to know people at a deeper level, building the bonds of community as people share and pray for each other, carrying each other's burdens. Some chavurot are geared to a specific age group or stage of life in order to meet the needs of each individual. Regardless of size or focus, each *chavurah* must have a trained leader who is able to facilitate the group and keep it focused on the primary values of the community.

PERSONAL TALMIDUT
Individually

"We proclaim Him, admonishing every man and teaching every man with all wisdom, so that we may present every man complete in Messiah." - Colossians 1:28

Through one on one discipleship, you and your team have the opportunity to address the unique, individual needs of each person in your congregation. As you teach and disciple, be mindful of those who do not catch on as quickly as others. A good shepherd never outruns the flock; he will not go faster than the slowest sheep in order that none of them be lost. So, in one on one discipleship, do not move too fast. The important thing is not how fast you can get through the material, but how well you can make disciples. For one man I discipled, it was necessary that we take several months on matters of assurance of salvation before moving on to other topics. This man

Notes:

137

Notes:

had so much sin in his past that it was extremely hard for him to wrap his mind around the fact that he was forgiven and would spend eternity with the Lord. I could not move on with him until he grasped this fact, because if he did not have assurance of his salvation, he could not have assurance of anything else. Just as some kids take longer to learn how to ride a bike or tie their shoes, each person grows at their own rate. As leaders and disciplers, we must be careful not to judge, but to be patient with each person!

We must also be ready to explain the purposes of discipleship. People learn at their point of need, and if they do not see the relevance of something, they will regard it as irrelevant and not worth their time. In discipling individuals, you need to spend time discussing the relevance of these things. Let each person know how important it is to learn these basic spiritual disciplines for their walk with the Lord.

THE PEOPLE FOR DISCIPLESHIP

"I am writing to you, little children, because your sins have been forgiven you for His Name's sake. I am writing to you, fathers, because you know Him who has been from the beginning. I am writing to you, young men, because you have overcome the evil one. I have written to you, children, because you know the Father. I have written to you, fathers, because you know Him who has been from the beginning. I have written to you, young men, because you are strong, and the word of God abides in you, and you have overcome the evil one." – 1 John 2:12-14

We find in this passage that in every community there are three basic groups of people, each with unique needs that need to be addressed through discipleship. As we disciple people from each of these groups, our goal is to present all of them complete in Messiah. Though we touched on this briefly during the Gathering Stage, here we will go deeper into how to disciple people from each group.

UNDISCIPLED BELIEVERS

Undisciped believers, are *"little children"* to whom John is referring. New believers are certainly in this category, but so also are people who have been believers for many years, yet have never been through any kind of discipleship. These people are tossed to and fro by every wind of teaching, and are in no way grounded and rooted. Instead, they are forever moving from one group to another, picking up bits of information here and there and combining them to form their own ideas. These people need to be stabilized so that they can become healthy, functioning members of the Body of Messiah (Ephesians 4:14-15). Undiscipled believers need to go through basic discipleship in foundational matters of faith, improving the soil so that the seed can grow unhindered (Matthew 15:13, Luke 8:14).

In congregation planting, I assume that each person coming into the congregation is undiscipled, and so have foundational discipleship as a required part of the membership process. Though there are certain exceptional people for whom exceptions can be made, for a genuine believer, the process of discipleship is a joy through which we grow deeper into the things we love. I find that the most mature believers make the best students, as they submit themselves under the Lord's discipline. A good teacher loves to learn, and will forever be asking questions in order to grow even more.

Whether they are new or not so new in the faith, undiscipled believers need to be instructed in foundational matters such as...

THEIR RELATIONSHIP WITH MESSIAH

Undiscipled believers need to be taught what it means to be in a relationship with Messiah. Religion, the external expression of our faith, is always a poor substitute for relationship. From the very beginning, we see that relationship is intrinsic to who God is and to who He designed us to be. Genesis 1:26 tells us that God created us in His "image" and "likeness." These two words show us the two purposes for which God created humanity: to relate to Him and to represent Him to others. Created in His likeness, we are like God, and therefore can relate to Him at a level that no other creature can. Likeness refers to similarity; just as two sisters are similar but are not the same. We are like God in many ways. For instance, all people desire to be loved. This is because God is love. Because we are created in His likeness, we must love and be loved in order to be healthy people.

Created in God's image, we represent Him. Like a lake which reflects a clear image of a majestic mountain, we serve to reflect God, to represent Him to others. Yet, because of sin, we misrepresent the Lord. Sin breaks the relationship we were created for, but through Messiah, we are being restored into His image so that we can again relate to God and truly represent Him to

Notes:

others. Relationship is key to representation. We represent the living God as we relate well with others. Through broken relationships, people misrepresent God. Discipleship helps people understand how to have healthy relationships with God and with others in order to represent Him, whether at home, in the community, or at work.

Discipleship sessions on relationship with Messiah can cover such topics as:

- ✡ Lesson 1: The assurance of our salvation in Messiah, 1 John 5:13
- ✡ Lesson 2: Prayer, 1 Peter 5:7
- ✡ Lesson 3: God's Word, Psalm 119:9, 11
- ✡ Lesson 4: Our fellowship with other believers, Hebrews 10:25
- ✡ Lesson 5: Our witness to unbelievers, Psalm 107:2

ASSURANCE OF SALVATION

Assurance of salvation is essential for everything else in life. Generally, people judge this by their own feelings or emotions, but these can come and go. As a discipler, you must make sure that your disciple has a better foundation. Through faith in Yeshua, we can have complete assurance of our salvation (I John 5:13). As you meet with the person, teach them to base their assurance, not on their experiences, but upon the Word of God. Though some people have had amazing experiences, these can be distracting if they are not reflective of Scriptural truth. The enemy comes even as an angel of light (2 Corinthians 11:14), so we must not believe every spirit, but test them carefully (1 John 4:1). As people share their experiences with you, be sensitive and caring, but help them by pointing them to the truth of God's Word, the Lamp by which to evaluate our spiritual experiences. It is incredibly limiting to depend on one's own experience as a foundation for our entire walk with God!

As people gain this spiritual assurance in Scripture, they will gain confidence in the Lord. Our emotions may be here today and gone tomorrow, but in Him we have an anchor for our souls (Hebrews 6:19). Emotions can provide false assurance, but also can falsely condemn. When a person is struggling, feeling guilty and telling themselves that they are junk, they must realize that it is their sin that brings the junk; God did not create them with it. Rather than merely affirm a person who is struggling in this way, telling them that they can overcome it, point them to the grace of God, for this is their greatest need. Remind them of who God says they are: His child

Notes:

(1 John 3:1). He does not see us as sinners, but forgives and forgets when we confess our sin (Jeremiah 31:34). He can no more remember the sins for which we have been forgiven than deny the very death of the Messiah for those sins. There is no condemnation in Messiah Yeshua, and this includes no self-condemnation. Yeshua took our punishment and therefore we do not have to beat ourselves up. People need to be told the truth about these things, and will not find it except from the community of which they are a part.

PRAYER & THE WORD

Instruction on prayer and the Word should focus on application, for the purpose of discipleship is not merely to teach people about these spiritual disciplines, but to train them in actually doing them! Prayer and the Word cover our vertical relationship with God. Prayer is us talking to God and Scripture is God talking to us. Disciples need to be taught how to confess their sins to God in prayer (1 John 1:9), so that nothing hinders their relationship with Him (Psalm 66:18). Make sure that the person is comfortable with the truth that all Scripture is inspired by God (2 Timothy 3:16), even those parts which they may not yet understand. As you go over these essential disciplines of our faith, challenge the disciple to spend five minutes each day in prayer and ten minutes in the Word. Aim for reachable goals, which they can grow in as they mature in their faith.

FELLOWSHIP

Sessions on fellowship and witnessing cover our horizontal relationships with others. Through fellowship, we relate with those inside the Body of Messiah. Through sharing our faith, we relate with those outside.

As a person is being discipled, ensure that they are attending services regularly, fellowshipping with other believers, for this is essential to their growth. If this was Yeshua's "custom" (Luke 4:16), it needs to be ours as well. As believers, it is essential that we are in regular fellowship with the Lord as well as with one another (Hebrews 10:24-25).

WITNESSING

Among believers, witnessing is not something that is natural, assumed, regular, or in many cases done at all. As such, some may object to the time

Notes:

141

Notes:

taken in discipleship on this aspect of our walk with God. However, we cannot allow what others do or do not do to serve as our teacher. To illustrate this point, let me share a story: During World War II, as Italy was taking over various sections of North Africa, men from one of these African countries captured a group of Italian soldiers and brought them to their tribal leader. The men wanted to torture the soldiers, but their leader would not permit it. "But," the men protested, "They've done it to us!" In response their leader gently told them, "But they are not your teachers." We have a Master in heaven, and we follow His teaching. As His disciples, we see what God's Word says to do and do it even if it is not commonly done.

People must be taught how to witness, and encouraged to look to the Lord for enablement, acting on faith rather than fear. Through their good works, they can serve as a practical witness, earning the right to be heard (Matthew 5:15-16). With friends, they can be a personal witness, sharing Messiah one on one (John 1:45). At times, God may give them an opportunity to be a public witness (Luke 24:46-48), and all of us can be a persuasive witness (2 Corinthians 5:10-11), pointing others to the truth. Again, start with small goals, encouraging the person to start praying for one friend, neighbor, or co-worker with whom they can share the Good News, planting seeds, and praying for God to give the increase.

THE BIBLICAL TEACHINGS OF MESSIAH

Undiscipled believers must also be discipled in the biblical teachings of Messiah (2 Peter 3:18). It is essential that people be grounded and rooted in the truth, able to understand the primary teachings of Messiah well enough to be ready to give a defense for them, and be able to teach them to their own physical and spiritual children. Believers need to understand for themselves what God's Word says on primary matters such as why Yeshua is Lord, or why we follow the written Scripture alone as authoritative. As they study and memorize what Scripture teaches on these topics, they grow in their ability to explain them to others. Beware of simply teaching people to give the right answers, repeating what you say, for this is not true discipleship.

Discipleship sessions on the biblical teachings of Messiah can cover such foundational issues as:

✡ Lesson 1: The written Word, 2 Timothy 3:16
✡ Lesson 2: The suffering Messiah: Messiah is good, Isaiah 53

✡ Lesson 3: The divine Messiah: Messiah is God, Isaiah 9:5/6; Colossians 2:9
✡ Lesson 4: The Triune Nature of God, Matthew 28:19
✡ Lesson 5: *Ruach HaChodesh* (The Holy Spirit), John 14:17
✡ Lesson 6: The background and meaning of *Zikkaron* (The Lord's Supper) & *Tevilah* (Immersion)

Notes:

Through these vital matters, people grow in their faith in our foundation. They are then equipped to look at tradition and decide which customs will best help them to express their faith, rather than simply practice external things which they may not understand.

THE PRACTICAL LIVING FOR MESSIAH

As they are being rooted and grounded on a solid biblical foundation, these believers must also be taught in the practical matters of how to live for Messiah day-to-day, loving one another, parenting their children according to God's Word, managing finances, dealing with death in the family, etc. There are materials available for teaching on these matters, but they are not exhaustive. Part of shepherding the flock is speaking to specific issues which may not be in the books.

Discipleship sessions on practical living for Messiah can cover such topics as:

✡ Lesson 1: Messianic Jewish or Gentile identity
✡ Lesson 2: Finding a congregation
✡ Lesson 3: Sharing Messiah with family members
✡ Lesson 4: Observing the holidays and holy days at home
✡ Etc.

GROWING BELIEVERS

The second group of people in 1 John 2:12-14 are the *"young men,"* those who are strong and healthy. These are the growing believers in your community. Though these people may have already been through formal discipleship, they need continual guidance and encouragement in their role as lifelong disciples of Messiah.

Notes:

SERVICE TO MESSIAH

Growing believers need to learn about serving the Lord and be given opportunity to do so, for it is through service that they will grow. Positions of service should be reserved for growing, discipled believers. A brand new believer should not be involved in any heavy service during their first year to ensure that they not confuse their service with their salvation, based solely upon the work of Yeshua. In managing various ministry teams, leaders need to be mindful of this precaution.

As growing believers serve, they must be taught how to do so properly and wisely, doing everything out of a motive of love. In Acts 6, Stephen and the other six men were "just" serving food, but they were chosen because they were filled with the *Ruach* and with wisdom. Everything we do in the community is about people, not about food, chairs, or equipment. Those in our congregations who serve behind the scenes in various capacities must be taught that everything they do is in order to care for people; that people are their priority.

TSURIS IN MESSIAH

Growing believers also need to be taught how to deal with *tsuris* (problems). This side of heaven, we will all encounter all kinds of problems in life. People need to be taught how to live faithfully through these problems and to honor the Lord, not revert to Plan B (Be miserable, Be selfish, etc.) God only has one plan for us in our difficulties, to trust Him and walk with Him through the problems. This is the reason why we fear no evil in the shadow of death: He is with us! (Psalm 23:4). These things must be taught, as this is certainly not our natural response to problems.

(See Appendix 4 for more information on congregational counseling)

PARENTING FOR MESSIAH

As they embark on the journey of parenting, all believers, particularly those who did not grow up in a believing home, need training and support in how to be godly parents (Proverbs 22:6). Many people have had very poor modeling as to what this looks like. By default, they depend on the tools they learned from what they experienced growing up, and do not know what Scripture has to say on this subject. These believers need to be re-parented themselves, learning new tools from God's Word in how to love and care for their own children in a proper, godly way.

In raising children, you are raising leaders, for once they grow up and say "I do," they will become leaders of a new home. As you parent them, you are passing on values which they will bring into their own home one day. In a sense, through parenting, you are planting another congregation. When your children are young, you need to have a vision for them, understanding the important role you play in their lives. When you tell them today that they cannot walk across the street without holding an adult's hand, it is because you know that one day they will be taking their own child's hand, protecting and training the next generation.

MATURE BELIEVERS

The third group of people in 1 John 2:12-14 are those who are mature, the "*fathers*" of whom John speaks. The hallmark of maturity is when a person begins to care for others more than for themselves. Love fulfills all Torah (Romans 13:10), and everything we do in life is to live out God's greatest commandment to love (Matthew 22:36-40). Loving, mature believers are ready to be leaders who in turn will care for and disciple others.

LEADERSHIP INVOLVEMENT

"*... let us press on to maturity, not laying again a foundation of repentance from dead works and of faith toward God*" – Hebrews 6:1

If a father has three children, how many would he desire to become mature? All three, of course! In Messiah, every single believer is designed for maturity, and through His Word, we press on to the mark of this high calling. God is not like our mom who may have let us get away with not cleaning our room, or like our teacher who gave us an "A for effort." He loves us too much to let us get away with foolishness. How do people grow to maturity? As we teach them, setting the expectation for our community, and sharing our vision with them for all to grow as leaders.

Though not everyone will become a leader in the congregation, every person in the community is called to take a stewardship role over his or her own heart, living as a Spirit-led believer, following Yeshua. From this, each man will be equipped for his calling to lead in his own home, and some will be called to take a leadership role in the congregation.

Notes:

Notes:

_____

_____

_____

_____

_____

_____

_____

_____

_____

_____

_____

_____

_____

_____

_____

Have the vision for leadership involvement, for every member of your community to be growing as leaders. As you instruct them in this expectation, you must inspect as well, asking how they are implementing the teaching, reading the Word and praying with their families, being faithful servants in the congregation, etc. Be mindful as you do this, however, to ask yourself the same questions, renouncing in yourself before you denounce in others.

LEADERSHIP DEVELOPMENT

"… we are no longer to be children, tossed here and there by waves and carried about by every wind of doctrine … but speaking the truth in love, we are to grow up in all aspects into Him who is the head, Messiah." – Ephesians 4:14-15

As we have discussed, when we first make a contact with a person, whether outside the congregation or at a service, our goal is to love them and share Messiah with them. When by God's grace, this person accepts Yeshua into their life, we rejoice at their salvation! At this point in their life, we know something that they do not yet know. We know what lies ahead for them according to God's Word, for we have been there before. We know that from the day of salvation until the day they go home to be with the Lord, they will be growing more into the likeness of Messiah. We know that one day, they will be a leader!

Likewise, in parenting, we do not raise children, but leaders who will grow up to become great men and women of God. Before a child has any idea what they want to be when they grow up, we must have the vision for them that they will become leaders. If this is God's plan for them, why would we have any other? Cast a vision for your children, believe God for them, and instill in them these things.

So, when a person is saved, immediately get them started with discipleship. Once they are discipled, Lord willing, they will become a member of the congregation. If they choose to do so, they will then grow into leadership. Because we have been there before, we will be able to guide and encourage them along the path. Leaders come from a congregation's membership, members from those who are growing disciples, and disciples from those who were initially contacts.

(More principles concerning leadership development can be found on pages 160-169).

LEADERSHIP REPLACEMENT

"Moses My servant is dead; now therefore arise, cross this Jordan, you and all this people, to the land which I am giving to them, to the sons of Israel." - Joshua 1:2

No one is irreplaceable. Eventually, you will need a Joshua, for even Moses went on to be with the Lord! In light of this, you must be making disciples along the way and developing new leadership. We need to be ready to pass the baton, for this is part of a leader's responsibility as we move ahead with the Lord. Make sure that you have systems in place that are transferable, and not dependent on your personality or own specialized way of doing things. Be wise about these matters, for Scripture assures us that our disciples will follow the very pattern that we live.

As we conclude this section on discipleship, let us consider one last illustration. In the movie, "The Karate Kid," young Daniel asks Mr. Miagi to teach him karate. Mr. Miagi agrees under one condition: that Daniel never question his methods. When Daniel shows up ready to learn karate, Mr. Miagi has him paint his fence, showing him the precise motion to use for the job. After days of doing similar chores, Daniel is finally fed up, and asks, "I thought you were going to teach me karate, but all you've done is have me do your unwanted chores!" At this point, Mr. Miagi responds, "I have been teaching you karate; defend yourself! When Miagi thrusts his arm at Daniel, he instinctively defends himself with an arm motion exactly like that used in one of his chores. After Daniel successfully averts several more blows, Miagi simply walks away, leaving Daniel to discover what the master had known all along: skill comes from repeating the correct but seemingly mundane actions.

As we plant congregations, we are not looking for people who can hit home runs, but for those who can hit singles and doubles consistently. We do not look for leaders who meet the world's expectations, but for those who are mature and reliable, who know how to deal with real life issues. Leadership is not a matter of personality, but responsibility, and these leaders are developed through the basics of discipleship. Through discipleship, we grow in assurance of our salvation in Messiah, and in the spiritual disciplines of prayer, the Word, fellowship, and sharing our faith. As we consistently implement these spiritual disciplines, they form the functional habits and mature character that make us more than conquerors in Messiah.

Notes:

147

If you find yourself running into issues as you attempt to institute discipleship in your congregation, see Appendix 2.

For guidance when there is a need to disciple more than one person at a time, see Appendix 3.

Notes:

For information regarding the system and function of congregational counseling, see Appendix 4.

MEMBER MAKING SYSTEM

Figure 6:3

This next system which we will consider is a result of the preceding. We make contacts in order to make disciples, and we make disciples who will then serve as functioning members of the Body of Messiah. The specific people who will become members, however, is God's business, for He adds to the Body as He wills. Our job is to make disciples and His job is to figure out what to do with them.

Membership is a biblical concept, however, in many congregations, it is viewed as old-fashioned or legalistic. In fact, many believe that the Bible teaches against the idea of membership. This, however, is simply not true, for, as we will see, from the giving of Torah through the time of the first century Body of believers, membership was simply a normal way of life.

Though various terms may be used and "membership" systems look different, eventually a leader will find committed, trustworthy people whom he will place in positions of responsibility in the congregation. At this point, if a congregation does not have specific standards for membership, issues may arise as others wonder why they are not also permitted to serve in the congregation.

WHY MEMBERSHIP?

FOR RIGHTEOUSNESS

Notes:

"You shall do no injustice in judgment; you shall not be partial to the poor nor defer to the great, but you are to judge your neighbor fairly." - Leviticus 19:15

"You shall have just balances, just weights, a just ephah, and a just hin; I am the LORD your God, who brought you out from the land of Egypt." - Leviticus 19:36

The Torah tells us that we must have equal weights and measures, and to do otherwise is wrong in the sight of God. This standard of equality must be carried out in our congregations, serving to demonstrate the fact that God loves us all, and loves us all the same. The opposite of this godly measuring system is favoritism. Favoritism is foolishness, and we need not look further than the lives of the Patriarchs to find that it does not work out well! Equality must first be implemented at home, for if you allow yourself to have favorites there, you will also have favorites as a leader in the congregation. If at home you are only loyal to those who obey your every command, you will do the same in the congregation. This must not be so, for we are called to love each person equally.

A membership system allows you to set the same biblical standards for everybody in the community, ensuring that no one gets special privileges simply because you connect well with their culture or personality. All must be discipled in the same way, with equal weights and measures before they are permitted to serve. Each member of the congregation should be held to the same standards as well as to the same values and benefits, regardless of whether they are Jewish or Gentile. As we accept all people on the same basis, we model Messiah's acceptance of each one of us.

Your community standards for membership should not be dependent on circumstances. If a person has a bad day, they are not exempt from keeping the standards. Work to make sure you have equal weights and measures across the board so that no one can accuse you of playing favorites. As you develop your community's standards of membership, realize that not everyone in the congregation is going to understand them. You must objectify these things in order to clearly communicate them to your community and to those who are interested in becoming a part of it.

FOR UNITY AMIDST DIVERSITY

Notes:

"But thanks be to God that though you were slaves of sin, you became obedient from the heart to that form of teaching to which you were committed ..."
- Romans 6:17

In the Hebrew Scriptures, it was assumed that all members of the community of Israel both agreed with and heeded the Torah of Moses, otherwise they were put out of the community, outside the camp (Deuteronomy 13:5; 17:12; 21:21; 22:21). In this regard, the town functioned as a sort of congregation. The elders of each town handled benevolence, discipline, blessing, and teaching at the local level (Deuteronomy 13:12-18; 14:28-29).

By the time of Yeshua, in a sense, the synagogue represented the town or community (John 9:22; 12:42; 16:2; Acts 15:21). When people moved from one congregation to another, it was a normal precaution for letters of commendation to be sent ahead of them (1 Corinthians 16:3; 2 Corinthians 3:1; 8:18-24). The leaders knew the people in their communities, for they recognized when 'unbelievers' entered in (1 Corinthians 14:23-25). If a person found themselves cast out from their synagogue, as the blind man whom Yeshua healed in John 9, they were left without help or connection. Membership in a community was a serious, very real matter.

All throughout Scripture, membership through commonly held beliefs and values was the norm, and in God's eyes, it is still an ordinary thing. In order for a community to be healthy, its members must be in agreement (Amos 3:3), trained in the same values. Though diverse, we are unified in the primary values of our community.

FOR STABILITY TOWARD SUCCESS

"Obey your leaders and submit to them, for they keep watch over your souls as those who will give an account. Let them do this with joy and not with grief, for this would be unprofitable for you." – Hebrews 13:17

As a leader, whether in the home or in the community, you will be asked to give an account for the service that you provide for those under your care. This is why God commands people in the congregation to "obey" their leaders, following their instructions, and "submit" to their position as leader over them.

Both dads and elders, in their calling as leaders, are to keep watch over souls. Leaders are constantly running interference as they pray and care for each member of their flock. However, as they do this, they are not only talking to God about each person, they are also actively involved in their lives, asking how they are doing, making sure they do not turn to the left or to the right, and ensuring they stay close to the shepherd. This is what it is to keep watch over the souls of those entrusted to you.

But how do you know whose souls you are responsible for? How does a person know which leader to obey and submit to? We see the answer clearly throughout Scripture. In the Torah, elders were responsible for their towns (Deuteronomy 24, etc.), and therefore had to know who the members of their town were. When Ephesians 5:22 tells wives to be subject, it is only to their own husbands. In 1 Timothy 3:4, we see that men have a stewardship for their own home, not everyone's home. In 1 Timothy 5:9, needy widows were put on "the list," in order to be cared for by their own congregation. Just because a person is a congregational leader does not mean they can ask every person they meet on the street about their prayer life. They also cannot be responsible for the personal growth of every individual who visits the congregation or attends sporadically. Rather, they are responsible to shepherd, instruct, and serve those who have submitted to their care and authority. In Hebrews 13:17, it is implied that the leaders knew those they were responsible to watch over, and the congregation knew who their own leaders were in order to obey and submit to them.

THE NECESSITY OF MEMBERSHIP THEN & NOW

As you read through Paul's letters, the phrase, *"Do you not know?"* appears again and again. Paul was like a mother pulling her hair out as she watches her child running into the house with muddy shoes for the hundredth time. Because Paul had instructed the congregations in God's Word, they should have known what was expected of them. Our membership is a result of our discipleship, one leading naturally to the other. Paul could not expect people to do what he had never taught them. A leader who implements member-

Notes:

Notes:

ship but not discipleship in his congregation will be frustrated, finding few people willing to step up to the responsibility of accountability and service.

If everyone coming into your congregation came from the same background where they were taught godly values, a membership system would not be necessary; however, when you have people coming from many different backgrounds, a membership system is absolutely necessary!

Paul realized this as he engaged in ministry to the pagan world. In the Jewish community, having moral and ethical values was normal, as people were raised with the morality and ethics of Torah. In the Gentile world, however, people did not understand what morality and ethics were. Many Gentiles who were coming to faith did not understand that in following Yeshua, they had to leave their pagan ways behind them. As a result of this issue, by the end of the 1st Century, the membership process in a congregation was two years long. During this time, under the tutelage of one of the congregational leaders, a person was taught the basics of the faith, being immersed after one year of training and only permitted to take the Lord's Supper if they were living out a testimony demonstrating their walk with the Lord at the end of the second year. (*Keith Drury, "Church Membership in the Early Church," drurywriting.com*)

Our culture today is much like that of the first century pagan world, not holding to community-enforcing Biblical values, but reinforcing all the wrong values to our children through the media. As a congregational leader, you must realize that people coming into your community are not good to go. Even if they came from a different community, they do not understand what it means to walk with Yeshua until they are taught. Therefore, if you bring them into a membership simply because they confess Yeshua as Lord, you are going to run into problems. Just because a person believes in Yeshua does not mean they are not still involved in gross moral sin (1 Corinthians 5:1). People must be taught what it truly means for Yeshua to be Lord over their time, relationships, abilities, skills, thought life, etc.

So how do we go about member making? Before making members, one must first make disciples of all who wish to join the congregation. If the potential member is an individual whom you personally led to the Lord, you know where they are spiritually. However, if the person was a believer before they got to you, you have no idea what they know, but yet you are responsible before God to keep watch over their soul. Discipleship is vital!

Membership is simply identifying those disciples who are committed to be a part of your community, under your care.

THE SYSTEM OF MEMBER MAKING

There are certain goals by which we can evaluate and integrate new members into the life of the congregation.

AGREED VALUES

"Can two walk together, except they be in agreement?" – Amos 3:3

First of all, it is essential that we ensure each new member agree with all of the congregation's values. Some may think that this is asking too much; do members really need to agree with every one of the values? Before asking anyone to agree with them, assess your primary values and remove any that are not this important.

The membership system in the congregation is simply a continuation of your core group development. In your membership classes, you will be discussing the vision for your congregation and the values involved in it. Potential members need to truly understand your values, not simply agree with them, for some may be quick to assent just so they can become a member. Those who wish to join your congregation must understand the reasons why you hold to certain beliefs and not to others. The classes will help them to appreciate what they are committing to, and bring them to a point of decision. Are these the values they will commit to live by?

One way to assess a person's understanding is through a membership application in which each of your congregation's Articles of Faith is listed. After each one, the person can indicate their agreement by checking "yes," "no," or "not sure." After a person fills out the application, their answers can be further evaluated through an interview with a leader in the congregation. During the interview, this leader needs to be on their game, taking note whether the person's body language matches up with their written response. If the person checked "no" next to any Article, they need to meet with a leader who can study further with them on the matter they disagree with. Do not view disagreement as a threat, but rather as an opportunity for further discipleship, taking the person through Scripture to show them where the congregational values come from. Perhaps the information was not pre-

Notes:

sented clearly enough when the person heard it the first time and further clarification is needed.

The level of dedication and commitment each person has to the congregation will reflect their understanding of the goals and direction of the congregation. It is necessary that a potential member understand that membership means agreeing to regular attendance, service, tithing, and other investments necessary for the success of the congregation. Therefore, it is not possible for a person to join your community while remaining a member elsewhere. Membership takes commitment, and dual membership is a divided commitment.

Therefore, do not be in a rush to bring people into membership. If they do not totally understand and agree with your values, or seem wary of the commitment required, hold off on making them members for as long as it takes for them to understand and agree, ready to commit to live out these values as a member. Patience is needed in this process as each person learns at a different rate.

ACTIVE SERVICE

"from whom the whole body, being fitted and held together by what every joint supplies, according to the proper working of each individual part, causes the growth of the body for the building up of itself in love." - Ephesians 4:16

The leadership must make sure that through discipleship, each part of the Body becomes functional to do the work of service. The result of discipleship is not merely well-taught people, but empowered servants who are not just hearers but doers of the Word. Yeshua said in John 13:17, *"If you know these things blessed are you who do them."* Implementation is what Scripture is all about; the blessing is only found in the doing.

When a person wishes to join your congregation, but is not interested in serving, your response to them should be, "If this is your desire, then you cannot be a member here." If this seems harsh, let us understand that in order for a congregation to be healthy and functional, the members must serve; this is why they are members. People who do not serve are not members. If some members are not serving, their membership should be suspended, for active members serve. From the very beginning of the membership process, ensure that this expectation is made clear.

Notes:

154

Once a person becomes a member, they need to immediately be placed into service in some capacity. As they begin to serve, provide them with various opportunities to develop in their gifts in the Lord. A new member should be eased into service, not given too much responsibility during their first year. They need to be given time to demonstrate faithfulness in the small things before being entrusted with larger tasks.

Though many congregations do not require their members to serve, this is vital to the health and function of not only your congregation, but also for the members themselves. It simply is not healthy for a discipled believer not to be serving. People will not be spiritually-minded and growing in godliness if they are not serving. Paul taught in 2 Thessalonians 3:10 that whoever is not willing to work does not get to eat either! We are building a testimony to the glory of God as we serve together, helping to "push the truck up the hill." People need to realize that serving in the congregation is hard work, but worth all the effort they invest, for it is a calling from the Lord.

Be careful, though, not to be legalistic or judgmental about this. To feed their families, some may not be able to come to services every Shabbat. In these instances, remember that the Torah was given to a redeemed people, not to redeem people. In bondage, we were not able to keep Shabbat. A free people lives according to God's truth, but not everyone in our community is able to be that free.

AFFIRMED BY MEMBERSHIP

"I commend to you our sister Phoebe, who is a servant of the congregation which is at Cenchrea; that you receive her in the Lord in a manner worthy of the saints, and that you help her in whatever matter she may have need of you; for she herself has also been a helper of many, and of myself as well." – Romans 16:1-2

Before welcoming new members into service, it is wise to perform a background check on each individual. This is particularly important in order to reveal any background involving crimes against children, for pedophiles look for children's ministries that are not properly handled. Likewise, others may have ulterior motives in wanting to work with finances. This precaution is not intended to prevent repentant individuals from becoming members, for we believe in redemption and forgiveness. If a person has

Notes:

Notes:

_____

_____

_____

_____

_____

_____

_____

_____

_____

_____

_____

_____

_____

_____

_____

repented of past sins, we need to believe them, and forgive them as the Lord has! However, this does not mean that they should be allowed to serve in their former area of struggle. For the sake of testimony and security, place people in the ministries that will best help them to avoid temptation and ensure no charge can be made against the congregation. A leader must handle these matters wisely as one responsible to watch over the souls of those under his care.

Another step before affirming a new member is to involve the counsel of current members. At least two weeks prior to the presentation of potential new members, send a notification email out to the membership giving them an opportunity to voice any concern about those coming into membership. We must vet potential members and address any concerns that come up, so that at their presentation before the community they can be wholeheartedly affirmed by all members of the congregation.

At the membership presentation, once this affirmation has taken place, it is important to pray over the new members as a community, for we know that the point of commitment is the point of attack; the enemy does not concern himself with the uncommitted believer. For Adam and Eve, commitment to follow one little mitzvah was enough for the enemy to bring temptation their way. In light of this, the new members should expect to face temptation in various areas as they commit to walk in obedience to the Lord. As you present the members, make sure that the children of the congregation can be present as well, for it is important that they understand the commitment that is taking place. As the service concludes, welcome the new members with plenty of hugs, affirming their commitment in the Lord.

LEADER MAKING SYSTEM

Figure 6.4

FOR ANYONE & EVERYONE

"If anyone aspires to the office of overseer, he desires a noble task." - 1 Timothy 3:1

As we consider the system of leader making, a proper understanding of leadership is essential. As stated before, every single believer in Yeshua is called to be a leader, though each of us have different areas of stewardship. It may only be your own life over which you have stewardship responsibility as a Spirit-led believer, but even so, you are responsible before God for the plans and decisions you make.

If leadership is a possibility for *"anyone,"* then it is a possibility for everyone. The only thing holding a person back from being a leader is vision according to God's will. Our vision for our lives is too small; God knows what He has for each of us, and faith believes His will, not our own. The enemy does not want to stop us from doing our will, but God's will, so he tempts us to give in to complacency. This is spiritual warfare. In light of this battle, we must press on, moving forward to the high mark to which God has called us.

In leader making, we have vision for those under our stewardship. We see our growing disciples as future leaders who will one day become great men and women of God. As congregational leader, cast this vision for each person in your congregation. Though geared toward leaders in a congregation, the principles in this section are also valid for leaders of a home; remember, as you raise your children, you are actually raising leaders.

CALLED TO SERVE

"But the greatest among you shall be your servant." – Matthew 23:11

Just because a person has an "alpha male" personality, it does not automatically mean he will be a good leader. He may be strong-willed and stubborn, but not necessarily a leader unless he has been discipled as such. Leadership is not a matter of personality, but a matter of responsibility before God. This high calling has more to do with having the right heart attitude than the "right" set of traits. Like Samuel, we must learn that *"God sees not as man sees, for man looks at the outward appearance, but the Lord looks at the heart"* (1 Samuel 16:7). For leadership roles, we must look for people

Notes:

157

of character, whatever their appearance or personality, willing to step up to their God-given responsibility.

A leader must be prepared to serve, for as we lead, we represent Messiah, the greatest Servant of all! A servant-leader accepts and handles his (or her) responsibility with maturity; first in the heart, then in the home, and finally in the congregation (1 Timothy 1:5; 3:5, 15). If you are a parent, for better or worse, you are a leader. As we honor Yeshua in our hearts and homes, we also honor Him in the congregation, and accept the responsibilities He has placed before us.

Any authority a leader has is only to be used for the sake of serving others, never for ourselves. Through every aspect of His life, Yeshua demonstrated this for us. When the enemy asked Him to turn stones into bread (Matthew 4), Yeshua refused to use His miraculous power and authority for Himself. Later, however, He would freely use it to feed 5,000 hungry people. At Yeshua's death, people tempted Him to prove His identity as the Son of God by using His power to save Himself. However, because He was the Son of God, He refused to do this, using His power not to save, but to willingly sacrifice Himself, leaving an example for leaders to follow. We lead in the steps of our Messiah who emptied Himself, coming as God in the flesh to serve rather than be served, ultimately giving His life for the sake of His loved ones. Proper leadership is always servant-leadership.

QUANTIFYING QUALIFIED SERVANT-LEADERS
A plurality of elders

Although it is true that we are all equal before God, this does not mean that we do not need to appoint leaders. Without proper leadership, chaos ensues, and those with stronger personalities will always win. Every ministry in the congregation must be headed up by leaders who are prepared to shoulder the responsibility, take the blame, and direct the team, keeping things running smoothly. Each team leader is there not only to "get stuff done", but to care for the team. Though they are not the primary congregational leader, they each take the role of a shepherd over their particular ministry team.

This system of leadership is normative throughout Scripture. As we mentioned previously, before there were synagogues, there were elders in every community (Deuteronomy 19:12; 21:3-6; 19-20; Ezra 10-14). As synagogues came onto the scene, each had its own elders as well (Luke 7:3-5). In each of

Notes:

the Messianic congregations, elders were to be appointed (Acts 14:23; 20:17; 1 Timothy 5:17; Jacob 5:14; 1 Peter 5:1,5). This was the norm, as someone must be willing to step up and take responsibility for issues that arise. Elders are necessary, so do not wait for the perfect ones to come your way. Work with what you have and trust the Lord.

✡ *There is a "first among equals"* ✡

In Scripture, we see that there was a plurality of elders, but always a first among equals. Amongst the *shlichim* (the Apostles), Peter was the recognized leader (Acts 2:14). As such, he stepped up and took on matters of responsibility. We see very clearly that within the *shamashim*, Stephen was first among equals (Acts 6:5, 8). In the group of elders leading the congregation in Jerusalem, Jacob was the one in charge (Acts 12:17). Even in heaven we see one of the elders stepping up as leader to tell John to stop weeping (Revelation 5:5).

Although we may be called by many different titles, one thing is clear: the elder in charge is to be a servant to all the others (Matthew 20:25-28). An elder is given authority only to serve, and his title simply helps to point people towards the right person to blame if there is a problem. Elders live to serve, and in doing so fulfill their calling before God.

As a result of sin, however, people are continually looking for validation, and many believe that this will be found in a title such as "elder." Focusing on something so insignificant as a title, though, will only lead to failure. We must recognize that the highest title we will ever receive is that of "child of God." To hold this title is an honor far greater than any of us will ever deserve. If a person is not satisfied with this title, they will not be content with anything else and will become like a dog chasing its tail, on a continual search for validation. A person who is given a title must rely not on the title, but on *Ruach HaKodesh* for empowerment.

NORMAL GROWTH IN THE CONGREGATION

A leader does not simply show up, he or she is carefully developed from within the congregation. This process of growth is what we expect as the "norm." Though there will be exceptions to this rule, do not allow these to become your precedents. In the normal method of spiritual growth in the congregation, contact making leads to disciple making which leads to mem-

Notes:

159

ber making which leads to leader making. Our leaders come from within our membership. This is a biblical, though frequently unpopular, framework.

Notes:

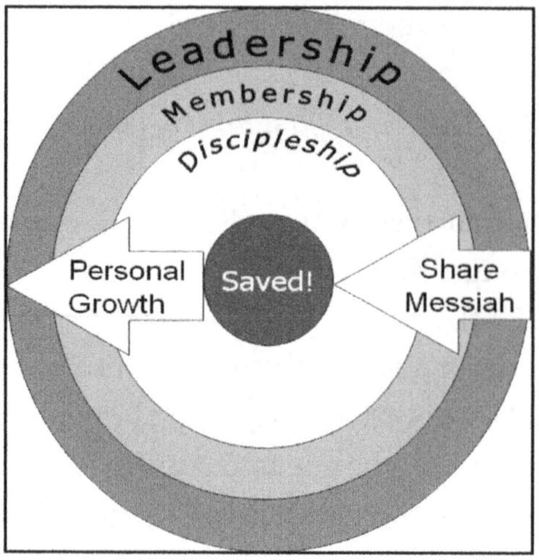

Figure 6.5

Once, an elder from a very well-known Messianic congregation moved to the area in which I was serving as a congregational elder. He visited our congregation and after the service approached me and introduced himself, explaining who he was and asking in what capacity he could serve. When I began to explain our membership process, he interrupted me repeating that he had been an elder at his previous congregation. I responded by restating our requirement that all people wishing to serve in our community must take our membership classes. He could not wrap his mind around this, yet begrudgingly agreed to try out our membership class. However, as the class progressed, he was still not able to understand why we did things so differently than his previous congregation. He felt it was demeaning and humiliating that he be required to go through membership as a seasoned elder. As a result, he chose to move on from our congregation. We parted on good terms, and he went on to find a place where he felt more appreciated. Though some may see this as a great loss, we trust the Lord's will. This is His business. Our job is to have standards that are wholesome, fair, and even-handed.

THE PRINCIPLE OF LEADERSHIP DEVELOPMENT

"The things which you have heard from me in the presence of many witnesses, entrust these to faithful men who will be able to teach others also." - 2 Timothy 2:2

LEARN FROM GOOD PEOPLE

Leaders are developed through one-on-one training. Paul told Timothy to entrust the things which he himself had personally taught him. Timothy was also comprehensively trained, *"in the presence of many witnesses."* Timothy's training did not consist of teachings which were meant only for himself, but of primary issues that everyone needed to know, matters which Timothy would later pass on to others. Timothy was authoritatively trained, *"from me."* This was direct discipleship.

As you train a person to be a leader, you need to be able to personally ask them, "How is it going? How are you doing in this area?" and respond appropriately. This is what Paul was doing as he wrote 1 and 2 Timothy, using his authority to provide help and guidance for Timothy in how to better lead his struggling congregation. As you develop leaders, you must continue to be there for them, mentoring them, coaching them, and providing support for them through the ups and downs of leadership.

LOOK FOR GOOD PEOPLE

Being a believer for many years does not in itself qualify a person for leadership. Once there was a man who was fired from his job after twenty years of work. In shock, he asked his boss, "How can you fire me after twenty years of service and experience?" The boss responded, "Twenty years? You merely have had one year of experience twenty times!" We need leaders who are grounded and rooted in the truth, continually being conformed to the image of Messiah.

As you choose people from your discipled membership to help share in the work, you need to look for faithful servants who have "CASH" (**C**haracter, **A**ttitude, **S**kills, and **H**abits).

CHARACTER & ATTITUDE

In 2 Timothy 2:2, the word *"faithful"* implies both **C**haracter and **A**ttitude. Look for people of character, who will hold firm to their integrity in any situation, as well as those who have the right attitude, who trust the Lord, and believe God rather than complain. Do not seek out those who appear wise, for they may merely be wise guys. *"The fear of the Lord* (the right attitude) *is the beginning of wisdom"* (Proverbs 1:7). Look for people who have a rev-

Notes:

_____

_____

_____

_____

_____

_____

_____

_____

_____

_____

_____

_____

_____

_____

_____

erence for God, people with the fear of the Lord in their eyes, who are living for Him. These are the people to invest in and to raise up as leaders, for they are the ones who have true wisdom.

SKILLS & HABITS

Notes:

Next, the word "*able*" in this verse implies the need for competency; leaders must also have certain **S**kills and **H**abits. Though it is not necessary that a person possess all that is necessary for the task at the beginning, skills are easier to teach than habits. For those with poor habits, who may be unable to arrive anywhere on time or are sporadic in their prayer life, re-parenting in the form of discipleship is needed.

A wise leader first looks for discipled people with signs of CASH, and then trains them from there. Beware of being need-driven, accepting anyone who shows interest in helping you. Remember, your role as a leader is to build people up. If you do not have enough people for the task at hand, pare down your program so that people are not overwhelmed, and so you do not need to lean upon those who are not yet discipled. Make sure you evaluate each volunteer properly by your values, taking great care not to succumb to being need-driven.

THE PRACTICE OF LEADERSHIP DEVELOPMENT

If a new believer or newcomer to your congregation shows signs of CASH and displays potential in a certain area, it may be tempting to give them a title and immediately place them in a position of leadership. This is very unwise, however, for leadership is far more than a title, and disaster will ensue if a person is not adequately prepared for such a position. Imagine if one day your five-year-old showed interest in cooking, and even exhibited some skill as he helped you stir the brownie mix. "This is wonderful," you might think, "I'll put him in charge of cooking dinner!" Of course no parent would actually assent to this, for at this point, all the child is ready for is a simple task: perhaps next he could set the table! All future leaders, whether young or old, need to be developed step by step. Remember, we want people to grow slowly, for though weeds spring up quickly, fruit trees take years to develop before they can produce good, mature fruit.

"TARP" is an acrostic that will help us to understand the four-fold process by which we develop leaders, from the initial phases of training to maturity.

This system can be used in the congregation as well as in the home, for both a parent and an elder have the same goal: to raise godly leaders.

TASK GIVEN: ORIENTATION PHASE

Be direct

As a person in your community grows in their walk with the Lord through the process of discipleship and membership, they will eventually be ready to be entrusted with a task. At this point, the trainee is not expected to know what they are doing; they are there to learn. Although they may not yet have all the skills needed for the task, these things can be developed if they have the right character and attitude. However, if at this point they attempt to tell you how to run things, judging everything you do in light of their previous congregation, this is a red flag. Look to develop people who are not already "wise," but who fear the Lord, desiring to serve Him with a humble and teachable heart.

When you give a person a task, you must first provide orientation as to what will be expected of them, just as an employee is required to go through orientation at the start of a new job. At this point, it is essential that the steps of the job be clearly explained and expectations laid out. It is likely that the person desires to provide quality work, but if the expectations are unclear, it will lead to confusion and frustration for both of you. If a trainer is not direct at the right time, they will most likely become overly direct at the wrong time. It is wrong for a trainer to leave a trainee to their own devices but then become upset when they do not live up to the unspoken expectations. In order for the training to be a success, directly inform the trainee up front what will be expected of them.

Allow me to illustrate how this works: Perhaps as a new planter, you have the task of setting up chairs for the service (along with everything else!) One day, the person you are discipling comes along with you and watches as you set up the chairs. As you work, you ask him if he can help out. When he agrees, you explain step by step what needs to be done (the number of chairs to be set in each row, how wide each aisle needs to be, etc.) After completing the task, you ask if he can help out with this on a regular basis, giving him the details of when he will need to arrive and what will be involved in the completion of the task each week. You now have a new assistant, ready to move to the next phase of leadership development.

Notes:

ASSISTANCE REQUIRED: EXPLANATION PHASE

Be thorough

As the person continues to assist regularly, allow them time to adjust to their new role. Over time, assess their level of dedication to the work and whether they are able to keep their commitment to regular service. As the person takes ownership of their new responsibility, they may begin to ask questions: ("Why do we set the chairs up this way? Why don't we put them in a circle instead?"...) Encourage such inquiries, viewing them as a sign of growth rather than as a threat to your authority. If the person grew up in a dysfunctional home or came from a spiritually dysfunctional congregation, they may be hesitant to ask questions. Assure such people that they are in a safe environment where their questions are expected and welcomed.

As questions are raised, be thorough in your responses, taking the opportunity to further explain the values which underlie every task in the congregation. Do not defer to an "easy" answer such as, "That's just the way we do it here," or "Because I'm the leader and I said so," but explain carefully ("We set them up this way because we value God's Word and want everyone to be facing toward the Word of God at the front of the room.")

If you do not know the answer to the person's question, let them know that you will find out and get back to them about it. This is very important, for trainees need to know and understand the value of their service. They cannot assist if they do not fully understand what they are assisting to attain. Leadership development requires deep investment in people. This time of explanation is a valuable opportunity to more deeply communicate the values of your congregation to its future leaders.

RESPONSIBILITY DEVELOPED: PARTICIPATION PHASE

Be creative

Over time, if the person has proven to be a trustworthy and dependable assistant, he may now be ready to handle a greater position of responsibility, given charge over the task.

When a person agrees to step up in this way, it is important that their natural creativity be encouraged and that they be given freedom to present their own ideas of how to improve the system. People mature as they take this stewardship responsibility over the task entrusted to them. It must be under-

Notes:

stood that healthy things grow, and that without creativity, the community will fossilize over time. As leaders, we need to be continually evaluating our systems and making changes in order to be more effective in glorifying God and reaching out to lost people around us. At this point, a trainer should empower a trainee in their God-given creativity, not presuming to have all the answers, but leaving the door open for growth, encouraging the trainee as a partner in ministry.

However, as you discuss these matters together, continue to ensure that the person has a deep understanding of the values behind their role, for people in service are not here to change the values of the congregation, but to understand them and contribute to the work of the congregation more effectively and efficiently. As our methods of ministry grow and change in order to meet the needs of our ever-changing world, we must ensure that our values stand firm, for God's Word never changes. Through this process of growth, pray that the Lord gives each new leader creativity stemming from an unwavering commitment to the mission and values of your community.

POSITION ESTABLISHED: DELEGATION PHASE

Be steady

As the person takes on their new role of responsibility, a leader is born. It is at this point that they receive a title serving to define their new responsibility. ("You are now the 'chairman'!")

In developing leaders, we must be careful not to bestow a title too quickly, withholding this until it actually describes the responsibility which the person is already ably handling. For instance, an individual should not be given the title of *shamash* until they have consistently demonstrated faithfulness in service. A person should not be made an elder until they have shown wisdom, counsel, and clear direction in the Word of God for the community and congregation. Ideally, when a person is given a title, people should say, "Wasn't he already a *shamash*? I was sure that he was!" The congregation should be able to observe the person's faithful dedication to the responsibilities of ministry, carried out as if he had held the title all along.

As you confer this title, make sure the person fully understands the responsibility that comes along with it. If they are wary of this responsibility, encourage them. Remind them that as the congregational leader, you are the one to whom the blame will ultimately fall. Explain that because you laid

Notes:

Notes:

hands on them, you will take responsibility for their welfare, ensuring that they do not get hurt.

At this stage, you must take the role of cheerleader in the new leader's life, encouraging and supporting them in their position. Though this may not connect naturally with your personality, you must not allow your personality to dominate you, but be dominated only by the lordship of Yeshua. Just as a parent's voice continues to be important in the life of their adult child, your voice is powerful as you communicate messages such as "I know you can do this;" "God is with you," "You are more than a conqueror in Him..." All leaders need mature, stabilizing authority in their life reminding them that there is always someone there for them who believes in them, and that they can have victory in every situation because God is with them. In the ups and downs of ministry, all of us need steady reminders of how God has answered prayers in the past, and how He has enabled us to step up and handle difficult situations in the present. You must remind them of the truth that God has given them, *everything pertaining to life and godliness* (2 Peter 1:3). Indeed, they have everything it takes, but it will take everything they've got.

As you encourage those whom you have trained, you must believe God's Word, first for yourself and also for them, and have a vision of victory for them. If a leader does not believe the people in his congregation are more than conquerors, he will not be very affirming of them. With God's perspective, a trainer is able to give grace rather than judgment when a trainee makes a mistake, for they understand that we all make mistakes. Good leadership does not fix blame, but fixes problems, acting with maturity and consistency on behalf of those under their stewardship. People need to be given permission to fail, for they will never succeed if they are afraid of failure. As they make decisions, they will make mistakes; this comes along with responsibility. When this happens, process the mistake with them, explaining how the situation should be handled according to God's Word, and encourage them to keep moving ahead.

As the new leader takes on this active role of service in the congregation, he or she should be encouraged to recruit and train new assistants to help with the task and learn the values behind it. In this way, we develop a self-sustaining system, continually developing and training new leaders from within the community, for in God's Word we see that a true leader does not make followers, he makes leaders.

Here is a visualized way to explain this training plan through which leaders are developed:

STEPS	INITIAL —	INVESTING —	GROWTH —	MATURITY
For Trainer	Be Direct	Be Accurate	Be Creative	Be Steady
For Trainee	Orientation	Explanation	Participation	Delegation
Activity	Task	Assistance	Responsibility	Position

Figure 6.6

Through this framework, we see the proper order for leadership development in a congregation. As you develop leaders, do not give in to the temptation to take shortcuts. Even if a person has great skills and may even have been a leader in another congregation, this does not mean that they are ready for a position of leadership. Skills and gifts are irrelevant if they do not contribute to the mission of the congregation. All people must go through discipleship and membership in order to be taught in the values of the congregation, and then use their skills to further the will of God in that setting.

As leaders are developed, they will serve in various roles within the congregation, whether as elders, deacons, or overseers involved in administration and management.

CAREFUL SERVANT-LEADERSHIP TRAINING PRINCIPLES

"Do not lay hands upon anyone too hastily and thereby share responsibility for the sins of others; keep yourself free from sin." – 1 Timothy 5:22

Raising up leaders is a great privilege, but also a serious responsibility. As we develop leaders for service in the congregation, we must be careful, for we will be held responsible for those we commission for service. In leader making, seek the Lord throughout the entire process, and remember these principles we have discussed:

Notes:

167

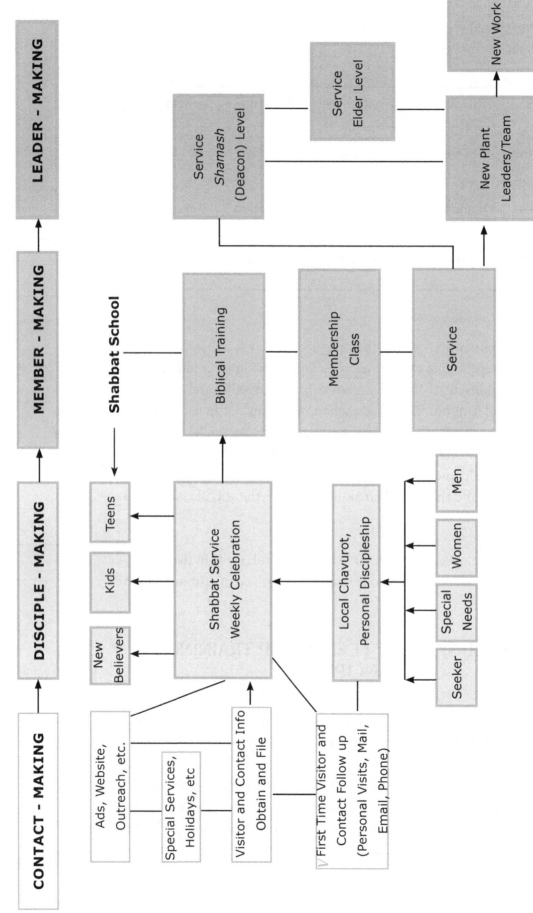

Figure 6.7

✡ Be careful: Do not judge according to the flesh, but recognize that all are called to leadership.   Leadership is a vision of maturity for all believers (1 Timothy 3:1).

✡ Be careful: Recognize that leadership is not a personality trait, but is a responsibility taken; a responsibility to serve. (Matthew 20:26-28).

✡ Be careful: Do not be need-driven or people-pleasing, but be people-oriented. We are called to equip people for service (Ephesians 4:12) and develop them in service (Ephesians 4:16). As we raise up leaders, we need to make certain they are growing properly, and care more about their growth than about getting the job done.

✡ Be careful: Remember that leaders must model the values which we want others to have (Hebrews 13:7). We must be servant-leaders to the servant-leaders in our communities!

As we conclude this section on the ministry of the Word, consider this flow chart (Figure 6.7), further detailing the progression of contact making, disciple making, member making, and leader making in a congregation.

Notes:

_____

_____

_____

_____

_____

_____

_____

_____

_____

_____

_____

_____

_____

_____

_____

_____

CHAPTER 7

THE MINISTRY OF OVERSEER

"And God has appointed in the congregation, first apostles, second prophets, third teachers, then miracles, then gifts of healings, helps, administrations, various kinds of tongues." – 1 Corinthians 12:28

The ministry of prayer and the ministry of the Word are absolutely primary in a Messianic congregation as we live out Yeshua's work as our *Kohen Gadol*, as well as His work as the Living Word, our greatest Prophet. These two responsibilities are what we live for: to worship the Lord through prayer, and to raise up great men and women of God through the ministry of the Word.

Many leaders, however, have little time to focus on these primary ministries as there are frequently too many other tasks vying for their time. This is where the final responsibility of a Messianic congregation comes in: the ministry of overseer, through which we live out Yeshua's work as King.

The ministry of overseer, which includes the work of administration and management of the congregation, serves to assist the congregational leader and other elders in their calling to focus on the ministries of prayer and the Word full-time. Indeed, the purpose of the overseer ministry is to ensure that these vital responsibilities remain the focus of the congregation.

As previously stated, administration serves to provide structure for the congregation, as a skeleton provides structure and balance for the body. Admin generally takes place behind the scenes, and when successful, is nearly invisible. In fact, in a very healthy congregation, the only time the ministry of overseer is perceived is when the announcements are made during a service. Though they maintain a low profile, those who serve in this role are absolutely essential, bringing stability to the congregation, and providing ground for healthy fellowship, enabling the congregation to move forward in achieving its goals.

An illustration to help us better understand this vital role is found in 1 Corinthians 12:28. The Greek word used for "administration" in this verse is *kubernesis*. In Acts 27:11 and Jacob 3:4, a similar word derived from the same root is used to speak of the pilot of a ship. On a ship, the captain sets the destination, but the pilot is the one who actually navigates the way through storms and obstacles. Likewise, in a congregation, the congregational leader determines the ministry's strategic direction, but the administration are the ones who steer the "ship" in order to reach the goal.

OVERSEEING & FELLOWSHIP

"and I pray that the fellowship of your faith may become effective through the knowledge of every good thing which is in you for Messiah's sake." - Philemon 6

As events are planned, roles are delegated, and classes are set up, a wise overseer ensures that congregational activities center around only those things which promote true fellowship in the community.

Today the term "fellowship" is used so loosely. People label their get-togethers as "fellowship" when really all they are doing is socializing, hanging out together eating dinner or watching a sports game. There is nothing wrong with these things, but socializing is a result of fellowship, not true fellowship itself. The Greek word for "fellowship," *koinonia*, comes from the root word "common." Believers have Yeshua in common with one another; thus, our fellowship is about Him. True fellowship is enjoyed in those things which are primary, not secondary. (For more information on primary and secondary matters, see page 42).

In Scripture, we see that those who know Messiah have fellowship with the Lord (1 Corinthians 1:9, Philippians 3:10, 1 John 1:3, 6-7, etc.) Believers also have fellowship with the Lord's people (2 Corinthians 6:14, Philippians 2:1-2). We fellowship together when we worship (Psalm 55:14), when we study the Word (Acts 2:42), when we witness (Galatians 2:9, Philippians 1:5), and when we support and minister to each other (Romans 15:26, Hebrews 13:16).

Notes:

In light of their role to ensure that the essential priorities of a congregation are kept in focus, an overseer must use discretion when scheduling congregational "fellowship." Those things which do not contribute to genuine spiritual fellowship for the congregation need not be allotted time and resources in the agenda of the congregation.

Notes:

THE OFFICE OF OVERSEER IN SCRIPTURE

Throughout Scripture, we see the importance of the role of overseer as it is lived out in relation to the ministries of prayer and the Word. In both the New Covenant and the Hebrew Scriptures, this is a normative pattern presented for the people of Israel, for community and congregational life. This model serves as a paradigm for congregational life today.

OVERSEER IN THE TORAH

"Moses' father-in-law said to him, 'The thing that you are doing is not good.'"
– Exodus 18:17

After the people of Israel had safely crossed the Red Sea, Moses' father-in-law, Jethro, came for a visit. After rejoicing together over all that God had done for Israel, Jethro stayed around to watch Moses work. When he saw all that Moses was doing for the people all day long, Jethro stated the obvious in the form of a question, *"Why do you alone sit and all the people stand about you from morning to evening?"* (Exodus 18:14) In response, Moses told his father-in-law, *"Because the people come to me to inquire of God when they have a dispute ... "* (Exodus 18:15-16) Jethro identified a problem here and told his son in law, *"The thing you are doing is lo tov (not good). You will surely wear out both yourself and the people who are with you, for the task is too heavy for you; you cannot do it alone."* (Exodus 18:17-18)

Jethro then offered his counsel on the matter, first reviewing with Moses the good that was presently being done. Moses was already successfully leading the people in prayer as the "people's representative before God." (Exodus 18:19) He was also leading in the ministry of the Word, through instruction and application, *"teaching them the statutes and the laws, and making known to them the way in which they are to walk and the work they are to do."* (Exodus 18:20)

However, Moses was also singlehandedly attempting to address every issue that arose in the community. Though this may have seemed necessary, in reality, it was burning Moses out. Jethro goes on in verses 21-23 to propose a solution. He instructs Moses to select *able men who fear God... and hate dishonest gain* from among the people, and appoint them to share the responsibility of judging the people, taking on the brunt of the work that Moses had been doing. Here again we see the vital role that delegation must play in a leader's life.

Once people are trained up as leaders in the values of the community (notice how Jethro emphasized the ministry of the Word before mentioning delegation), they are now able to assist you in leadership, particularly in areas of administration. As other leaders stepped up to share the responsibility, Moses was not stepping down. He would still be there to supervise these leaders and address the most difficult cases that came up among the people, but he would now be *able to endure* as he ministered in his areas of primary responsibility.

OVERSEER IN THE NEW COVENANT

Over 1,500 years later, we see this same pattern as we study the development of the congregation in Jerusalem through the book of Acts. In the early stages of the congregation seen in Acts chapters 1-5, the only people involved in service were the apostles. As leaders, they ably handled all of the congregational responsibilities including prayer, teaching, outreach, handling of finances, etc.

This system worked for a while, but as the congregation grew, the needs soon outnumbered the personnel. As greater administrative needs arose, the apostles were not taken off guard. They had anticipated growth and had been training people to assist in leadership responsibilities so that they could focus on their primary ministries of prayer and the Word (Acts 6:2). So, in Acts 6-11, we see that some of the work was delegated to new leaders: Steven and his team leading in practical service, Phillip reaching out to people in the surrounding areas, and Barnabas stepping up to work alongside Paul in ministry. Finally, in chapter 12, Peter passed the baton of leadership completely over to Jacob and his team. At this point, local leadership took over and Peter moved on to further ministry.

Notes:

_____

_____

_____

_____

_____

_____

_____

_____

_____

_____

_____

_____

_____

_____

_____

_____

173

MINISTRY THROUGH MANAGING

Acts 6:1-7

As we continue our study on the ministry of overseer, we will focus in on Acts 6, and the situation which led to great growth of the congregation in Jerusalem. The apostles' response to the situation at hand models for us the godly outlook of a mature servant-leader, and the wise delegation of the ministry of overseer.

THE TRIAL OF VILLIFIED LEADERSHIP

Acts 6:1

"Now at this time while the disciples were increasing in number, a complaint arose on the part of the Hellenistic Jews against the native Hebrews, because their widows were being overlooked in the daily serving of food." – Acts 6:1

LOVE IS TESTED

Just when everything was going well for the apostles, this complaint threw a wrench into the system. The widows among the "Hellenistic," or Greek-speaking Jews, were not being served in the daily distribution of food, and this group of believers was upset over it.

At this point in Acts, the ministry was focused on the Jewish people of the apostles' own community. This complaint brought a new question to the forefront: did God care about the Greek-speaking Jews as well? The apostles' leadership was being tested. How would they react? First, they recognized God's greater purpose in permitting this trial. The event expanded their vision for the new congregation, and they stepped up to respond to the complaint with love.

From the apostles' example, we are reminded to never despise problems, for they are very important in the plan of God. Every "problem" we face as leaders is a test of love. Like a father taking time to help his child who struggles with her homework day after day, we love those under our care and do not give up on them. In God's eyes, it is always too soon to quit. We must persevere in love as people complain, fail, misunderstand, and need to be reminded of the truth over and over again. Looking to Yeshua will bring the victory through these tests of love!

Notes:

PROBLEMS REVEAL PRIORITIES

"each man's work will become evident; for the day will show it because it is to be revealed with fire, and the fire itself will test the quality of each man's work." – 1 Corinthians 3:13

Notes:

Problems will always reveal your true priorities. When everything is going well, you may be able to do all the things you set out to accomplish. However, when you do not have enough time, money, personnel, or space to do it all, you must choose where your focus will lie. This is seen in the home as well as in the congregation. When everything is going well at your home, your children may think that movies are just as important as food. That is, until the budget becomes too tight to have both. As you make these decisions, your leadership roles will continually be tested.

✡ 1st reason for failure: People cannot express their concerns

In some congregations, people have nowhere to go with their concerns. If they speak up about those things which are important to them, they may feel that they are being judged by others as having a rebellious spirit. This is not healthy, for each person in the community needs to be able to express their concerns to the leadership, and, in response, be shown love, care, and kindness. Having no platform for people to voice their concerns will ultimately lead to failure in the congregation.

✡ 1st step toward victory: A venue for problems to be aired

The first step towards victory, then, is providing a venue for problems to be addressed. Our righteousness is not found in solving problems but in addressing them, and a leader must be a safe harbor to whom people can come to discuss their problems. If a person cannot bring their concerns to their leaders, they will revert to gossiping or complaining. A congregation needs to have a system set up so that people can voice their concerns and complaints to the leadership just as the Greek-speaking Jewish people did.

THE TRUTH OF VICTORIOUS LEADERSHIP

Acts 6:2-6

As the apostles moved forward in addressing the problem, we see how they acted upon three matters which are vital for the ministry of overseer: prioritization, delegation, and supervision.

175

VICTORIOUS LEADERS PRIORITIZE

"So the twelve summoned the congregation of the disciples and said, "It is not desirable for us to neglect the Word of God in order to serve tables." – Acts 6:2

Notes:

The apostles discerned that they could not stop serving the Word in order to serve tables. This was a courageous response, to be able to say "no" in order to say "yes" to their primary calling. This is not easy to do when a felt need is expressed in your community. In these cases, it may appear that the most loving thing to do would be to say yes to everything! However, to say "yes" would hinder the apostles from meeting the community's deeper needs. The people's request for food to be brought to their widows was important, but it was not the priority of the elders.

Those entrusted with overseeing the work set the priorities for the work. Just as parents are the ones to set the priorities in a home, elders set the priorities in a congregation. Unfortunately, many elders do not have a firm grasp of what their primary responsibilities are, and therefore end up doing all kinds of different things in order to keep busy. It is essential that elders realize that there are higher priorities and lower priorities in ministry, and be able to make the distinction.

"But we will devote ourselves to prayer and to the ministry of the Word." – Acts 6:4

In verse 4, we see the reason why the apostles could not take time to serve tables: they were devoted to the higher priorities of prayer and the Word. As we have discussed, prayer undergirds the congregation, and the Word enables the growth of the congregation. In light of these, the overseer ministry provides healthy fellowship in the congregation through the establishment of healthy structure, enabling the vital ministries of prayer and the Word to continue.

Leaders are the ones to establish which priorities are essential; they draw the line for what is primary. In doing so, they must also enforce the priorities they have established, for they will be tested on them every single day. Consistency in this area is vital. You have a stewardship role over your flock. If a parent allowed their child to pick and choose which rules should be enforced, the result would be chaos. Those under leadership do not have the authority to throw out the priorities they do not agree with.

✡ 2nd reason for failure: Lack of stewardship priorities

Congregations that do not have clearly set stewardship priorities are a disaster waiting to happen. Failure will ensue if there is no distinction set between lower and higher priorities.

✡ 2nd step toward victory: Prioritizing values to vision

For victory, leaders must hold firmly to their priorities, learning to graciously say "no" to lower priorities in light of the higher priorities that have been established. These higher priorities are those to which we must be devoted. In Acts 6:4, the word "devote," *proskartereo*, means to "attend continually." Paul uses this word in Colossians 4:2 when he exhorts believers to, "*Devote yourselves to prayer.*" (See also Romans 12:12, Acts 1:14, 2:42).

VICTORIOUS LEADERS DEPUTIZE

"*Therefore, brethren, select from among you seven men...*" – Acts 6:3a

Though it was not in their realm of priority, the apostles did not dismiss the problem at hand, nor did they speculate as to the motivation of those who conveyed the message. Rather, in taking action to address the complaint, the apostles trusted the complainers. This was not a loyalty group, but a values-oriented group. If a person in your congregation brings a complaint to your attention, do not take it personally. Listen to them, discern the relevance of the complaint in light of your primary values, and care about the people involved.

The apostles took responsibility to address the need, yet did not take the responsibility of the solution on themselves. Instead, they delegated this tactical role to others who would become *shamashim* in the community. Prioritization leads to delegation.

"*... men of good reputation, full of the Spirit and of wisdom, whom we may put in charge of this task.*" – Acts 6:3b

The apostles determined specific qualifications for the new leadership position that was being developed. The people proposed to fill a leadership position must be tested, shown to be individuals of good reputation who are

Notes:

177

controlled (full of the Spirit,) and capable (filled with wisdom). The apostles determined these qualifications, and then brought them before the entire congregation.

✡ 3rd reason for failure: Lack of appropriate delegation

Notes:

Some leaders fail because they do not have anyone on whom they can trust to delegate tasks. This situation can stem from a variety of reasons. If a leader has unrelenting standards, requiring everything to be done exactly the way he likes it to be, then no one but himself will ever be good enough for the task. Also, if a leader is unclear as to the qualifications needed for the position, he will never find anyone suitable enough for the job.

✡ 3rd step toward victory: Teach clearly & entrust to others

In order to have trustworthy people to whom you can delegate tasks, you must develop them in trustworthiness. After this, you need to clearly communicate your expectations, and then step back and allow them to accomplish the task. (For specific guidelines on how to delegate, see page 183).

VICTORIOUS LEADERS SUPERVISE

"... whom we may put in charge of this task." – Acts 6:3b

The apostles took responsibility for the work. Leaders are the ones who are ultimately responsible for the implementation and quality of the work done in the congregation. The apostles stepped up to this role, supervising the men placed in charge of the work, in order to make sure the widows were being properly cared for. This is what leaders do; they take a supervisory responsibility for their entire community. In so doing, leaders do not blame others. Any leader who throws someone else "under the bus" is not being a leader. If the person to whom the task was delegated fails, it is because the leader made a bad decision in putting that person in charge.

When you place a person in a leadership position, you support them in their position and the decisions they make within it. If they fail, you are the one to blame. As the responsible party, people need to address these issues with you.

178

"The statement found approval with the whole congregation; and they chose Stephen, a man full of faith and of the Holy Spirit, and Philip, Prochorus, Nicanor, Timon, Parmenas and Nicolas, a proselyte from Antioch." – Acts 6:5

The apostles also took responsiblity for the witness. In light of the careful way they responded to the people's request, all were in agreement with the idea to delegate the ministry of serving tables.

When people bring a concern to an elder, they want to know that their voice is heard, that they are cared for, and that their problem will be addressed. They do not expect elders to take care of everything on their own, but rather to use their position to address issues. In this case, the apostles' solution proved to be more effective than it would have been had they taken on the responsibility themselves. The men chosen to work with the widows were not only men of righteous character, they were also equipped practically for the job. They each had Greek names, and would be able to communicate with the Greek-speaking widows in Greek.

"And these they brought before the apostles; and after praying, they laid their hands on them." – Acts 6:6

Finally, the apostles took responsibility for the workers. By laying hands on these men, they were publically committing to take a supervisory responsibility for them, identifying with them in their service.

As you commission people for service in your congregation, remember that in doing so, you are taking responsibility for them. Be wise about this, and lay hands on no one quickly (1 Timothy 5:22).

✡ 4th reason for failure: A lack of responsibility, accountability and supervision

When a leader does not take a supervisory responsibility for the work, witness, and workers under his care, implementing a reporting system in order to stay informed of their progress, it will lead to failure.

✡ 4th step toward victory: Good people need good supervision; bad people need better

Notes:

All of us are bad people who are saved by grace. Because of this, we all need God's supervision! Left to our own devices, we would not fare well. People mature in Messiah as they are properly supervised. Rather than being confining, it is only through guidance that the flock knows where they are going.

Notes:

THE TRIUMPH OF VINDICATED LEADERSHIP
Acts 6:7

"The Word of God kept on spreading; and the number of the disciples continued to increase greatly in Jerusalem, and a great many of the priests were becoming obedient to the faith." – Acts 6:7

THE RESULT OF THE WORKERS

Through the wise handling of the issue at hand, the apostles were enabled to continue in their primary ministry. As a result, the Word of God kept spreading because the ministry of the Word was not hindered. Though the enemy had attempted to bring division, God's Will prevailed.

When the enemy wants to attack a congregation, he will frequently target the leadership. This is because he knows that if he can hinder the leadership from doing their job, everything else will fall apart. Zechariah 13:7 states, *"Strike the Shepherd that the sheep may be scattered."* For the sake of the flock, we in leadership must be on our game, knowing and doing our job, handling issues as they arise, and looking to Messiah for wisdom and strength.

THE RESULT OF THE SPREADING WORD

As they continued to spread the Word, the number of disciples kept multiplying. If a congregation wants more disciples, they must prioritize the spreading of the Word. As more are saved and discipled, the congregation will grow. This is what we are working towards, not so we can have a mega-congregation, but so we can move forward to the day when all Israel will be saved!

THE RESULT OF THE WISE HANDLING OF THE SITUATION

Directly after this situation was resolved, a great number of *kohanim* came to faith in Messiah. The priests served in leadership themselves, and could readily recognize problems, for they experienced them all the time at the Temple. However, they could also see when problems were handled wisely and lovingly. These priests were drawn to the faith as they observed how the apostles dealt with the problem at hand. As we love one another through our everyday problems and difficulties, wisely addressing the issues that come up, others are watching. Will they be drawn to the Lord?

✡ 5th reason for failure: remaining ingrown

Remain ingrown and you will fail. The salt must be gotten out of the salt shaker. Some may think that merely focusing inward on one's own congregation will ensure its health; however, this is far from the case.

✡ 5th step toward victory: reaching out

After handling internal issues, bringing stability to areas of difficulty through dependence on God's grace, then, by the same grace of God, reach out with the Good News to others.

Good leadership casts a vision for this, encouraging others to use their gifts and reach out, trusting that failure is not going to be the last word on their lives. In order to ensure that each ministry in the congregation is moving forward in this way, make sure that each has a mission statement that is working toward the overall mission of the congregation, otherwise it is just taking up ground. Applied trust permits growth and unity.

MESSIANIC LEADERSHIP EMPOWERMENT

Empowering people through delegated responsibility

"Therefore, brethren, select from among you seven men of good reputation, full of the Spirit and of wisdom, whom we may put in charge of this task." – Acts 6:3

People will step up to take responsibility in various roles as they are empowered to do so. The Messianic congregation is the empowerment zone, and Messianic leaders are here to empower people, reminding them that they

Notes:

_____

_____

_____

_____

_____

_____

_____

_____

_____

_____

_____

_____

_____

_____

_____

can do all things through Messiah who strengthens them. We must believe what God says about those who are His, and challenge those in our care to believe His Word as well, reminding them that God will give all the resources they need to accomplish His purposes.

Notes:

Assure people that the congregation is a "safe zone" for them, a place where they do not have to be afraid of making mistakes, but can "spread their wings" as they grow in fulfilling their calling. Encourage people to try new things, neither avoiding nor planning on problems, but embracing them as they come, trusting in Yeshua, and in so doing, to learn and grow. There has only been one fool-proof plan, and He died in our place. Therefore, we surrender all our plans to Him, realizing that through weakness His power is made perfect. He thinks our weaknesses are wonderful, and we trust Him with them. Though it can be humbling to realize that our high point of ministry may be something we never planned on, we want Him to be the One to receive all the glory.

People who are empowered have:

✡ A sense of meaning

As you empower others to serve Messiah in their calling for Him, you are blessing them! Empowered people care about the tasks entrusted to them as they are given real ministry responsibility, and step up to be involved in the work of God. As they become more involved, their service for Yeshua becomes more and more important to them.

✡ A sense of competence

Empowered people feel confident about their ability to do the work at hand. They know they can follow through on their responsibility as the *Ruach* enables and blesses them.

✡ A sense of liberty

Empowered people feel free to make choices concerning the work because they are not micromanaged. They are told what needs to be done, and are then given freedom to be creative in how they get it done. Be careful not to limit creativity, attempting to make the task mechanistic. Give people freedom in the implementation of their responsibility and trust those you train, realizing that they may find an even better way to get the task done.

✡ A sense of impact

Empowered people feel that they have influence in their congregation when others listen to their ideas and appreciate their service. It is important that each member of the Body have a voice in the congregation. If people do not feel this way, it is an indication that something is wrong. We need to listen to and appreciate what each part of the Body brings to the table!

Notes:

THE MINISTRY OF DELEGATION

As we have touched on previously, delegation is the act of giving another person responsibility and authority to get a job done in an atmosphere of trust within a defined area of freedom. Although it may be tempting and at times easier to do everything yourself, this is not what a congregation is about. When God chose Abraham, He could have stopped there, being satisfied with his faithful service, but instead He chose to make him into a great nation, for God is worthy of the praise of many. Through delegation, we recognize this and empower people to step up to the calling of God on their life, having a vision for their growth.

A growing congregation is called to care for and help many people. In order to do this well, there needs to be a team approach, for one leader to put twenty people to work rather than attempt to do the work of twenty people! In my experience, it seems that the recruitment and subsequent care of volunteers is one of the most neglected yet most vitally needed areas of ministry in a healthy congregation.

As you prepare to delegate, consider the means by which you will recruit people to help fill a needed role. Perhaps you could send out an email to the membership explaining the need. Another option is to make an an-

183

Notes:

nouncement during your services and later to hold a meeting in order to explain the mission and vision of the ministry and provide more specific information for those who show interest.

As you develop leaders and recruit volunteers, it is vital that delegation be handled with wisdom and care. Proper delegation must include:

✡ Explained responsibility
When delegating a task, clearly tell the person all that will be expected of them, leaving no surprises. Ask follow-up questions to ensure that they understand, and let them know that they can come to you at any time if they have questions or concerns.

✡ Enough authority
In bestowing authority, you are simply granting the person access to the resources they will need in order to get the job done. Emphasize that we utilize our authority for the glory of God and for His work, never to serve ourselves.

✡ Explicit accountability
A person must understand that they will be held accountable for the accomplishment of the task. Let them know this up front; not to frighten them, but to equip them to be ready to be asked about it.

FREEDOM TO SERVE

"So if the Son makes you free, you will be free indeed!" - John 8:36

"As free people ... live as servants of God." - 1 Peter 2:16

God has set us free from sin through faith in Yeshua. Though many attempt to use this freedom for their own purposes, true fulfillment is found only as we use our liberty in order to fully serve Him! To help us understand this concept, think about a train which desires to be free from its tracks. If it tries to leave the tracks, it may think it is free, but will soon find that it is going nowhere fast! The train is only free to move as long as it stays on the rails. Our freedom is only found as we stay in the Will of God; we are not free apart from Him.

As God's servants walking in His Will, it is clear that we are to use our freedom to "do His business" until He returns (Luke 19:13). Ministry leaders are to empower those under their care in this truth, equipping them and encouraging them as they mature through delegated service. A person will be confident to move forward in their delegated role as they understand the parameters within which they have freedom to work. It is essential that each ministry leader explain these parameters and the concept of the "area of freedom" up front to every new servant who joins their team. Consider this diagram to help explain this concept of Messianic empowerment:

Figure 7.0

AREA OF FREEDOM

The box in the middle of the chart represents the area of freedom that every member, as well as each leader, in the congregation has. Each shares the same freedom and the same limitations to govern the boundaries of their freedom, relative to the area in which they serve.

SCRIPTURE/ETHICS/VALUES/LAWS

These are the unchangeable boundaries that no person or leader in the congregation is permitted to cross. In our freedom, we cannot go against Scripture, ethics, our congregational values, or the laws of the country and state.

POLICIES & PROCEDURES

These are the guidelines by which a congregation is run. For instance, it may be a policy in your congregation to provide a receipt for all expenditures made using the finances of the congregation. It is expected that all members, including elders, adhere to congregational policy. Policies are in place in order to aid in getting the work of a congregation accomplished.

Notes:

PLANS & BUDGETS

These are the means that each ministry leader is given to equip those serving on their team, so that the congregation does not spend money which they do not have, nor go beyond the resources allotted to them.

Notes:

JOB DESCRIPTIONS / FELLOW SERVANTS

Each ministry leader in the congregation has a job description and each has fellow servants who serve as their peers in ministry. In order for the congregation to function smoothly, dialogue and feedback are continually needed between people serving together. Each ministry needs to be asking each other how they are doing, inquiring as to whether they are running into problems, and being sensitive to prayer needs. Although each may live out their role somewhat differently, it must be recognized that fellow servants are also doing God's work, and that each has the same Holy Spirit leading and enabling them.

Leaders must make sure that each person is given the authority and encouragement to go to the very edge of their box, using every inch of space available within their defined area of freedom, every dollar that is budgeted, and every resource designated to use. Leaders need to give people freedom to make decisions on their own, not insisting that they confer with the congregational leader each time they would like to do something that is already under the covering of their authority.

A well-defined area of freedom will enable each ministry to succeed in moving forward to fulfill their calling, helping them not to feel overwhelmed as they understand the stewardship allotted to them.

CAN "BOXES" GROW?

"The first servant appeared, saying, 'Master, your mina has made ten minas more.' And he said to him, 'Well done, good servant, because you have been faithful in a very little thing, you are to be in authority over ten cities.'" – Luke 19:16-17

Absolutely! A congregational leader must have a vision for each person's "box" to grow as they expand the horizons of their ministry. Though the side of the box defined by our responsibility to Scripture, ethics, values, and laws cannot change, the other three sides are open to expansion. As ministries grow and needs increase, more funds can be budgeted. If policies and procedures are not helping to get the ministry's work accomplished, these also can be changed. Ministry leaders can adjust in order to help other ministries who may be struggling. Job descriptions likewise can be tweaked in order to better define a growing ministry.

If a ministry leader would like to go beyond the parameters of their box as a result of ministry growth, they can talk this over with the congregational leader and formulate a plan for their box to grow. For instance, if the contact making team planned for 100 people to respond to an outreach, but 200 people responded, this is wonderful! You can adjust the plan and find more money to give to a ministry that is blossoming.

Often times, the secular world understands this concept of thinking and acting "outside the box" better than believers do, in that they tend to make better use of the resources at their disposal, coming up with new, innovative ways to further their personal and career goals. Encourage your people to step up as followers of Messiah, not being fearful to use what they have been given, but rather to be faithful as they press on in Yeshua, in whom there is no condemnation.

As each "box" within the congregation grows, the congregation will grow as well! True growth happens as individuals and ministries grow, not as more people are found to attend your services. It is possible that God may bring a revival and cause your congregation to grow in this way, but is it probable? Perhaps God is waiting for you to first use the resources you have already been given!

CAN "BOXES" SHRINK?

"Another came, saying, 'Master, here is your mina, which I kept put away in a handkerchief; for I was afraid...' He said... Take the mina away from him and give it to the one who has ten minas.'" – Luke 19:20-24

Some people may be hesitant to use all the freedom allotted to them, perhaps afraid that if they spend all their money, someone may be upset with them, or that if they use all their space, people will judge them. These thoughts may be reflective of the home the person grew up in, where their parents were perhaps overly protective or rigid. Encourage people to come to you

Notes:

quickly if they are feeling overwhelmed with their responsibilities so that you can work through these things with them, for we each have a stewardship responsibility over our "box."

If the person is overwhelmed and feel they can no longer handle their task, do not judge them, but give the responsibility to another person who will move forward with the work so that it will be able to continue. We must wisely use the freedom given to us in order to further the work of God of which we are a part.

The ministry of overseer works alongside the ministries of prayer and the Word to bring health and balance to a congregation. This role is vital to the healthy functioning of a congregation and, when wisely managed, can facilitate great victories for the Lord!

Ministry/ System	Contact-Making	Disciple-Making	Member-Making	Leader-Making
Ministry of Prayer	Praying for and with contacts	Training believers in prayer and worship	Teaching members to pray for each others' needs and worship in unity	Leading in public prayer and worship
Ministry of the Word	Proclaiming the Word of salvation	Teaching believers to study and memorize Scripture	Training and evaluating disciples on values, theology, and beliefs	Training and coaching leaders in the ministry of the Word
Ministry of Overseer	Organizing the finding, filing, and following-up of contacts	Organizing opportunities for public and small group growth	Organizing membership classes, training for immersion, evaluations, member service, and care	Appointing *z'keinim* and *shamashim*

Figure 7.1

PART 3

PLANNING
FOR A HEALTHY
CONGREGATION

CHAPTER 8

THE PRAYERFUL & PRACTICAL PLANNING PROCESS

"But I will come to you after I go through Macedonia ... and perhaps I will stay with you, or even spend the winter... for I hope to remain with you for some time, if the Lord permits ..." – 1 Corinthians 16:5-7

Whether you are at the beginning of the congregation planting process, or already a seasoned congregational leader, in order to attain and sustain health in each of the vital ministries of your congregation, planning is essential, for when you fail to plan, by default, you plan to fail.

Planning is a decision-making process through which ministries develop their objectives and strategies, and then build action plans in order to achieve them. In planning, we make present decisions which will affect our future activities.

In Scripture, we see that planning is normative. Even the apostles had to plan in order to continue in effective ministry. This is demonstrated throughout Paul's writings. As a mature believer, Paul knew the importance of planning and took a stewardship responsibility over it. However, things did not always work out according to his plan (Romans 1:10-13; 15:22-24). As he planned, Paul knew that his steps were ultimately ordered by the Lord (Psalm 37:23). Like Paul, as we develop plans, we hold them with open hands and say, *"If the Lord permits."* (1 Corinthians 16:7, James 4:15) We plan while continually trusting in His grace to be our sufficiency as we move forward.

WHY SHOULD WE PLAN?

"In this case, moreover, it is required of stewards that one be found trustworthy." – 1 Corinthians 4:2

Through planning, we structure our community, involve our people, and manage our resources to achieve our goals for the Lord. We plan in order that we may be good stewards of the resources over which God has entrusted us. As leaders, we are to be faithful overseers over each area of ministry in our congregation, seeking to represent Yeshua in His roles as Prophet, Priest, and King.

Faithful stewardship means:

- ✡ Faithfully praying: Being dependent on Yeshua
- ✡ Faithfully planning: Making decisions for Yeshua
- ✡ Faithfully practicing: Acting with diligence in Yeshua

Leaders also have a stewardship to promote unity and trust within the congregation. Planning develops this unity and trust as it brings people to the same page regarding your common goals.

WHAT DOES PLANNING ENTAIL?

"When Gideon heard the account of the dream and its interpretation, he bowed in worship. He returned to the camp of Israel and said, 'Arise, for the Lord has given the camp of Midian into your hands.' He divided the 300 men into three companies, and he put trumpets and empty pitchers into the hands of all of them ..." – Judges 7:15-16

After bringing everything to the Lord in prayer, it is time to plan. In planning, a group of people comes together, assesses their resources, and then makes a decision about how to best utilize their resources in order to accomplish ministry goals within the calling God has for them. Planning is not developing a wish list, but making decisions that will be acted upon. Action must follow a decision, for no plan ever works on its own; rather, you must work the plan! Just as victory is not won in a huddle, but on the field, a plan is accomplished as it is put into action. When leaders are pro-active in planning for their responsibilities, they are more likely to be effective, and less likely to be merely reactive to the problems which inevitably arise.

Notes:

193

HOW DO WE EFFECTIVELY PLAN?

BASIC PLANNING

Notes:

In everyday life, we are constantly making plans even though we are usually not aware of it. Whether planning for a shopping trip or getting ready for a long day at work, people plan by continually addressing three simple questions:

- ✡ Where do we want to go?
- ✡ Where are we starting from?
- ✡ How do we get from here to there?

Though these questions are straightforward, the more people there are involved, the more intentionally and carefully they must each be considered. As many people are brought together for a common purpose, it takes time to strategically plan, but this is essential if you all want to arrive on the same page, aiming for the same goal.

The principles which we will cover in this section regarding planning are commonly taught in the business and management world, but are easily adapted to congregational planning. In light of our vital calling, Messianic congregations should certainly not set the bar lower than any secular business or corporation would, but must press on to the mark, taking a stewardship responsibility over that which God has entrusted to us.

PLANNING IN MESSIANIC CONGREGATIONS

Regularly scheduled planning meetings are necessary for a congregation to function in a healthy and effective manner. These meetings are needed on a more frequent basis during the planting process, but are just as essential once the congregation is established. In an established congregation, it is important to set aside a couple of days each year for the express purpose of prayer and planning.

In preparing for a planning meeting, bring together your core group or group of ministry leaders who are reliable and dependable. In order to avoid confusion, there should not be more than seven to ten people involved in a planning meeting. Those involved in the planning process must be only those who are committed to seeing the plan through to completion. Do not include people who do not plan on staying around to see the plans fulfilled.

As you meet together with your group, it is helpful to have an easel or white board handy so that you can write down ideas as they are raised and post them around the room for all to see and be able to participate in the discussion. Remembering your stewardship to promote unity and trust, make sure that people are heard as they propose and discuss ideas.

The beginning of a planning meeting should be spent taking time to look at the biblical paradigm of congregational health (See page 112). As mentioned previously, just as a doctor evaluates health based on what a healthy individual looks like, we must also have a plumbline by which to discern congregational health, rather than evaluate on the basis of how healthy we feel.

As we look at this paradigm, first focus on what is currently working well. Encourage people in how God is blessing their ministry. This is vital for the health and unity of the group, as the enemy works to discourage and divide. For the things that are going well, take time to praise God and thank Him!

Then, remembering our charge to represent Messiah as Prophet, Priest, and King, evaluate which areas require more attention, and focus in on two or three that will be most strategic. As you concentrate on these pertinent issues, you will be able to develop year-long goals in order to address them (1 Corinthians 16). Through this discussion, do not become discouraged by the needs, but rather recognize that through your assessment, you are growing and moving forward. No one does everything perfectly except for God, and we are all developing, finding ways to do things better, learning to delegate more, and plan more effectively. So do not condemn yourself, for there is no condemnation in Messiah Yeshua.

Also, do not measure yourself according to what other groups do. We each have our calling, and comparing ourselves to others is not of God. He has a work for you to do. Press on to the mark, trusting and believing Him. Although it may be tempting to measure your community by the number of people you have, this is not the measurement God uses. Yeshua addressed His followers as a "*little flock*" (Luke 12:32). God is not ashamed of a remnant and neither should we be. Beware of falling into the worldly mindset that "bigger is better."

Notes:

Remember that righteousness is seen not in being perfect, but in addressing issues and praying for God to give the increase. As we follow the Lord, we will encounter many problems, for we are going against the grain of this world. This can be very difficult, but it is never cause for despair because we know Someone greater than the problems! (1 Samuel 17:37, 45; John 16:33)

Notes:

As you work through these things in a planning meeting, it is helpful to have a structure by which you can order and direct the process.

Allow me to present a framework designed to assist in specific congregational planning. Through this structure, we will cover seven areas which require clarity in order to produce accomplishment:

✡ 1. *What are we about?* Review Mission, Vision, and Values

✡ 2. *Where are we now?* Conduct a Situational Analysis

✡ 3. *Where do we want to be?* Develop Objectives

✡ 4. *How will we get there?* Develop Strategies

✡ 5. *Who will be responsible?* Formulate an Action Plan

✡ 6. *How will the plan be managed?* Develop a Reporting System

✡ 7. *What about unforeseen problems?* Make Course Corrections

1. WHAT ARE WE ABOUT?

Review Mission, Vision, and Values

The first step in planning is to come back to the foundation, and take time to review your congregation's mission, vision, and values. This is essential, for before you can move ahead, you must all be on the same page about why you exist, where you are going, and how you will get there. Reviewing these matters will help stabilize the planning process, enabling you to plan in light of these major matters, rather than the needs of the moment.

MISSION: WHY WE EXIST

"Brethren, I do not regard myself as having laid hold of it yet; but one thing I do: forgetting what lies behind and reaching forward to what lies ahead, I press on toward the goal for the prize of the upward call of God in Messiah Yeshua." – Philippians 3:13-14

What defines us as a Messianic community? What is our testimony, our calling, what we are here for? What are we trying to do? Why are we different from other congregations? (For more on the mission of a Messianic congregation, see page 14).

VISION: WHERE WE ARE GOING

"For those whom He foreknew, He also predestined to become conformed to the image of His Son, so that He would be the firstborn among many brethren" – Romans 8:29

What do we ultimately want to "grow up" to be in Yeshua? (For more on vision in a Messianic congregation, see page 35).

VALUES: HOW WE WILL GET THERE

"A new commandment I give to you, that you love one another, even as I have loved you, that you also love one another. By this all men will know that you are My disciples, if you have love for one another." – John 13:34-35

How will we righteously get from here to there? How can we best love each other along the way? (For more on values in a Messianic congregation, see page 41).

A proper understanding of your congregation's mission, vision, and values lies at the root of problem solving in a congregation. All the problems your congregation is facing can be traced back to a misunderstanding or failure to live out one or more of these three things. As a leader looking over the messy-ness of your Messianic community, you can evaluate the cause of your problems, and find answers to questions such as, "Why are we not achieving any of our goals?" In order to do this, tools are needed to help ascertain and evaluate the matter objectively.

Notes:

Here is an evaluatory tool detailing the connection between congregational problems and the interaction of mission, vision, and values. Prayerfully make use of this paradigm in your planning as you determine the root cause of the issues you may be facing:

Notes:

_____

_____

_____

_____

_____

_____

_____

_____

_____

_____

_____

_____

_____

_____

_____

_____

_____

_____

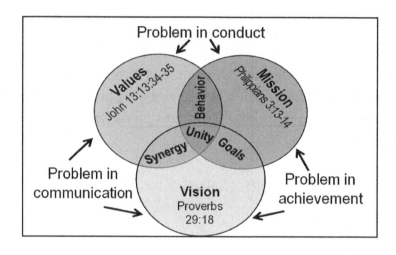

Figure 8.0

PROBLEMS OF ACHIEVEMENT

Is your congregation struggling to move forward in getting things done? Do great ideas keep coming up but never translate into action? Does each leader seem to be moving in a different direction? If this is the case, you are facing a problem of achievement. Problems of achievement stem from a disconnect between your mission, why you exist, and your vision, where you are going. Mission and vision overlap to form your goals. As these two areas are clearly understood, you will be able to move forward in forming and implementing goals for your congregation.

PROBLEMS OF CONDUCT

Do people in your congregation struggle to get along? Are they acting out of a "me first" mentality? These issues reveal a problem in conduct. If people do not understand your mission, why you exist, they may mistreat each other based on unhealthy past experiences. If they do not understand your values, how to love each other along the way, they will not understand how to act in a healthy way towards others. Mission and values overlap to form behavior. As these two areas are understood, behavior will improve as well.

PROBLEMS OF COMMUNICATION

If people in the congregation are having trouble communicating with each other, misinterpreting nonverbal cues, and misunderstanding what others are trying to say, you have a problem in communication. Problems of communication show a misunderstanding of your vision, where you are going, and your values, how to love each other along the way. As these two things are understood, it brings about synergy, as people learn to collaborate, respect each other, and work together, finding common ground as they move to accomplish your vision.

When a congregation has healthy goals, behavior, and synergy, it leads to unity in the community!
However, this is only possible as everyone understands why we are here, where we are going, and how we are getting there, called to love each other along the way.

As you use this tool to help diagnose the type of problems you are facing, ask yourself, "Which of these root matters are people not understanding? What have they forgotten? What needs to be reiterated and reviewed? What needs to be more clearly communicated?" All problems, whether in achievement, conduct, or communication, can be addressed as you wisely discern the root cause of the issue.

Once you determine where the problem lies, remember that it is the responsibility of leadership to address the issue. Though you may not be able to resolve it, you must not remain silent, for when proper leadership under-reacts, improper leadership will over-react (Genesis 34). Through teaching, discipleship, and counseling, review and re-teach your mission, vision, and values, and then leave the results in God's hands, seeking His guidance and help.

2. WHERE ARE WE NOW?

Conduct a Situational Analysis: "SWOT"

"Then Joshua the son of Nun sent two men as spies secretly from Shittim, saying, 'Go, view the land, especially Jericho.'" – Joshua 2:1a

"Then the two men returned and came down from the hill country and crossed over and came to Joshua the son of Nun, and they related to him all that had

Notes:

199

happened to them. They said to Joshua, 'Surely the LORD has given all the land into our hands; moreover, all the inhabitants of the land have melted away before us.'" – Joshua 2:23-24

Notes:

_____

_____

_____

_____

_____

_____

_____

_____

_____

_____

_____

_____

_____

_____

_____

Once you have reviewed what you are about as a congregation, it is time to determine how you are presently doing, asking yourselves, "Where are we now?" In planning, it is essential that you know where you are starting from before you attempt to move forward. If I were to meet a friend for lunch in the center of the city, and was trying to give him directions, it would not be helpful to instruct him to drive north if he is coming from the north side, even if this is the direction I must take as I live on the south side. Different starting points require different strategies.

In order to figure out your "starting point," you need to carry out a situational analysis of your community, determining what is going well and what will need some work. This includes both an internal assessment of your communities' strengths and weaknesses as well as external assessment of any opportunities or threats you may be facing. The acrostic "SWOT" will help us in this process:

STRENGTHS:

First, determine your strengths: the abilities, resources, and crucial assets you have which significantly impact you, and praise God for them. If a person is hurting, it is easy for them to allow their pain to dominate them. If our congregation is struggling, we must be careful not to let pain become the driver. Remember the good things that have happened. Has God given victories before? He can certainly give victories now!

In assessing strengths, ask yourself, What are we doing well? What experiences do we bring to the table? Though God is not dependent upon our experiences, we may be able to utilize them for His work. Recognize that you can utilize your areas of strength in order to address your areas of weakness.

WEAKNESSES:

Now, assess your weaknesses, the inabilities or lack of resources that significantly impact your ministry. What are we not doing as well? What weaknesses do we need to compensate for? For instance, we might desire to have a live worship team, but if we do not yet have musicians, we may need to utilize recordings instead. What are our limitations regarding time? Some people on the team have more time to give to the ministry than others and this needs to be taken into consideration. Also, how are we limited by the space available to us? In considering these things, recognize that you may not be able to accomplish everything you would like to do.

As you work through an internal assessment of your community, evaluate each specific ministry within your fellowship or congregation by the same value system, pinpointing areas of strength and weakness. At this point, it is helpful to put together a list of what is not working well in the congregation and then discern the top two or three areas on which you will focus during your planning meeting.

OPPORTUNITIES:

Looking outward now, what opportunities do you see around you? What are some situations that could significantly help your ministry to succeed? Opportunities may include local community events, neighborhood buildings that become available, a new bus service, etc. Perhaps there is a new synagogue or Jewish community center close by which could provide more opportunities for witness. Each of these potential opportunities need to be evaluated as to how they can be utilized to expand the work of the congregation.

THREATS:

Threats are situations around you that can significantly hinder your ministry from succeeding. Threats are external to the congregation, but they have potential to impact the proper functioning of the Body.

These may be anything from a changing economy to "anti-missionary" protests outside the building. When major events happen around the world, you as a congregation cannot ignore them, but must figure out how to address them in your community. All threats need to be evaluated as to how much of a hindrance they will pose to the proper functioning of the congregation.

Notes:

Part of your discussion on where you are now should also include a review of how you got to be there. It needs to be understood that your present state is partly a result of past decisions, just as your future state will be a result of your present decisions. Take some time to review these past decisions, being careful as you do so that you are not doing this to affix blame, but to fix problems.

Notes:

3. WHERE DO WE WANT TO BE?

Develop "SMART" Objectives

"Now there was a disciple at Damascus named Ananias; and the Lord said to him in a vision, 'Ananias.' And he said, 'Here I am, Lord.' And the Lord said to him, 'Get up and go to the street called Straight, and inquire at the house of Judas for a man from Tarsus named Saul, for he is praying" – Acts 9:10-11

In Alice in Wonderland, Alice asks the Cheshire cat, "Which way should I go?" The cat answered, "I don't know; it depends on where you want to end up." If you do not have a goal in your ministry, your direction will be very unclear. It has been said, "You'll never leave where you are until you decide where you'd rather be."

A goal is the primary result which you must accomplish in order to fulfill your mission and vision. Objectives are the specific ways you plan to achieve your primary goal. In other words, objectives are your metrics and goals are the values you are working toward achieving.

To communicate its purpose, a goal is specific and succinct. The goal of Hope of Israel Congregation, a Messianic congregation I planted in Charlotte, NC, states, "Our goal is to develop Messianic *talmidim* who serve as witnesses to Israel by being involved in planting new Messianic congregations and on behalf of Israel by serving the Body of Messiah in our area in its calling to make the Jewish people desirous of Messiah."

Based on your situational analysis, take time to review your goal and then formulate new objectives in order to get you to where you want to be.

OBJECTIVES IN PLANNING

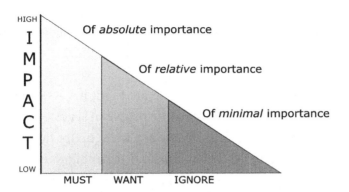

Figure 8.1

Notes:

In planning meetings, it is helpful to have a brainstorming session as you develop objectives. But what do you do if every person present comes up with ten ideas each? Because we value the input of each person, we must work through each of these ideas and evaluate their importance.

This diagram will help you in the organization of proposed objectives. As you can see, those ideas which are determined to be of very minimal importance need to be ignored. On our "wish list" are all those ideas of relative importance. But which ideas do we actually implement? Those which are of absolute, or primary, importance. Use this framework as you discuss the ideas which arise, and aim to agree on two to three things on which to focus attention.

"SMART" OBJECTIVES

At times, it can be difficult to determine which ideas are of minimal, relative, or absolute importance. How do we formulate objectives which will actually help us to reach our goal? Let us learn from Nehemiah, administrator par excellence. In the thirteen chapters of the book of Nehemiah, sixteen prayers are recorded. This is what godly administration looks like! Through his planning, Nehemiah models for us how to set "SMART" objectives: those that are **S**pecific, **M**easurable, **A**greed upon, **R**ealistic, and **T**ime-related.

SPECIFIC

Notes:

"Then I said to them, "You see the bad situation we are in, that Jerusalem is desolate and its gates burned by fire. Come, let us rebuild the wall of Jerusalem so that we will no longer be a reproach." – Nehemiah 2:17

The clearer the bull's eye, the more likely you are to hit it. As general ideas are brought up, such as, "We want to see more people in service every week," follow-up questions must be raised: "What are we actually talking about? What people?" Objectives need to be clear and unambiguous, free of clichés. Specific objectives will tell a team exactly what is expected, who will be involved, where the task will happen, and which attributes are important.

These five "W" questions can help in setting specific objectives:

* ✡ **What**: What do we want to accomplish?
* ✡ **Why**: What are some specific benefits that would be accomplished through this objective? This clarifies values, helping everyone to understand the correlation between held values and action.
* ✡ **Who**: Who will be involved? Who is impacted, and who will be the point person?
* ✡ **Where**: Where will this objective be taking place, or what space will be needed for it?
* ✡ **Which**: What resources will be used for the project? Which local laws and restrictions need to be taken into account? Identify requirements, restrictions, and resources.

MEASURABLE

"So I went out at night by the Valley Gate in the direction of the Dragon's Well and on to the Refuse Gate, inspecting the walls of Jerusalem which were broken down and its gates which were consumed by fire. Then I passed on to the Fountain Gate and the King's Pool, but there was no place for my mount to pass. So I went up at night by the ravine and inspected the wall. Then I entered the Valley Gate again and returned." – Nehemiah 2:13-15

Concrete benchmarks are needed to measure progress towards the attainment of a goal. If an objective is not measurable, it is not possible to know whether a team is making progress towards successful completion. A measurable objective will help a team stay on track, reach its target dates, and experience the joy of achievement on the way to reaching the ultimate goal. With measurable objectives, you will be able to address questions such as: How much? How many? How will I know when it is accomplished?

AGREED UPON

"I told them how the hand of my God had been favorable to me and also about the king's words which he had spoken to me. Then they said, 'Let us arise and build.' So they put their hands to the good work." – Nehemiah 2:18

Do not drag people into a plan kicking and screaming. In a planning meeting, it is very important that each person be given a chance to contribute to the discussion. To make sure this happens, go around the room and ask individual people what they think about the idea at hand. Some may need to be encouraged to speak up, but this is the time in which to speak. No one wants to be told six months later, "I was sure that plan wouldn't work!" As objectives are discussed, it is essential that decisions only be made when people are on the same page. Objectives of absolute importance are those that are seen as most important to the group as a whole. An objective will be put into action if those on the team believe that it is worth doing.

REALISTIC

"And I said to the king, 'If it please the king, let letters be given me for the governors of the provinces beyond the River, that they may allow me to pass through until I come to Judah'" – Nehemiah 2:7

As an objective is developed, we must ask if it will actually be able to be carried out. It is wonderful to come to an agreement, but agreement does no good if the plan is not realistic to begin with. To determine if an objective is realistic, ask practical questions such as, "Do we have the resources it will take to see this through to completion?" You cannot plan beyond the resources which are under your control. While an objective should stretch a team in order to achieve it, it should not be extreme. The objective must be neither out of reach, ("Too idealistic") nor too far below the community's standard ("Who would want to do that?") A realistic goal is one that will seem reasonable and relevant to all involved.

You must consider this point carefully so as not to waste money on projects that may not be reachable. All things are possible with God, however, we should not make plans on what is possible; but on what is most probable.

TIME-RELATED

Notes:

"Then the king said to me, the queen sitting beside him, 'How long will your journey be, and when will you return?' So it pleased the king to send me, and I gave him a definite time." – Nehemiah 2:6

It is very important to set a time frame for the completion of objectives, providing the group with a set target deadline. It is natural for a group to dream, but then fall into procrastination, and end up doing nothing. Setting a target date for completion helps a team to focus their efforts and grounds them in the real world. Many people will only do something if they know that on a specific date they will be asked about their progress; this is why teachers give exams. A time-related objective will establish the sense of priority needed to complete the task.

4. HOW WILL WE GET THERE?
Develop Strategies with "POP"

"Let them construct a sanctuary for Me, that I may dwell among them. According to all that I am going to show you, as the pattern of the tabernacle and the pattern of all its furniture, just so you shall construct it." – Exodus 25:8-9

Now that we know where we want to be, we must figure out the means by which we will get from here to there. It is time to develop a strategy. Strategy formulation is the process of realistically outlining how a ministry proposes to achieve their objectives and goals to fulfill their mission and purpose. This will entail utilizing your "SWOT" resources to develop strategies to accomplish your "SMART" objectives.

So how do we do this? Allow me to introduce you to "POP," (**P**roblem, **O**ptions, **P**lan), who will be of great help to you as you form strategies as a group.

PROBLEM

As you consider the objectives you would like to see accomplished, ask yourself what problems are standing in the way of their accomplishment. When a problem arises in your congregation, you must ensure that you fully understand the problem so that you can strategize to fully resolve it as you move forward in accomplishing your objective.

To do this, first assess if the situation which you are facing is a true problem or merely an inconvenience. Anything that is keeping you from achieving the goal to which God has called you to do is a legitimate problem which must be addressed. An inconvenience will not stand in the way of your goal. For instance, if it is raining outside, it may be inconvenient, but it does not hinder you from working inside and accomplishing your objectives for the day. If it is concluded that you have a real problem on your hands, the next step is to meet with your team to make a list of all aspects of the problem. As you do this, list every way you can think of that the issue is currently impacting your ministry, being careful not to miss any aspect.

Next, prioritize the aspects of the problem that are key hindrances. Pray for discernment as you identify those things which are of most concern and on which you will focus first so as not to let anything hinder the fulfillment of your calling.

OPTIONS

Now that you fully understand the problem, it is time to move forward towards a solution. To do this, make another list, this time of all the possible ways to address the issue.

Looking at your list of options, discuss each idea, listening carefully to what each person has to say on the matter. In this discussion, recognize that God can use any person who is filled with *Ruach HaKodesh* to be the one to propose the best solution. Encourage people to be willing to think outside the box, utilizing their God-given creativity in order to formulate the best solution to the problem.

Each proposed idea will have various ramifications, and all of these must be thoroughly discussed. Take time to ask questions such as, "Who and what would this solution impact?" "Is there any possibility anyone would be hurt by it?" Who would we need to talk to before putting this idea into action? Remember that people are our greatest priority; never make any plans or decisions that will impact others without first talking with them about it.

Notes:

207

PLAN

After all this discussion, now list the solutions in the order that will best achieve the results you are looking for, leading to the fulfillment of your goal. As you put together the best options in order to address the problem, you are forming your strategy by which you will achieve your objectives.

The role of an elder at this point is not to come up with all the ideas, but to double check that all areas of the problem have been adequately addressed. Rarely do the elders come up with all the good ideas. It is their role to encourage and empower people to step up in bringing their ideas to the table while they step back and trust God. Recognize that this is not about the elders, but about what is best for the entire community.

Now it is time to decide which of these possible solutions is most likely to address and resolve the problem, and then begin to formulate an action plan!

DEFINING STRATEGY & PURPOSE

PURPOSE	Defined purpose	Dynamic distractions	Motivated overcomer
	Undefined purpose	Discouraging delays	Indifferent Planning
		Undefined strategy	Defined strategy
		STRATEGY	

Figure 8.2

Eventually, you may be presenting your plan to others outside of your planning meeting. In order to bring your team to the same page, it is essential that your strategy be clear and well-defined. However, along with the presentation of your strategy, you must also effectively express the purpose behind it.

Notes:

Purpose provides meaning, worth, and intention. Purpose answers the question, "Why?" Never tell people "how" until you tell them "what," and then do not tell them "what" until you first tell them "why." Leaders have to explain why the issue at hand is important before explaining how it needs to be addressed. Purpose is provided by both the clarity of the vision and the perceived urgency of the call. Is the message clear? Is it urgent? If it is unclear, people will not understand what the issue is. If it is not urgent, it will not be considered a priority.

Strategy, as we have noted, is the process by which the group will achieve its specific goal. Strategy answers the question, "How?" Strategy is developed by our fully utilized resources to achieve objectives according to our applied values.

When both your purpose and strategy are undefined, you will be met with discouraging delays.

When you have a clear purpose, but undefined strategy, you will run into dynamic distractions as people try to come up with ways to meet the goal and may end up majoring in the minors.

A defined strategy but undefined purpose will lead to indifferent planning. Though the strategy is clear, people do not understand the reasons behind the proposed plan and do not see why it is important, so they lack the motivation to implement anything.

Lastly, when there is both a defined purpose and defined strategy, others will be motivated to be overcomers, ready to work with you on putting the plan into action. They are ready to roll because they clearly understand both the purpose and strategy.

5. WHO WILL BE RESPONSIBLE?

Formulate an Action Plan

"And Yeshua sent Peter and John, saying, 'Go and prepare the Passover for us, so that we may eat it.' They said to Him, 'Where do you want us to prepare it?" and He said to them, 'When you have entered the city, a man will meet you carrying a pitcher of water; follow him into the house that he enters ...'" - Luke 22:8-10

Notes:

_____

_____

_____

_____

_____

_____

_____

_____

_____

_____

_____

_____

_____

_____

_____

_____

209

After determining a workable strategy, a specific action plan is needed in order to carry it out. An action plan answers the specific questions of "*Who* will be doing *what* by *when* with *how much*?" A plan on its own does no good unless there is a person who is designated and equipped to see it through to completion.

Notes:

An action plan:

- ✡ Designates *who* will be responsible to carry out the plan.
- ✡ Identifies *what* must be done to accomplish the plan.
- ✡ Sets the timeframe as to *when* the plan will be completed.
- ✡ Allocates the *resources* needed to fulfill the plan.

Once you have addressed these important questions, everyone will know what to expect as the action plan is put into motion. The delegated individuals are then commissioned to follow-through with the implementation of the plan. As the action plan is delegated, it is best to ensure the point person understands precisely what needs to be accomplished, and then leave it to them to determine the specific steps they will take to do it. For example, if you have delegated a person to be in charge of preparing the *oneg* for a special event, they should be able to choose which stores they will go to and the specific types of food they will buy. Remember, proper delegation must include explained responsibility, enough authority, and then explicit accountability.

6. HOW WILL THE PLAN BE MANAGED?

Develop a Reporting System

As the plan is put into action, a reporting system is needed to ensure that results conform to the plan, for as we have noted, people do not do what you expect but what you inspect. This is wise ministry guidance.

Never make an action plan without also implementing a system to manage its progress. Even for the simplest of plans, it is essential to follow-up frequently with the person responsible for its completion, ensuring that they have sufficient time and resources to accomplish their goal, and that they have not run into any hindrances. A leader does this not to intimidate the person, but to support them in their ministry. If they run into problems, leaders are there to help and affirm them. The goal of a reporting system is to help people, not to call them on the carpet.

This is the role of an elder, to help people succeed, making sure the congregation is running smoothly and in order. When the Temple was standing, this was what the high priest did all week long, making sure the Temple was functional so that people could worship God without distraction. We serve God by obtaining and sustaining health, continually assessing the functionality of our systems.

IMPORTANCE OF GODLY LEADERSHIP GUIDANCE

"I will instruct you and teach you in the way which you should go; I will counsel you with My eye upon you." – Psalm 32:8

In Nehemiah 4-5, we see how Nehemiah guided his people as they built the walls of Jerusalem. As a godly leader, he did not only instruct them when they first took up their task, but continued to be with them in the midst of it, inspecting their progress, addressing problems, praying for them, and encouraging them not to give up in the midst of adversity. He knew exactly what each of his teams were doing and what their needs were because he was in continual communication with each person.

In light of Nehemiah's example, we see that godly leadership guidance…

 ✡ Measures activities against goals: "We should be doing this by now"

"For though by this time you ought to be teachers, you have need again for someone to teach you the elementary principles of the oracles of God, and you have come to need milk and not solid food." – Hebrews 5:12

 ✡ Measures results against objectives: "We should have done this by now"

"For if we had not delayed, surely by now we could have returned twice." – Genesis 43:10

 ✡ Provides testing of assumptions: "What happened this week?"

"Bring the whole tithe into the storehouse, so that there may be food in My house, and test Me now in this," says the Lord of hosts, "if I will not open for you the windows of heaven and pour out for you a blessing until it overflows." – Malachi 3:10

Notes:

✿ Allows for corrective action / assumption adjustment: "How do we adjust to reach our objective?"

"Come now, you who say, 'Today or tomorrow we will go to such and such a city, and spend a year there and engage in business and make a profit.'" – Jacob 4:13

Notes:

✿ Encourages growth in gifts, skills and results: "I will succeed as I adjust and develop"

"Now as to the love of the brethren, you have no need for anyone to write to you, for you yourselves are taught by God to love one another; for indeed you do practice it toward all the brethren who are in all Macedonia. But we urge you, brethren, to excel still more... We urge you, brethren, admonish the unruly, encourage the fainthearted, help the weak, be patient with everyone." – 1 Thessalonians 4:9-10; 5:14

✿ Provides a needed link between the plan and daily work: "We see how our work is connected to a plan."

"Obey your leaders and submit to them, for they keep watch over your souls as those who will give an account. Let them do this with joy and not with grief, for this would be unprofitable for you." – Hebrews 13:17

REPORTING MEETINGS & STRUCTURE

"When they had arrived and gathered the assembly together, they began to report all things that God had done with them and how He had opened a door of faith to the Gentiles." – Acts 14:27

WHY ARE REPORTING MEETINGS NEEDED?

A reporting system is the normal process by which the progress of plans is evaluated. As a plan is put into action, we now need to evaluate its progress through regularly scheduled meetings in order to know if things are working well and if any adjustments are needed. In some cases, this can work through the internet or video-conferencing, depending on the people involved and the nature of the specific plan, but usually meetings work best when all can be present in person.

WHEN SHOULD REPORTING MEETINGS TAKE PLACE?

Reporting meetings should be scheduled relative to the timing and progress of the action plan. It is important that they be arranged when everyone who is involved in the plan can be there. Monthly meetings are usually sufficient, but in some cases, they may need to be held more often. Even if the plan will take a year to accomplish, it is important to assess its progress along the way, not waiting until the last day only to find a major problem that could have been averted.

WHERE SHOULD REPORTING MEETINGS BE HELD?

These meetings should be held in a central location that is convenient and comfortable for all. If the building in which you are meeting for services is available, this can be an ideal spot. Make sure your meeting location has sufficient space for parking and is accessible for any who may have a disability.

WHO SHOULD BE AT A REPORTING MEETING?

Everyone involved in the implementation of the plan should be at each meeting. All attendees will need to be notified about what will be expected of them in a timely manner prior to the meeting, as well as made aware of the agenda items for the meeting. A person gifted in administration should be delegated to handle the administrative scheduling and coordinating for the group.

WHAT TOPICS SHOULD BE COVERED DURING A REPORTING MEETING?

No one appreciates it when a meeting is prolonged unnecessarily. Therefore, you will want to make sure the meeting agenda is focused on what really needs to get done. A good format for a reporting meeting commences with a call to order, followed by a time of prayer, a report of the ministry's progress, a discussion about any needed course corrections, as well as a time to review future responsibilities and / or activities before the meeting is adjourned. Keeping minutes which can later be distributed to all involved parties is always wise, especially if any financial decisions are to be made. Before concluding a meeting, make sure to discuss the next meeting date and proposed topics for its agenda.

Notes:

213

Notes:

_____

_____

_____

_____

_____

_____

_____

_____

_____

_____

_____

_____

_____

_____

_____

_____

During a reporting meeting, the group will discuss what aspects of the ministry have gone well, as well as address issues and provide necessary course correction. It is important to take time during these meetings to appreciate those who have faithfully followed through with their responsibilities. Those who have overcome unexpected difficulties in order to accomplish the goal at hand should receive special recognition. Although we live to hear the words, *"Well done, good and faithful servant,"* from the One we gladly serve, it is the responsibility of leadership to appreciate the servants whom God chooses to use in the process. Appreciating and commending faithful workers is in itself a way of honoring the Lord who gives the increase.

HOW SHOULD A REPORTING MEETING BE CONDUCTED?

Even if people do not always agree with one another, all need to be treated with respect and love, each person being considerate of each other and addressing issues in an orderly and straight-forward fashion. By listening carefully to one another and waiting patiently until each person has expressed what they have to say, love is exhibited. Beware of merely waiting for a person to finish talking in order to jump in with one's own ideas.

7. WHAT ABOUT UNFORESEEN PROBLEMS?

Make Course Corrections

"Come now, you who say, 'Today or tomorrow we will go to such and such a city, and spend a year there and engage in business and make a profit.' Yet you do not know what your life will be like tomorrow. You are just a vapor that appears for a little while and then vanishes away. Instead, you ought to say, 'If the Lord wills, we will live and also do this or that.'" – Jacob 4:13-15

If, during a reporting meeting, it is revealed that the plan did not work out as expected, realize that this is a normal part of life. At this point, you need to be flexible, shifting your assumptions and being willing to modify the plan if needed. In doing so, be careful not to stop the action, just adjust as necessary. As you discuss these matters, remember that in the discussion you will be figuring out how to fix the problem, not affixing blame. Eisenhower once said, "A plan is not important. The planning is important because the people involved in the planning can then flex together."

WHAT IS AN ASSUMPTION?

An assumption is a temporary estimate of a very important probable development that cannot be predicted with accuracy, that is subject to no significant control (by us), and that will have major impact on future activities and results.

Notes:

In planning, we must make assumptions, for we never have control over all the variables involved. For instance, we may have assumed the point person would be present for the planned event, but then he came down with the flu. We may have assumed the specialty store would carry the item we needed, but arrived to find out it had been discontinued. We may have assumed the weather would be nice for our outreach, but that was before the hurricane hit, etc.

Unexpected difficulties come up all the time, for we are living in a world that is not user-friendly, and we have an enemy who is continually trying to lead us to stumble. So how do we go about developing and implementing plans when we cannot control all the factors involved? As we see in Jacob 4:13, we must always factor God into the equation as we plan, holding all things with an open hand, for God is in charge of all the things which we can only assume. Trust Him with these things, and recognize that problems are simply another way for Him to get you closer to where you need to be; moving from holding tight to your own plan to being in line with His.

And so we shift our assumptions. In light of the fact that we can only work with the resources over which we have a stewardship control, assumption shifts are a necessary part of reporting meetings. The key to keeping the plan on track in the midst of course corrections is to make the smallest change possible in light of the changed circumstance.

THE ASSUMPTIONS ADJUSTMENT

When assumptions shift, what should you focus on changing?

Notes:

_____

_____

_____

_____

_____

_____

_____

_____

_____

_____

_____

_____

_____

_____

_____

RESPONDING TO ASSUMPTION SHIFTS

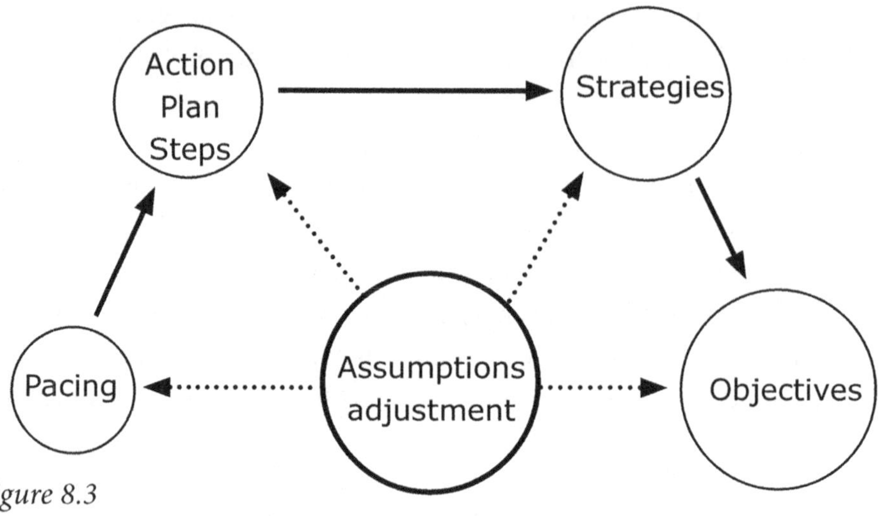

Figure 8.3

✡ *Pacing*: First, check to see if the pacing on a plan can be adjusted. Raise questions such as, "If we can't do it this week, then can we do it next week?"

✡ *Action Steps:* If the problem is more serious, the steps of your Action Plan may need to be adjusted. For instance, "If Chaim can't make it to set up on Friday, who can step up to be there?" "If we don't have the resources we need to accomplish the project, what else do we need to budget for?"

✡ *Strategies*: If, in our assumption shift, we must rule out the Action Plan entirely, then we may need to adjust our strategies. "What are some ways we can get back on track regarding our objective?" "What new approaches do we need to consider?"

✡ *Objectives*: Only when all other course corrections have been fully considered and deemed impossible should we consider changing the objectives themselves. Objectives are laid to reflect the values and goals of the congregation. However, perhaps the problem brings you to realize that you have been "guarding the wrong bridge." You may have a value system that reflects tradition or experience over Scripture. You must make sure that your objectives are leading you "by the Book," and if not, adjust accordingly.

Looking back over this section on prayer and planning for Messianic congregations, let us review the essential steps which must take place as we plan to move forward in achieving our objectives and goals in order to fulfill our mission and purpose:

1. Review mission, vision, and values
2. Conduct a situational analysis
3. Develop objectives
4. Develop strategies
5. Formulate an action plan
6. Develop a reporting system
7. Make course corrections

For a large, complex organism like a congregation, these are not simple steps, and you may find some overlap in how the phases interact. Through it all, remember that the most important goal of this process is to see leadership supporting and encouraging one another, growing together in unity and trust. Though the plans may or may not succeed, and though they may need eventual revision, it is of utmost importance that the people involved grow in unity and love for one another through the process. Together, as you plan for your congregation, remember in all things to continue to pray and praise Yeshua!

PLANNING FOR FUTURE GROWTH

Just as a person is designed to grow from birth to maturity and eventually to reproduce, once a Messianic congregation is established and functional, meeting its goals and stabilized as a self-propagating, self-supporting, and self-governing congregation, the leadership can begin to think about expanding the work. This mature congregation is now ready to reproduce, that is, plant new congregations in new areas, and as such the cycle begins again. This is exactly what happened in the congregation in Jerusalem. Once local leadership was entrusted with full management of the congregation, the Apostles and others were enabled to begin new congregations throughout the region (Acts 12:17, 15:22-23).

The vision to see strong Messianic congregations established, for the glory of HaShem and effective testimony of His faithfulness, must not end with us. We have a responsibility to share this vision with those in our stewardship, communicating the burden of God's heart for the lost sheep of the house of

Notes:

_____

_____

_____

_____

_____

_____

_____

_____

_____

_____

_____

_____

_____

_____

_____

_____

_____

Israel (Luke 19:41, Romans 10:21), and the necessity for all believers to be discipled in such a way as to best communicate our Messianic faith to the Jew first and equally to the Gentile.

Our calling is to pass on something better than we received, refusing to be content with peace in our time while allowing our children to suffer for our mistakes (2 Kings 20:19). We have a responsibility to pray for younger leaders, and come alongside them, passing the baton to the next generation who will pass it to the next and the next, *L'Dor VaDor*, until Yeshua's glorious return!

APPENDICES

SUPPLEMENTAL MATERIAL

APPENDICES
Supplemental Material

✡ *Appendix 1*
Teaching the Word: Preparation & Presentation

✡ *Appendix 2*
Understanding the Problems of Discipleship

✡ *Appendix 3*
Group Discipleship

✡ *Appendix 4*
Congregational Counseling

✡ *Appendix 5*
A Congregation's Relationship with the Greater Body of Messiah

✡ *Appendix 6*
Sample Constitution (Covenant, By-Laws, and Articles of Faith)

✡ *Appendix 7*
Sample List of Unifying Values

✡ Glossary of Hebrew Terms

✡ Additional Resources

TEACHING THE WORD: PREPARATION & PRESENTATION

Notes:

In Part 2 of this book, we considered the structure of the ministry of the Word through an overview of its four systems: contact making, disciple making, member making, and leader making.

However, the content of the ministry of the Word is the Word itself. Thus, it is necessary for us to briefly consider the matter of teaching in the congregation.

Some think of teaching as an activity reserved only for those of a certain class or gifting. However, even as all believers in Messiah are to be Spirit-led, so we are also all to be, in some respect, teachers (Hebrews 5:12). We can easily see how this applies to those who have children (Deuteronomy 6:7). However, all people, whether married or single, are called to make disciples (Matthew 28:19-20). However, Jacob says, "*Let not many of you become teachers, my brethren, knowing that as such we will incur a stricter judgment*" (Jacob 3:1). A teacher of the Word is called to provide not just any sort of teaching, but only sound teaching. In Ecclesiastes, King Solomon presents a key passage on this point:

"*In addition to being a wise man, the Preacher also taught the people knowledge; and he pondered, searched out and arranged many proverbs. The Preacher sought to find delightful words and to write words of truth correctly. The words of wise men are like goads, and masters of these collections are like well-driven nails; they are given by one Shepherd. But beyond this, my son, be warned: the writing of many books is endless, and excessive devotion to books is wearying to the body.*" – Ecclesiastes 12:9-12

We are called to bring the truth of the Creator's redemption into this world "*under the sun.*" The essential means by which we do this is through sound teaching of His revelation. This passage in Ecclesiastes lays out a methodology to guide us in doing so.

PREPARATION IN THE WORD

As we prepare to teach the Word, we must first make…

- ✡ **Observations**: We ponder and deliberate the meaning of the actual words of the Scripture we are studying. From this we discover…

- ✡ **Truths**: By asking questions, we search deeply for truths communicated through the words of Scripture. As we do this, we find the…

- ✡ **Theme**: This helps us to understand the message of the text as a whole. Finally, on this basis, we arrange an…

- ✡ **Outline**: We organize and prioritize the insights we have discovered, ready to share them with others!

Looking deeper into this passage, we see how Kohelet, the Preacher walked through each of these steps.

"In addition to being a wise man, the Preacher also taught the people knowledge." – Ecclesiastes 12:9a

Kohelet was wise. Wisdom is the application of knowledge; that which comes as we live out God's Word in our lives. The wise skillfully apply His truth as they live life day-to-day.

Wisdom must precede good teaching, just as money must precede benevolence. A teacher needs to be wise himself in order to share wisdom with others. This is the beginning, not the goal of growth. Solomon, despite his personal failings, must have retained the gift of wisdom, which he had requested and obtained for the benefit of his people (Proverbs 2:7, 1 Kings 3:9-12, 4:29-34).

The Preacher also taught the people knowledge. If a teacher is only wise for himself, he is not truly wise at all. The activity of teaching is the highest work of service (1 Timothy 5:17). Those taught are not necessarily the powerful, the wealthy, or the intellectual class. Yeshua died for all people, and we minister to all as well. So, prepare your teaching not merely for professors and scholars, but for *am ha-aretz* (the common people.) A teacher is not to be a miser in accumulating knowledge; instead he is to share it for the ben-

Notes:

_____

_____

_____

_____

_____

_____

_____

_____

_____

_____

_____

_____

_____

efit of others. The idea of the word for "knowledge," (*yadah*) is to know by experience. Thus the Preacher was giving people insight for living, not just information with no practical purpose.

Those taught should not be dependent on the teacher, but on the Lord. The Hebrew word for "taught," (*limad*), comes from the same root as the word, "learned," (*lamad*). This word literally means "to cause to learn," or to "facilitate" learning. To share wisdom for living is greater than giving people the correct answers; it is the difference between giving a man a fish and teaching him how to fish. *Limad* has the connotation of training as well as educating (this can be seen in the derived term for "ox goad," (*malmad*), in Hosea 10:11). To learn is to come to terms with the will and law of God.

"*... and he pondered, searched out and arranged many proverbs.*" – Ecclesiastes 12:9b

The Kohelet "pondered;" he was observing the text carefully (Psalm 1:2-3; Joshua 1:7-8). Pondering implies deep thought and consideration of the text, deliberating about the meaning of the words. The specific grammar of a passage and the context surrounding it are of profound importance in the quest to discover the meaning of a text.

The word for "pondered," (*izen*), comes from the word for "ear" or "hearing." The ear represents hearing and obedience, and is involved in important symbolic actions throughout Scripture. For instance, if a slave chose to remain in permanent service to his master, his ear was to be pierced through with an awl (Exodus 21:6, Deuteronomy 15:17, cf. Psalm 40:6). By this legal act, he was then bound to obedience for his entire life. At the priesthood ordination of Aaron and his sons, blood from the sacrificial ram was placed on the lobes of their right ears, as well as their thumbs and big toes (Leviticus 8:23-24, Exodus 29:20). Consideration of the Master's words proves submission to the Master. Rather than assume the words to mean whatever feels right to us, or to read into them whatever we need to make our point, we submit to the actual meaning of the text.

He then "searched out." A teacher searches deeply for truths in the words of Scripture (2 Timothy 2:15). Questions are his flashlight, through which he can look into the depths of the truth. The word for "searched out," (*chiker*), has the idea of "investigate" or "examine." It can refer to the initial phases of a search or the end result, the theme of a passage, but it always connotes

Notes:

225

a diligent probing. This word is used concerning investigating legal cases (Proverbs 18:17), the plight of the needy (Job 29:16), and the process of searching out a particular subject (Job 5:27; 8:8; 28:27). The work of preparation is difficult and involves diligent research.

Notes:

He also "arranged." The Hebrew word here, (*tiken*), means to "make straight." Through this, he "set in order," or "outlined." An outline is not formulated to set limits on the truth of the text, for there is always more in the Word than can ever be observed, let alone outlined! Rather, through outlining, the principles the student has learned becomes accessible, both for himself (or herself), and others.

Organizing the truths of the text in outline form is like making a map of the new territory we have discovered, so that the teacher might find his way back in again, and, this time, bring others with him. An outline prioritizes the insights according to the theme of the text.

"Proverbs," (*meshalim*), are wise instructions, truth in an applicable form. The root of the Hebrew word for proverb, (*mashal*), is to "represent," "be like," or "compare." We study the Word so that the truth might be proverbial in people's lives.

PRESENTATION OF THE WORD

When presenting a message, I counsel teachers to consider four steps through which they can effectively convey each of the points they wish to present from their outline. These steps are:

✡ **Explanation:** This entails explaining both the meaning and the message of the text, reflecting on the actual words, giving the historical background and genre of the text, and then explaining the meaning of the text in a way that is relevant to the listeners.

✡ **Illustration:** For more difficult points especially, a clear illustration will help to shed light on the message of the text, helping people to better understand and apply the teaching.

✡ **Application:** As you prepare your sermons, remember that people do not know what to do with them naturally. They need their hand to be held and to be given help in how to apply the teaching to their various walks of life, just as a parent walks with a child, not leaving them to fend for themselves.

✡ **Exhortation:** Through exhortation, a teacher drives a point home, communicating the vital and urgent nature of the message delivered, and motivating the people to implement what the *Ruach* has revealed to them through the teaching.

Notes:

"The Kohelet sought to find delightful words and to write words of truth correctly." – Ecclesiastes 12:10

"Delightful words" are not only practical, but creatively presented. We seek to communicate effectively so as to impart to others the spiritual nourishment we have already received from the Word (1 Timothy 4:6). Taking care to find the most fitting words through which to do this is both pleasurable and meaningful. As Proverbs teaches us, *"Like apples of gold in settings of silver is a word spoken in right circumstances"* (Proverbs 25:11).

Again, the Preacher "sought to find" delightful words, seeking them as a shepherd would seek after lost sheep (Psalm 119:176). The Hebrew word for "find," (*baqash*), means to "discover and take hold of," to "grasp in order to apprehend," even to "conquer." This work aptly expresses the idea of, "finding a needle in a haystack." Finding the right word along with a good illustration serves to communicate effectively what the many wrong words could never do.

Accurate words are "written" (*katuv*) to objectify the truth. They are worth recording and marking down, getting out on paper (or on papyrus, or a computer screen; whatever you have to work with!) They are "words of truth" (*div'rei emet*), in that they reflect the character of God. The Lord says, *"Let him who has My Word speak My word in truth."* (Jeremiah 23:28) They are also to be presented "correctly" (*yoshar*), that is, presented as accurately as possible to God's will. This word refers to straightness and uprightness in one's explanation. Yes, accuracy (the godly teacher), clarity (the good teacher), and creativity (the great teacher) are all part of the ministry of a teacher of the Word, however, before all there must be accuracy. Now, this certainly does not mean that the Preacher confused truth with dullness (10a). Rather, he wrote "in an attractive style" (CJB). This being said, creativity must not be prioritized over accuracy (2 Timothy 2:15).

APPROPRIATION OF THE WORD

"The words of wise men are like goads, and masters of these collections are like well-driven nails; they are given by one Shepherd." – Ecclesiastes 12:11

Notes:

Appropriation is about getting the ball across the goal line, making clear what the results of understanding the Word are to be (application and exhortation). The "words of wise men"...

Intensify: They motivate a person to live faithfully. As a farmer would use "goads," sharp sticks in order to motivate oxen to pull the plow, a wise man's words provoke others unto love and good deeds (Hebrews 10:24). Wise teachings are to goad their listeners to action.

Clarify: They focus one to live steadfastly, like a carpenter's well-driven nails. Solid teaching should stabilize others to persevere in God's Word throughout their life.

To become a "master" (*baali*) "of these collections" means to possess or own them. The collected wise words of God (the Scriptures) are integrated into the teacher's soul, and become part of his value system and thought process. Those who have mastered these collections of wisdom are like well-driven, firmly established nails. Once, I was helping a contractor friend build a store. When he saw me hammering, he commented, "Sam, your hammering is like bolts of lightning; you never hit the same spot twice." We want to avoid the crooked nails which result from such hammering. Teaching from the *bema* is to incisively and decisively speak the truth in love and refute the gainsayers. Masters of these collections are founded upon the rock (Matthew 7:24-25). They help the *talmidim* to be planted by living waters and firmly established in the truth (Psalm 1:2-3).

Glorify: They unify the listeners to live agreeably, like a shepherd gathering a flock. The teaching should gather people to follow the "One Shepherd" forever. A master of God's words is a mature teacher who rightly divides the Word of truth. There may be many masters, but there is only One Shepherd. All masters learn the truth of God's Word, and therefore all glorify the One Shepherd (Chagigah 3b).

We are to convey His values and vision to the flock. Every book in the Bible, from Genesis to Revelation, is all from One Shepherd. If the flock is to move forward in unity, He alone must be our focus. The wise draw their wisdom from the Shepherd of Israel, the one true God (Genesis 49:24; Psalm 23:1; 80:1).

LIMITATION IN THE WORD

"But beyond this, my son, be warned: the writing of many books is endless, and excessive devotion to books is wearying to the body." – Ecclesiastes 12:12

The work of preparing and presenting the Word is not to be "endless." Eventually the plane must land! "Beyond this," beyond the practical and edifying ministry of teaching people the truth of God, lies vanity.

Understand that there is always much more work that can be done; a person can write sermons or books endlessly. Let us be careful to not make writing a goal in itself; this is vain conceit as anything other than what helps us to rejoice in and obey God is vanity (12:13-14). Do not go further than what is useful and profitable for the people. Writing without providing application to your content is endless; such people never get anywhere. They are, *"ever learning but never coming to the knowledge of the truth"* (2 Timothy 3:7). Limitation provides focus, fulfillment, and closure.

The work is not to be "wearying to the body." Great study is a labor for the flesh, with application as the end goal. There is hard work in teaching (1 Timothy 5:17). Devotion in this area is needed, but to be too excessive is enervating to the soul, not spiritually energizing. As the Lord loves a cheerful giver, so once it ceases to be cheerful, stop giving! The goal of learning is living and giving, not simply a greater understanding of information.

The teacher must keep his eye on the ball. The goal of ministry is to help and encourage people to obey God and to follow His Word (Ecclesiastes 12:13). Everything will be evaluated and judged according to truth of God's Word as to whether or not it accomplished the purposes of God (Ecclesiastes 12:14; 1 Timothy 1:4).

Notes:

APPENDIX 2

UNDERSTANDING THE PROBLEMS OF DISCIPLESHIP

Notes:

———————————

———————————

———————————

———————————

———————————

———————————

———————————

———————————

———————————

———————————

———————————

———————————

———————————

———————————

———————————

———————————

The impact of discipleship reaches much further than the life of one individual believer, for *talmidut* is vital to the health of the congregation as a whole. Through discipleship, a congregation grows up into a mature and functional community.

This issue is so vital that we must recognize and counteract whatever hinders a congregation from engaging in discipleship. Here, we consider a list of excuses that leaders can tend to make which hinder the functionality and maturity of their congregations.

SAM'S TOP 10 LIST OF EXCUSES
for Not Making Disciples

10. UNTRAINED LEADERSHIP: *"I was never taught that"*

✡ *The Excuse:*

Many leaders simply have not been trained in the process of disciple making, and in fact, may never have been discipled themselves. They may feel that because they have not gone through the elements of discipleship, such as memorizing Scripture, they do not have the moral right to ask others to do so.

✡ *The Solution:*

If you are untrained, we are here to help. Please contact Word of Messiah to let us know how we can best serve you in this area. Do not allow pride to limit you to the confines of your own experience and keep you from asking for help. As a leader, step out and model the values of your community. If you want disciples, then first choose to be one. Encourage your community in the fact that we are all disciples. Refuse to stop learning and growing as His servant.

230

9. TRADITION: *"That's not how we do it here"*

✡ *The Excuse:*

Some leaders reject the idea of discipleship because it has never before been done in their community. They are concerned about introducing something new as people may be set in their ways and accustomed to the manner in which things have always been done.

Notes:

✡ *The Solution:*

Beware of accepting tradition over truth. Compare your method of ministry with what the Word of God teaches. Ask yourself, "If that's not how we do it here, then how do we do it?" God's Word teaches people to imitate the lives of faith their leaders live, not merely what they teach (Hebrews 13:7). If you are teaching your congregation about prayer, are you prepared to tell them about your prayer life? Are you living out your teaching in the way you interact with your spouse and raise your children? We must model the values we want others to have, and then guide them in how to live these values out through discipleship.

When introducing discipleship in your community for the first time, do not take things too quickly. Realize that the process may take a while, especially if you have an established congregation; big ships turn much more slowly than small boats. For those who object, explain to them what Scripture says about the matter and the reasons why you are making the change.

8. FEAR OF FAILURE: *"What if no one shows up and it flops?"*

✡ *The Excuse:*

Many people are afraid of failure. Leaders struggling with this fear have said, "When we brought up discipleship in the past, no one was interested." Therefore, they do not make the effort to begin discipleship for fear it will fail.

✡ *The Solution:*

If you are struggling with this fear, ask yourself, "When your kids were young and did not want to eat their veggies, did you tell them, 'That's ok; eat all the candy you want?'" Of course not! Though your community may not see the immediate value of discipleship, love them too much to let them have their own way. Train them up in the way they should go.

231

Notes:

_____

_____

_____

_____

_____

_____

_____

_____

_____

_____

_____

_____

_____

_____

_____

_____

_____

_____

In confronting your fear, believe God's promises as you obey His Word. Do not ever keep what God has not given to you, and realize that He has not given you a spirit of fear (2 Timothy 1:7)! Yeshua taught that anything not planted by the Lord "*must be uprooted.*" (Matthew 15:13). Surrender your fears to God, for if you do not deal with them, they will be passed down to your children. Be wise in this matter for their sake, and realize that if you are not willing to fail, you will never succeed. Do not be afraid of failure or allow it to characterize yourself or anyone else. Remember that God loves and accepts us at our worst, and this is how we must love others. Realize that we are all growing into the people of character we are called to be.

7. REALIST: *"That won't work here"*

✡ *The Excuse:*

Some simply say that as they consider all the factors that are involved, discipleship just will not work in their community.

✡ *The Solution:*

Though this may appear to be a realistic viewpoint, in reality it is veiled cynicism. Beware of deceiving yourself in this way, but recognize these ideas for what they are: symptoms of unbelief and hardness of heart. If you are concerned that discipleship would not work in your community, ask yourself why you feel this way? Discipleship is a part of many communities, though it may not always be conducted in the same way. Make modifications to adjust the system of your community. In finding discipleship material, be careful of getting hung up on minor details such as jargon; adjustments can be made as you choose to make discipleship a priority in your community.

6. CORPORATE EXPECTATIONS: *"That is not part of the requirements here."*

✡ *The Excuse:*

In congregations which have paid staff, and in those which are influenced or run by an external authority, leaders may be opposed to beginning a discipleship program if it is not already part of the established framework of the congregation.

✡ *The Solution:*

Those who are thinking in this way must re-assess the system by which their congregation is run. If it does not take Yeshua's command to make disciples into consideration, something is wrong with the system. If you are making concessions on the basis of money or authority, you must step back and ask yourself whom you are really serving, and take heed lest you be serving men rather than God (Acts 5:29). Think back and ask yourself who first called you to be in ministry. If it was not God, then perhaps you need to find a different job! Ministry is not a job, but a sacrifice, a labor of love. This is what the calling is all about. It is fundamentally different than the world's system or a religious system. Draw the line: are you a "corporate man" or are you God's man?

5. QUANTIFIER: *"If it can't be measured, it can't be managed"*

✡ *The Excuse:*

The impact of a discipleship ministry is not easily quantified. Those leaders who are looking for certain specific results are suspicious of a program which does not appear to meet their expectations. A ministry which does not deliver in this way may find itself on the bottom of the priority list.

✡ *The Solution:*

As you plan for a discipleship ministry, you must trust the Lord, not rely on what can be measured.

Be careful not to let the values of the world we live in color our view of the things of God. God does not promise quick results and big numbers, and you must refuse to allow these worldly values to drive your ministry. As the prophet Samuel learned, God does not evaluate as people do (1 Samuel 16:7). We follow God's commands, and leave the results up to Him, faithfully planting seeds, watering them with prayer, and trusting God to provide the increase. The goal of discipleship is to develop godly people, long-term. Though some grow faster than others, we can trust the Lord for the increase.

Just as a person would never guess that a tree could come from a small acorn, you may be surprised by what God has in store as you trust Him!

4. TOO FUSSY: *"No materials are good enough for me."*

✡ *The Excuse:*

Of course we want the materials we use to be good, but some are looking for

Notes:

them to be perfect. They become focused on the fact that the available materials do not spell certain words like they spell them in their community, or get caught up in other such parameters, and so refuse to use any materials at all.

Notes:

✿ *The Solution:*

If you are in this predicament, step out and write your own materials! Or find something that is not too "bad." The important thing is that you use something; do not wait for perfection to come along, as everything will fail to live up to your expectations in some way. Be careful of being so "right" that it makes you unrighteous, and beware of majoring in the minors! Lead your community in the primary matters, and be careful of making a big deal about something that is simply your own preference.

3. TOO BUSY: *"We'd have to hire someone to do that."*

✿ *The Excuse:*

For many leaders, the thought of adding one more thing to their schedule is completely overwhelming. This can be the response of a person who views discipleship as just "one more thing" demanding their time.

✿ *The Solution:*

If you find yourself too busy for discipleship, ask yourself: "What am I busy doing?" In your busyness, remember what you are working towards and re-prioritize according to God's Word. Do not allow the congregation or anyone else to determine what you should be focusing on. This is determined by God. In His Word, we see that we are here to do outreach and make disciples, and this is how we need to use our time. If your goal as a leader is to have a healthy community, realize that discipleship is essential in the realization of this goal. Do not be too busy to be effective. Make your punches count.

2. COMPLACENT: *"We're doing just fine; if it ain't broke..."*

✿ *The Excuse:*

Some congregations do not have discipleship because they believe that people are discipled by osmosis, "catching it" simply by being in attendance. These leaders are not open to starting something new because they figure that they are doing well as long as more people are coming in the front door than are going out the back.

✡ *The Solution:*

Once again, if you find yourself thinking this way, you need to recognize these thoughts for what they are: laziness. Ministry is a place not for lazy people, but for people who want to serve God. As a leader, you must model the values which have to do with honoring the Lord. Repent of the sin of laziness, and refuse to maintain a carnal status quo. Lead your community by taking the initiative to love people and make disciples for Messiah, to the glory of God. He is worth our all!

1. TRANSFER-GROWTH: *"Someone else probably took care of it."*

✡ *The Excuse:*

Often times, when a person moves from one congregation to another, it is assumed that they have already been discipled. Many leaders readily welcome these people into membership and even place them into positions of service without asking any follow-up questions.

✡ *The Solution:*

Though it may seem to make sense, this practice is very dangerous! Just because a person uses the right terminology does not mean that they have been discipled. Rather than assume this, you must have a system in place to screen potential members, otherwise you will not know what sort of people are joining your community.

Though many are concerned that having a discipleship requirement for membership will hinder their congregation's growth, this is actually the only way you will grow. Accepting undiscipled people as members will, in the end, actually stunt your growth. Do not be driven by numbers; God is not ashamed of a remnant and neither should we be. Also, do not be driven by need. As people come through discipleship and are ready to serve, be very wise about those whom you appoint for service; never take someone on board just because there is a need. Those wanting to serve in certain ministries, especially those working with children or finances, should be required to go through background checks. Be very wise on all these matters, protecting your flock against "fleece-covered wolves."

As you consider this list, realize that the genuine, most detrimental, #1 problem for discipleship is your own excuses. Though they may seem to be wisdom, each of these excuses will only serve to hinder your ministry. We must see these things for what they are and refuse to let them hinder us from moving forward in our high calling to make disciples!

Notes:

235

APPENDIX 3

GROUP DISCIPLESHIP

Notes:

At times, particularly at the start of a new congregation plant, you may find yourself with more disciplees than disciplers. One way to handle this situation is to disciple everyone together as a group. This can be difficult, yet all things are possible with God. However, before you step into this scenario, there are some practical issues that need to be addressed.

Successfully discipling more than one person at once depends upon your ability to manage the responsibility. Some parents have all they can deal with in raising one child, others are perfectly at ease with triplets. Consider the fact that, in discipling multiple people, you will not be able to give as much attention to each individual as you would meeting with them one on one. If you are discipling a group, you need to make sure that each person is doing their homework, and that they are all on the same page. Another issue is that some in your group may pick up the information faster than others. If the majority of the group is ready to move on, but the others are still working through the material, this can bring about an unhealthy situation. As the discipler, you must be careful that all are treated equally, and that those who need special attention will be able to receive it.

If you give birth to six children, you need to make sure that all are adequately fed and that all are growing; refusing to let the "runts" die. In fact, we are to give more honor to the weaker parts of the Body (1 Corinthians 12:22-24). The least of the brethren receive our special attention. Our goal is to ensure that each person become mature in Messiah, not just the stronger, quicker ones. Understanding the information quickly is not a big deal. The big deal is how you implement the information you learn!

Regardless of the number of people you are discipling, you must make sure that they all become grounded and rooted, not simply make it through the class. People will not learn from sitting through a class, but by implementing what they hear because they know they will be asked to give an account for it. Disciples need to understand that everything will be on the test, for once they leave the door, they will be tested. God expects us to invest what we receive, and does not share His Word with us so that we can hide it under a rock. We must make application, and teach others to do so as well.

236

CONGREGATIONAL "COUNSELING"

Congregational "counseling" is a normal facet of an elder's everyday responsibilities. However, here I have put the word in quotes because much of what is called counseling is really discipleship on point; meeting with a person in order to disciple them in a specific area of life. As a leader, this responsibility must be handled with great wisdom. First, a congregational leader should not expect to provide all the counseling needed in a congregation.

80% OF COUNSELING ISSUES

80% of all the typical counseling issues that arise in a congregation have to do with the everyday trials of life. As people go through adversity, whether it be loss of job, health problems, difficult family visits, etc., they need encouragement in how to trust Yeshua in the midst of these *tsuris*. Any Spirit-led believer who is grounded in the Lord can provide this type of counsel for a fellow believer. Though they may not be able to give advice on how to change the difficult circumstance, they can put their arm around their brother or sister and pray with them, exhorting them in the midst of the trial, saying, "Let's trust Yeshua together." It is important that a leader encourage people in the congregation to reach out in love and encouragement to one another in this powerful way.

15-18% OF COUNSELING ISSUES

About 15 – 18 % of counseling issues arise due to a lack of biblical instruction in specific areas. For those struggling with chronic marriage problems, the inability to keep a job, continual debt, etc., specific instruction is needed in God's teaching on these matters. This type of discipleship can be provided by elders or deacons in the congregation. In this respect, a congregational leader serves in the role of a general practitioner, not a specialist, and needs to find other leaders in the congregation who can also assist in meeting these needs.

Strong believers in your community who have skills in areas such as financial planning, marriage counseling, job searching, resume building, etc. can be of help for these people. For instance, a couple struggling in their marriage could be paired with an older, mature couple in the congregation for mentoring in what it means to build a healthy, godly relationship. As people come to you with various needs, it is essential to love them enough to take time for them, and be able to point them to a servant-leader who can best address their needs.

2 - 5% OF COUNSELING ISSUES

Finally, about 2 – 5% of counseling issues which arise have to do with people who are severely neurotic or psychotic. In these situations, it is wise to look for believing counselors in the community to whom you can refer. Realize that some situations will be above your pay-grade; you will not be able to do everything, and should not attempt to do so. In planting a new congregation, get to know the community around you and find godly counselors with whom you can partner. Be wary of allowing 1% of the people take up 99% of your time.

When people with psychotic or neurotic behaviors are causing problems in the congregation, it is necessary to take these people aside and say, "This is not a good meeting for you to be a part of, however, I would like to meet with you in a different setting." As you meet with them, assess whether the situation merits calling in outside help or not. At one congregation I was planting, there were several people with this type of need, who engaged in socially inappropriate, though not threatening, behaviors and were distracting others during the services. In order to help these people while being mindful of others in the congregation, we found a leader who was willing to meet with these people during our regular services and disciple them according to their needs. Through this important ministry, several people came to faith in Yeshua and grew to love and follow the Lord.

As we consider these matters, realize that we are to love all people the Lord brings our way, especially the least of the brethren. As a congregation, we will not be known by how we interact with the best of the people, but by how we serve the least. Remember that when we reach out to the least of the brethren, we are ministering unto Messiah.

Notes:

238

A CONGREGATION'S RELATIONSHIP WITH THE GREATER BODY OF MESSIAH

IDENTIFICATION WITH THE BODY

"There is one body and one Spirit, just as also you were called in one hope of your calling; one Lord, one faith, one immersion, one God and Father of all who is over all and through all and in all." – Ephesians 4:4-6

Messianic communities are a part of Yeshua's Body. Though established as self-supported, self-governed, and self-propagating, a Messianic congregation's Articles of Faith should evidence identification with faith in Yeshua as understood in evangelical circles. There is only one Body of Messiah, made up of Jewish and Gentile followers of Yeshua. As such, we all agree on the primary teachings of the faith regarding the Triune nature of God, the sin nature of man, the work of Messiah, salvation by faith in what Yeshua has done, the authority of Scripture, etc. These primary matters help clarify that which unifies a Messianic congregation with the greater Body, and identifies those who have deviated from the faith although they may call themselves- "Messianic" or "Christian."

In a Messianic congregation, there should be an attitude of affirmation of the Body, and a denouncing of any anti-church or anti-Gentile prejudice (Ephesians 4:1-3, 29). We are to love the entire Body of Messiah, and reject any sinful attitudes against them as these are improper for any believer to have, as well as contrary to our calling as a Messianic congregation. However, though we are to love everyone, a congregation should not have fellowship with those who would curse Israel or speak against its establishment (Genesis 12:3, Numbers 24:9; Romans 9:3). Such people are in error and our role concerning them is to seek to restore them to fellowship (Galatians 6:1).

COMMUNICATION TO THE BODY

"For just as we have many members in one body and all the members do not have the same function, so we, who are many, are one body in Messiah, and individually members one of another." – Romans 12:4-5

Notes:

A Messianic congregation exists to effectively communicate to others. First, we communicate to the Jewish community around us that Yeshua is the Messiah. However, we also serve to communicate to the larger Body of Messiah that God has not forsaken the Jewish people. As we successfully do this, the Body of believers in the area should view the local Messianic congregation as partners in their own testimony to the Jewish community. We serve as a resource for our brothers and sisters in Messiah, representing the truth that belief in Yeshua does not lessen one's Jewish identity. This outreach to the Body of Messiah can take place indirectly through website promotion or newsletters, or directly through relationship building over lunch or through presentations when invited to speak at church meetings, Bible studies, or conferences.

ACCESSIBILITY FOR THE BODY

"Otherwise if you bless in the Spirit only, how will the one who fills the place of the ungifted say the 'Amen' at your giving of thanks, since he does not know what you are saying? For you are giving thanks well enough, but the other person is not edified." – 1 Corinthians 14:16-17

Through regular services and special events, Messianic congregations provide occasions for all believers in their area to invite Jewish acquaintances to hear the message of Messiah. Make these opportunities accessible to those in local churches, promoting your special holiday gatherings, and encouraging others to invite their Jewish friends and neighbors to hear the Good News. In light of this, services should be conducted with visitors in mind, so that any person, whether Jewish or Gentile, can understand the message that is being presented (1 Corinthians 2:1-5, etc). Keep materials on hand to give out to visitors, and have resources available for people to use in outreach to their own Jewish friends and neighbors.

SERVICE IN THE BODY

"...I have become all things to all men, so that I may by all means save some. I do all things for the sake of the Good News, so that I may become a fellow partaker of it." – 1 Corinthians 9:22-23

Today, Messianic congregations recognize two realities. First, the majority of Jewish people who come to faith in Messiah do so through the ministry of sincere believers in churches, not through Messianic congregations. Secondly, of the many Jewish believers in churches around the country, few are discipled to remain Jewish or to raise their children as Jewish.

Messianic congregations can help bridge this gap by providing training for the larger Body of Messiah, helping churches to grow in sharing the Good News in a way that Jewish people can understand, as well as learn to effectively disciple new Jewish believers in their communities. As we serve the Body in this way, we equip them to help their Jewish brothers and sisters become rooted and grounded in their identity as followers of the Jewish Messiah, able to be a witness of God's faithfulness to the Jewish community as well as the general Body.

These training classes should be open to all, and, if possible, promoted throughout your area. Classes may include Jewish evangelism seminars, teaching on the Feasts of Israel, instruction on the Jewish context of the New Covenant, teaching on the calling of Gentile believers as seen in Romans 11, and other specific training in both evangelism and discipleship. These classes can be held at your congregation, or at interested churches in the area for Sunday school classes or mid-week meetings. Give different members of your community a chance to take part in teaching these classes, for all members need opportunities to grow in their ability to explain such core Messianic teaching.

ENCOURAGEMENT FOR THE BODY

"I say then, they did not stumble so as to fall, did they? May it never be! But by their transgression salvation has come to the Gentiles, to make them jealous." – Romans 11:11

We are called to minister but never to manipulate. Ministry is encouraging people in what they know they need to be doing. Manipulation is encouraging people to do what you want them to be doing. Many evangelical

Notes:

_____

_____

_____

_____

_____

_____

_____

_____

_____

_____

_____

_____

_____

_____

_____

_____

_____

churches in the area want to grow in being an effective witness to the local and worldwide Jewish community. These are the churches who need encouragement in the calling which they share with all Jewish and Gentile believers in Messiah, having equal partnership in Messiah's Great Commission (Romans 1:16, 11:11, etc). The larger Body of Messiah will more effectively communicate to the Jewish people as they understand the faithfulness of God's character as it pertains to both the Jewish people and the nations. As their understanding grows, they will grow to use their liberty in Messiah in order to more effectively testify to the Jewish people and to all people what the God of Israel has accomplished through salvation in Yeshua.

As we encourage and care for one another despite our differences, we reflect the culture of heaven. There was once a man who had a nightmare about hell. In his dream, he saw an abundance of wonderful food, but no one was able to get to it because they were forced to eat with six foot chopsticks and so could not get the food to their mouths! Next, the same man had a dream about heaven. There he was surprised to find the same situation: wonderful food, and six foot chopsticks! How could this be heaven? Because, in the second dream, the people were using the chopsticks to feed one another! Our care for one another testifies of God's program of restoration on earth. The commonwealth of Israel (the whole Body of Messiah) is meant to reveal the King of Israel's love for both the people of Israel and the nations.

SAMPLE CONSTITUTION
Including Covenant, By-Laws, & Articles of Faith

Notes:

COVENANT

Having been led, as we believe, by the Spirit of God to receive the Messiah Yeshua as our Savior and Lord, and on the profession of our faith having been immersed in the name of the Father, and of the Son, and of the Holy Spirit, we do now, in the presence of God, angels and this assembly, most joyfully enter into Covenant with one another, as one body in Messiah.
We agree, therefore, to be led by the Holy Spirit:

- ✡ To walk together in Messiah's love;
- ✡ To knit together Jew and Gentile in one local fellowship to worship the God of Israel;
- ✡ To reach out to the community with the love of God found in the promised Messiah of Israel;
- ✡ To be supportive of the State of Israel as exhorted in the Holy Scriptures and pray for the peace of Jerusalem;
- ✡ To strive for the advancement of this congregation in wisdom, holiness, and love;
- ✡ To promote its prosperity and spiritual growth;
- ✡ To sustain its worship, ordinances, discipline, and doctrine;
- ✡ To give it a sacred preeminence over all institutions of human origin;
- ✡ To contribute cheerfully and regularly to the support of the ministry, the expenses of the congregation, the relief of the poor, and the spread of the gospel through all nations;

We also agree:

- ✡ To maintain family and personal devotions;
- ✡ To faithfully educate our children in the Word of God;
- ✡ To seek the salvation of our kindred and acquaintances;
- ✡ To walk circumspectly in the world;

Notes:

✡ To be just in our dealings, faithful in our engagements, and exemplary in our deportment;

✡ To avoid all gossiping and inappropriate anger;

✡ To abstain from all forms of evil;

✡ To be prepared for the defense of the Good News;

✡ To extend love in removing all prejudices, especially anti-Semitism;

✡ To be zealous in our efforts to advance the kingdom of our Messiah;

We further agree:

✡ To watch over one another in brotherly love;

✡ To pray for one another;

✡ To aid each other in sickness and distress;

✡ To cultivate sympathy in feeling and courtesy in speech;

✡ To be slow to take offense, to be always ready for reconciliation and mindful of the restoration of our Messiah to secure it without delay.

✡ "To further clarify (but not delimit) the meaning of the above-stated covenant "to abstain from all forms of evil", we agree that the term "marriage" has only one meaning: marriage sanctioned by God, joining one man and one woman in a single, exclusive union, as delineated in the Bible; that God intends sexual activity to occur only between a man and a woman who are married to each other; that God has forbidden sexual activity outside of a marriage between a man and a woman; and that any form of sexual immorality or sexual activity outside of a marriage between a man and a woman, including without limitation, cross-dressing, promiscuity, adultery, fornication, homosexuality, bisexual conduct, transsexual conduct, polyamorous conduct, bestiality, incest, pedophilia, pornography or any attempt to change one's gender, or disagreement with one's biological gender, is evil, sinful and offensive to God.

We also agree that in order to preserve the function and integrity of the congregation as the local Body of Messiah, and to provide a Biblically accurate witness to the congregation members and to the surrounding community, it is imperative that all members of the congregation and persons employed by the congregation, including without limitation volunteers who are in a position of responsibility and authority over children and those employed as congregational staff, agree to and abide by the foregoing statement on marriage and sexuality and conduct themselves accordingly."

We moreover agree, that when we remove from this place, we will as soon as possible unite with some other congregation of like faith and practice, where we can carry out the spirit of this covenant and the principles of God's Word.

BY-LAWS

Notes:

ARTICLE I - NAME

The name of the congregation shall be [insert name]. The principal office of the congregation shall be located at [insert address].

ARTICLE II - PURPOSE

Our purpose is to maintain an indigenous, autonomous congregation under God; to promote the spirit of the early New Covenant congregation in the spreading of the Good News of Messiah Yeshua; to knit together Jew and Gentile in one local fellowship to worship the God of Israel; to maintain a testimony of the truth of the Good News and purity of the congregation (Matthew 28:18-20, I Corinthians 15:1-4); also to encourage our congregation planters at home and abroad, and to help them in their needs; to be supportive of the state of Israel as exhorted in the Holy Scriptures (Psalm 122:6). We want to maintain a standard of Biblical separation from worldliness and apostasy; and to actively, positively and assertively live for Yeshua.

The congregation, in recognizing its unique calling to reach out to all people, but especially to the Jew first (Romans 1:16), will have at its services a Jewish identity in worship; not to offend any Gentile brethren, but in order to reflect to the community the congregation's sensitivities and understanding of the Scriptures regarding Israel's Messiah who is the Savior of the world and to demonstrate as a congregation that God in Messiah has not forsaken His people Israel. The congregation, made up of Jew and Gentile alike, further understands that this testimony will always be secondary to the testimony of their love one for another to the Glory of God.

ARTICLE III - MEMBERSHIP

SECTION I - RECEPTION

Any person applying for membership with this congregation shall be exam-

Notes:

ined and recommended by the Membership Committee consisting of the *Z'keinim*, Congregation Leader, and other members approved by the Board of *Z'keinim*. Such person shall have first attended the congregation for at least four Shabbat services, give evidence of their salvation by personal testimony, shall have been immersed, be willing to serve in the congregation, and shall agree to uphold the Covenant of this congregation.

In furtherance of the foregoing, all such persons shall believe in Messiah Yeshua as Savior and Lord; shall actively pursue and continue in a vital fellowship with Messiah Yeshua in thought, word and deed; shall affirm all tenets of the Consideration of Values, Covenant, By-Laws and Articles of Faith; and shall offer evidence, by their confession and their conduct, that they are living in accord with their vital fellowship with Messiah Yeshua and with their affirmation of the tenets of the Consideration of Values, Covenant, By-Laws and Articles of Faith. Such persons shall attend membership classes and fulfill any prerequisites the Membership Committee deems necessary. Such applicants thus recommended shall be voted upon by the congregation and must receive a two-thirds majority of the votes cast.

This congregation will welcome into its membership by letter, any person giving evidence of salvation by a personal testimony and upon receipt of a letter of recommendation from any congregation maintaining the same or similar doctrinal stand. Recommendation by the committee will be made upon receipt of the letter and after investigation of the sending congregation. These will then be voted upon by the congregation and must receive a two-thirds majority of the votes cast.

SECTION II - CLASSIFICATION

✡ Active - A member shall be considered active if he regularly attends the services, gives evidence of his support of the Articles of Faith, is not under discipline, and has not been dismissed from membership.

✡ Inactive - After appropriate inquiry or examination by the Board of *Z'keinim*, a member shall be considered inactive if he does not regularly attend worship services (except if he is unable) or is under discipline. An inactive member shall forfeit the privileges of membership. Inactive members are to be advised in writing by the Board of *Z'keinim*. To be reinstated as an active member, an inactive member must follow the procedures for the reception of new members.

✡ Non-Participating Members - Members that are by necessity of circumstances not in the general area of the congregation for an extended period of time, will be able to maintain their membership. However they will be considered "non participating members" and will not be considered for quorum and will not have a vote.

SECTION III - RESPONSIBILITIES & PRIVILEGES OF MEMBERS

Notes:

Responsibilities:

✡ It shall be the responsibility of every member to attend all regular meetings and to manifest a keen interest in the up-building of the congregation.

✡ It shall be the responsibility of every member to practice stewardship of both talents and substance for the well being of the congregation. Every member, depending on their circumstances, is expected to be active in congregational service and tithing.

✡ It shall be the responsibility of every member to guard the testimony of the congregation and its leadership before non-members and each other by a spoken and unyielding loyalty to fellow members as an example of close fellowship with our Messiah Yeshua.

Privileges:

✡ It shall be the privilege of every active member 18 years of age and over to vote in the affairs of the congregation. All members between the ages of 13 and 17 may apply to the Board of Z'keinim for the privilege to vote.

✡ It shall be the privilege of every active member to hold office and serve on committees and boards.

✡ It shall be the privilege of every active member to use the facilities of the congregation for weddings, funerals, Bar/Bat Mitzvah and other related affairs upon approval by the Board of Shamashim/Deacons or Z'keinim.

✡ It shall be the privilege of every active member to receive all routine congregational communications, newsletters, etc.

✡ It shall be the privilege of every active member to receive advice and counsel from the Pastoral leadership of the congregation or its delegates.

✡ It shall be the privilege of all active members, to have their children dedicated to the Lord at a congregational service.

✡ It shall be the privilege of all active members to have the pastoral staff perform their wedding ceremonies following the required premarital counseling and agreement by the officiant.

SECTION IV - DISMISSAL

Notes:

✡ By Letter - Any member who wishes to unite with another congregation of like faith may, upon request of that congregation, be granted a letter of recommendation dependent on the approval by the Board of *Z'keinim*.

✡ By Erasure - Any member whose residence has been unknown to the congregation for one year or who has failed to attend for one year shall have his name erased from the roll. This will be done upon recommendation of the Board of *Z'keinim* and after sending a registered letter to his last known address. The congregation will then vote upon the erasure; a two-thirds majority of votes cast will complete the erasure at the congregational business meeting.

✡ By Removal - A friend of the congregation's (FOC) name is removed upon approval of the Board of *Z'keinim* when he ceases to regularly attend the services.

✡ By Death - The death of a member automatically dissolves membership

✡ By Expulsion - When the congregation, in the exercise of its constitutional authority in discipline, withdraws fellowship from one proven to be an unworthy member, his membership immediately ceases. This shall be done only after enjoining scriptural steps and in light of Galatians 6:1, Matthew 18:15-20, and I Corinthians 5:9-13.

✡ By Request - Any person requesting that his name be removed can be so removed by personal notification. The congregation may not accept the resignation from any member charged with conduct unbecoming a member or who is currently under congregational discipline until those charges have been investigated and that member cleared or the matter has been resolved.

ARTICLE IV - OFFICES & ELECTION

✡ A. Board of Trustees

The Board of Trustees shall consist of a minimum of three trustees made up of Congregation Leaders, *Z'keinim*, *Shamashim*, and those deemed responsible by the Board of Trustees. Trustees may serve maximum of two three -year terms before stepping down for at least one year.

Members of the Board of Trustees shall be active members of the congregation. New members of the Board of Trustees will be presented by the Board of *Z'keinim* to be voted on by majority vote of members present.

The extent of terms of membership of the Board of Trustees will be three, two, and one year terms for the first slate of Trustees.

The trustees will be responsible for the fiscal affairs of the congregation under the oversight of the Board of *Z'keinim*. They will prepare a yearly budget that will reflect ministry priorities of the *Z'keinim* that will be approved by two-thirds majority of the congregation at the yearly business meeting. They will also provide a quarterly financial report comparing actual giving and expenditures to the budget.

The Congregation shall have the following Officers who shall be elected in the manner described below:

The Congregational Leader shall serve as President and shall be chosen in the manner set forth in Article IV (B) below.

The following officers shall be elected by the Board of *Z'keinim* (Elders): Secretary & Treasurer.

The Board of *Z'keinim* may elect such other Officers including one or more Vice-Presidents, one or more Assistant Secretaries, and one or more Assistant Treasurers, as seems desirable, such Officers to have the authority and perform the duties prescribed from time to time, by the Board of *Z'keinim*. The following rules shall govern the term and duties of the Officers:

a. Election and Term of Office. The Officers shall be elected for terms of one year beginning on January 1 of each year and shall be elected by the Board of *Z'keinim* (except for the President - Congregational Leader, who shall be elected as set forth in Subparagraph (B) below) in December of each year to serve for the following year. The Board of *Z'keinim* shall promptly fill any vacancies in the corporate offices. Vacancies in any office shall be promptly filled.

Notes:

b. President. The President (Congregational Leader) shall be authorized to execute all documents and take all action which are required to be done by the President under the laws of the State of North Carolina. The President shall also have the duties of the congregational Leader as set forth herein.

Notes:

c. Secretary. The Secretary shall keep the minutes of the meetings of the members and the Board of Trustees in one or more books provided for that purpose; see that all notices are duly given in accordance with the provisions of these By Laws or as required by law; be custodian of the records and see that the Seal of the Corporation is affixed to all documents, the execution of which on behalf of the Congregation under seal is authorized in accordance with the provisions of these By Laws; keep a register of the post office address of each member which shall be furnished to the Secretary by each member; and in general perform all duties instant to the office of Secretary and such other duties as from time to time may be assigned by the Board of Trustees.

d. Treasurer. The Treasurer shall: 1) Have charge and custody of and be responsible for all funds and securities of the Congregation; keep and maintain adequate and correct accounts of the Congregation's properties and business transactions; bring reports and accounting to the leadership and members; receive and give receipts for money due and payable to the Congregation from any source whatsoever, and deposit all monies in the name of the Congregation, in such banks, trust companies or such other depositories as shall be selected by the Board of Trustees; 2) In general, perform all the duties instant to the office of Treasurer and such other duties as from time to time may be assigned by the Board of Trustees.

✡ B. Congregational Leader

The Congregational Leader will be a voting member of the Board of Z'keinim and will be responsible for the spiritual growth and welfare of the congregation. The Congregation Leader, a servant of God, must be in accord with the Constitution. In order to become Congregation Leader, he must be examined by the Board of Z'keinim and voted on by the congregation for a four-fifths majority of the votes cast at a congregational meeting for the calling of the Congregation Leader.

The Congregation Leader shall serve until his leadership is terminated by resignation or by request of the Board of Z'keinim and the congregation. If at any time the Congregation Leader's personal belief, preaching or conduct shall not be in full accord with the Constitution of the congregation, his services as Congregation Leader may be terminated by a two-thirds majority of the votes cast at any duly called congregational meeting. Congregational meetings, where the subject is the dismissal of the Congregation Leader, must be announced two weeks prior to the meeting date(s). The resignation of the Congregation Leader must be given to the Board of *Z'keinim* and congregation at least one (1) month prior to his departure. Upon removal or resignation of the Congregation Leader, the *Z'keinim* will move to establish a Congregation Leader search committee made up of *Z'keinim*, *Shamashim-Shamashot*, and other members of the congregation. The Congregation Leader at any annual meeting may call a confidence vote.

✡ C. Board of *Z'keinim*

The Board of *Z'keinim* will be the men responsible for the spiritual oversight of the congregation. *Z'keinim* will be selected by the Board of *Z'keinim* and affirmed by a two-thirds majority of votes cast at a congregational meeting. If a *Zakkein* is found to be spiritually unfit, a two-thirds majority of votes cast at a congregational meeting will dismiss him from the Board of *Z'keinim*. The extent of terms of membership of the Board of *Z'keinim* will be three (3), two (2), and one (1) year terms for the first slate of *Z'keinim*. *Z'keinim*, with the exception of the Congregation Leader, may serve maximum of two three (3) year terms before stepping down for at least one year.

Z'keinim will be responsible for the oversight of the Worship, Teaching, Outreach, and Administration of the congregation whether it is through visitation, discipleship, congregational discipline, Shabbat school, *Chavurot*, evangelism, congregational Web Pages, etc. The work of ministry will be accomplished by them generally through the delegation of those duties to other responsible members of the congregation.

Any account involving a member who is accused of violating the Consideration of Values, Covenant, By-Laws and/or Articles of Faith shall be directed to the Board of *Z'keinim* to be handled according to Scripture Matthew 5:23-24, 18:15-18, Galatians 6:1. In furtherance of the foregoing, all final decisions by the Board of *Z'keinim* regarding the interpretation and application of the Bible on a case-by-case basis, including without limitation such decisions pertaining to the morality, conduct and discipline of congregation members, will be accepted as final by the congregation.

Notes:

Notes:

_____

_____

_____

_____

_____

_____

_____

_____

_____

_____

_____

_____

_____

_____

_____

✡ D. Board of *Shamashim*

The Board of *Shamashim* will be the men responsible for the operational functioning of the congregation. The Board of *Z'keinim* will establish the Board of *Shamashim*. *Shamashim* will be selected in accordance with biblical standards (I Timothy 3, Acts 6). One becomes a member of the Board of *Shamashim* by being presented to the congregation by the Board of *Z'keinim* and affirmed by a two-thirds majority of votes cast at a congregational meeting. The extent of the term for membership of the Board of *Shamashim* will be two (2) years.

✡ E. Board of *Shamashot* (Deaconesses)

The Board of *Shamashot* will be the women responsible for helping *Z'keinim* with counseling, teaching, discipleship, and the operational functions of the congregation. The Board of *Z'keinim* will establish the Board of *Shamashot*. *Shamashot* will be selected in accordance with biblical standards (I Timothy 3). One becomes a member of the Board of *Shamashot* by being presented to the congregation by the Board of *Z'keinim* and affirmed by a two-thirds majority of votes cast at a congregational meeting. The extent of term for membership of the Board of *Shamashot* will be two (2) years.

✡ F. Shabbat School Superintendent

The Shabbat School Superintendent shall be selected by Disciple making *Z'keinim* or *Shamashim* / *Shamashot* and approved by the Board of *Z'keinim* and by a majority of votes cast at a special congregational meeting. The term shall be two (2) years.

✡ G. Missions Chairperson

The chairperson of the missions committee shall be selected by the Contact-making *Z'keinim* or *Shamashim* / *Shamashot* and approved by the Board of *Z'keinim* and by majority of votes cast at the annual business meeting. The term shall be for two (2) years.

ARTICLE V - ORDINATION & LICENSING

Ordination: When, in the judgment of the Board of *Z'keinim*, a man in this fellowship has been called of God to minister in the capacity of a pastor, evangelist, or missionary, it shall be the duty of the Board of *Z'keinim* to determine if the man is faithfully fulfilling the obligation of such a call and is worthy of ordination. It shall then recommend to the congregation the calling of a council to examine the candidate to be invited for said council and the congregational secretary shall send the invitation to each person of the council so invited. The council shall thoroughly examine the candidate as to:

Notes:

✡ His salvation experience.
✡ His call to the ministry.
✡ His view of Scriptural doctrine.

After which the council will deliberate and decide whether or not to recommend to the congregation his ordination. Upon recommendation of the council, the congregation will vote to affirm the ordination at the congregational meeting.

Licensing: Upon the recommendation of the Congregation Leader, the Board of *Z'keinim* may also present to the congregation any member of the congregation entering into full-time service and doing the required work of ministry for Messiah.

ARTICLE VI - CONGREGATIONAL MEETINGS

The annual congregational meeting shall be held the second Shabbat after Sukkot. A special congregational meeting may also be called by the Congregation Leader, the Board of *Z'keinim*, or upon the written request of seven (7) members of the congregation to the Board of *Z'keinim*, and must be announced by the Board of *Z'keinim* two (2) Shabbats before it is to occur.

Meetings to carry on routine business, such as voting on persons for membership, can be handled at any regular service of the congregation by a majority of voting members present. All duly called meetings are required to have been announced for two (2) previous weeks at regular services and need to have a quorum of one-third (1/3) of participating voting membership of the congregation.

ARTICLE VII - AMENDMENTS

This constitution may be changed or amended at any annual congregational meeting by a two-thirds (2/3) majority vote of ballots cast.

ARTICLE VIII - FISCAL YEAR

The fiscal year of the Congregation shall begin on the first day of January and end on the last day of December of in each year.

Notes:

ARTICLE IX - CORPORATE SEAL

The Board of Trustee shall provide a Corporate Seal, which shall be in the form of a circle and it shall have inscribed thereon the name of the congregation and the words "Corporate Seal."

ARTICLE X - FUNDS

No part of the net earnings of the corporation shall inure to the benefit of, its members, directors, officers, or other persons except that the organization shall be authorized and empowered to pay reasonable compensation for services rendered and to make payments and distributions in furtherance of the exempt purposes of the corporation.

In the event of dissolution, the residual assets of the corporation will be turned over to one or more corporations with similar purposes which are exempt as corporations described in Section 501(c) (3) of the Internal Revenue Code of 1986.

ARTICLES OF FAITH

1. We believe there is one God, eternally existent in three persons - Father, Son and Holy Spirit. We believe that God is all knowing, all-powerful, ever present, and changeless and that He is holy, righteous, faithful, merciful and loving (Deuteronomy 6:4; Isaiah 43:10-11; 48:16).

a. We believe that the Father is all fullness of the Godhead invisible. We rejoice that He concerns Himself mercifully in the affairs of men, that He hears and answers prayer, and that He saves from sin and death all that come to Him through faith in Messiah Yeshua (Exodus 4:22; Matthew 3:17; John 1:12, 3:16; 8:24, 58; Galatians 3:26).

b. We believe that Messiah Yeshua is the eternal and only begotten Son of God, conceived of the Holy Spirit, born of a Jewish virgin, Miriam. He was sinless in His life and He made atonement for the sins of the world by the shedding of His blood unto death. We believe in His bodily resurrection from the dead, His ascension, His high priestly work in Heaven for us, and His visible pre-millennial return to the world according to His promise. (Leviticus 17:11; Psalm 22:16; 110:4; Isaiah 52:13-53:12; Daniel 9:26; Zechariah 12:10; Mark 10:45; Romans 3:24-26, 5:8-9; 2 Corinthians 5:14, 21; 1 Peter 3:18; Isaiah 7:14, 9:6-7; Jeremiah 23:5-6; Micah 5:2; John 1:1, 8:58; 1 Timothy 3:16; Hebrews 1:2-3; 1 Corinthians 15:3-8; Hebrews 7:1-25, 8;1; 1 John 2:1).

c. We believe the *Ruach HaKodesh* (Holy Spirit) is a person of the Godhead; and as such, He possesses all the distinct attributes of Deity. He is ever present to glorify and testify of Messiah Yeshua. We believe that according to the *Brit Chadashah* (New Covenant), the *Ruach HaKodesh* permanently indwells regenerates, and seals the believer. He empowers, sovereignly imparting at least one spiritual gift to every believer for the purpose of edifying and equipping the Body of Messiah, guides, teaches, sanctifies, and fills believers, convicts the world of sin, righteousness, and judgment.

We believe the immersion of the *Ruach HaKodesh* is both initiatory and universal. Believers should therefore seek to identify, utilize and develop their God given gifts for service in the Lord (Genesis 1:2; Psalm 139:7-8; Nehemiah 9:20; 1 John 5:6; John 14:16-17, 15:26-27, 16:7-15; 1 Corinthians 2:10-11, 12:4-31; 2 Corinthians 13:14; Ephesians 1:13-14, 4:30).

2. We believe that the Bible is God's completed Word, that it was inerrantly written by divinely inspired men, that it is the supreme, infallible authority in all matters of faith and conduct, and that it is true in all that it affirms (Proverbs 30:5-6; Isaiah 40:7-8; Jeremiah 31:31; Matthew 5:18; 2 Timothy 3:16; 2 Peter 1:21).

3. We believe that humanity was created in the image of God. We believe that because of the original sin that all men are by nature and choice sinful and alienated from God. Man has no possible means of reconciling himself to God and that, by persisting in the sinful state of unbelief, man is justly condemned by God to eternal punishment. (Genesis 1:26-27, 2:17, 3:6; Isaiah 53:6, 64:6; Jeremiah 17:9; Mark 7:20-23; John 2:24-25; Romans 5:12-15; Ephesians 2:1-3).

Notes:

_____

_____

_____

_____

_____

_____

_____

_____

_____

_____

_____

_____

_____

_____

_____

Notes:

_____

_____

_____

_____

_____

_____

_____

_____

_____

_____

_____

_____

_____

_____

_____

4. We believe that man is reconciled to God, being justified by grace through faith in the atoning work of Messiah Yeshua. Being reconciled, man has peace with God and direct access to Him through Messiah Yeshua and has the hope of eternal glory in Heaven with God. Further, there is no way of salvation apart from faith in Messiah Yeshua for any person, Jewish or Gentile (Genesis 15:6; Habakkuk 2:4; John 1:12-13; 14:6; Acts 4:12; Romans 3:28; Ephesians 1:7; 1 Timothy 2:5: Titus 3:5).

We believe that all who have truly trusted in Messiah Yeshua are kept eternally secure by the power of God through the new birth, the indwelling and sealing ministry of the Holy Spirit, and the intercession of Messiah Yeshua (John 10:28-30, 14:16-17; Romans 8:38-39; Ephesians 4:30; 1 John 2:1; 1 Peter 1:23).

We believe that all who have trusted in Messiah Yeshua, though forgiven, still have to contend with the power of sin in this life. Each believer has the ability to choose sin or righteousness. God has made full provision for believers to live in obedience to Him through the complete atonement of Messiah Yeshua and the indwelling of the Spirit of God (John 17:17-19; Romans 6:1-11, 7:15-25, 8:11-13; 1 John 1:8-2:2).

5. We believe the Congregation is a living, spiritual body of which Messiah Yeshua is the head and all true believers are members. The body of Messiah Yeshua began at *Shavuot* (Pentecost) when believers were filled with the Holy Spirit after the ascension of Messiah Yeshua. It will be completed when the Messiah returns for His bride. The body of Messiah is distinct from Israel and is composed of both Jewish and non-Jewish (Gentile) believers made into one new man by faith in Messiah Yeshua (Matthew 16:18; Acts 1:5, 2:14-38; 1 Corinthians 12:13; Ephesians 2:11-15, 5:23-27; Colossians 1:18-20, 3:14-15).

We believe that the local congregation is an organized body of believers in Messiah Yeshua who have been through *Mikvah / Tevilah* (baptism) by immersion upon confession of faith and who associate for worship, fellowship, teaching, and service. We believe the local congregation is governed by its members through the *Z'keinim* (Elders) and is not ruled by any outside political authority. Its purpose is to glorify God through worship, instruction, accountability, discipline, fellowship and outreach (Matthew 28:19-20; Acts 2:42-47; Ephesians 4:11-13; Hebrews 10:19-25). We believe Messiah

Yeshua commands *Zicharon* (the Lord's Supper) and believer's *Mikvah / Tevilah* (baptism) by immersion for observation by the Congregation (Matthew 28:18-20; Luke 22:19-20; 1 Cor. 11:23-26).

6. We believe that Satan is the chief enemy of God and our souls, and that while he continues to rule this present world, Messiah Yeshua's atoning death and resurrection have defeated him. Satan will suffer eternal punishment by being cast into the lake of fire after the Messiah's one thousand year Messianic reign (2 Corinthians 4:4; Ephesians 2:1-3; Colossians 2:15; Revelation 20:10). Satan is the father of lies and anti-Semitism and hostility toward Israel. Believers can and should resist him and his demons by faith, applying Spiritual truth. We believe that though believers cannot be demon possessed, they can be demon oppressed (Genesis 3:1-19; Luke 10:18; John 8:44; Ephesians 6:10-19; James 4:7-8; 1 Peter 5:8-9; Revelation 12:13).

We believe in the God ordained ministry of holy angels to bring about God's intended plans and purposes and to minister to all believers (Isaiah 6:1-7; Daniel 10:10-21; Luke 15:10; Ephesians 1:21; Hebrews 1:14; Revelation 7:11-12).

7. We believe the people of Israel, comprised of the physical descendants of Abraham, Isaac, and Jacob, and are chosen by God. The Abrahamic Covenant expressed God's choice of Israel and His irrevocable, unconditional covenant to the Jewish people. Jewish believers have a unique two-fold identity as both the spiritual remnant of physical Israel and as members of the body of Messiah Yeshua. Non-Jewish believers become adopted sons and daughters of Abraham and partakers of the spiritual blessings of Israel and are therefore grafted into the Jewish Olive Tree for service.

We believe that it is the believer's duty and privilege to communicate the Good News of Messiah Yeshua to the Jewish people first, and also to the Gentiles, according to the Scriptures, in a clear yet sensitive way. It is also the believer's duty to support the God given rights of Israel to the land while opposing anti-Semitism according to the provisions of the Abrahamic Covenant. We believe God has a special purpose and role for the nation of Israel and the Jewish people. We believe in the full physical and spiritual restoration of Israel at the Second Coming of the Messiah as proclaimed in the Scriptures (Genesis 12:1-3; 17:7-8, 26:3-4, 28:13-15; Exodus 19:6; Amos 3:2; 9:8; Zechariah 12:10; 14:2-4; Matthew 23:39; John 4:22; Acts 3:19-21, 13:46;

Notes:

Romans 1:16, 9:3-5; 10:1-5; 11:2-5, 23-26, 28-29; Ephesians 2:14-19).

The Law is not, nor was it ever, a means of justification or sanctification, which come by grace through faith alone. Believers in Yeshua are under the New Covenant, which is not like the Mosaic covenant, and which the law of Moses eagerly awaited. However, both Jewish and non-Jewish believers have a stewardship to utilize the law of Moses as it is applied through New Covenant revelation. For non-Jewish believers as well as Jewish believers, observances such as the festivals and Shabbat are a means of expressing the faithfulness of God to His people (Deuteronomy 29:1--34:10; Jeremiah 31:31-33; Acts 21:24-25; Romans 6:14-15; 8:2-9; 10:4-9; 14:1-6; 1 Corinthians 9:20-21; 2 Corinthians 3:1-11; Galatians 3:3,11; Col. 2:16-17).

Notes:

_____

_____

_____

_____

_____

_____

_____

_____

_____

_____

_____

_____

_____

_____

_____

_____

_____

APPENDIX 7
SAMPLE LIST OF UNIFYING VALUES

————◇————

1. *We value the congregation, Matthew 16:18* - Disciples of Yeshua in mutual and loving accountability in the Lord.

2. *We value ministry by the fellowship, Ephesians 4:12* - The Congregation Leader's ministry is to prepare the believers for service.

3. *We value unity of faith, Amos 3:3* - The Bible is the final authority; the Articles of Faith articulates our unity of beliefs.

4. *We value diversity of service, 1 Peter 4:10-11; Luke 10:38-42* - The congregation gives opportunity to each member for service. Counsel and encouragement for ministry is provided (priesthood of every believer).

5. *We value leadership for effective ministry, Proverbs 29:18, 1 Timothy 3:5* - A congregational ministry is established when a leader is raised up. We only do those ministries when we have the personnel to properly accomplish the service.

6. *We value clarity and orderliness, 1 Corinthians 14:40* - Life and love are not well expressed in chaos; communication is a priority (Constitution, bulletins, budgets, etc.).

7. *We value the testimony of Messiah, Romans 1:16* - We exalt His Name above all others. Evangelism and outreach are taught, conducted and encouraged.

8. *We value a Messianic form of worship, Romans 11:1-2, 11-15, 17-24, 31* - As Messianic Jews and Messianic Gentiles we express our faith in a Jewish cultural religious context (terminology, holidays, etc).

9. *We value our kids, Psalm 127:3* - The congregation provides instruction in the faith in a Jewish frame of reference.

10. *We value discipleship, Matthew 28: 19-20* - We have personal and group discipleship for all. Members are disciples.

GLOSSARY OF MESSIANIC JEWISH TERMS

AM HA-ARETZ ("people of the land"): common people, later used in the Talmud to refer to uneducated, unobservant Jews

AMIDAH ("standing"): also called the *Shemoneh Esrei* ("eighteen") because of its eighteen blessings. The Amidah was originally composed both before and after the destruction of the Temple (70 CE). It is considered central to Jewish prayer.

AVODAH ("worship" or "work"): service to God, originally applied to Temple service.

BEIT TEFILAH ("House of Prayer"): originally referring to the Temple; a prayer and worship center (Isaiah 56:7)

BEMA ("high place"): pulpit or raised platform

BIRKAT HAKOHANIM ("The Blessing of the Priests"): Aaronic Benediction, taken from Numbers 6:24-26

BRIT CHADASHAH ("New Covenant"): the Apostolic Writings, often called the "New Testament." This term is from Jeremiah 31:31.

BRIT MILAH ("covenant of circumcision"): ceremony of circumcision performed upon Jewish males on the eighth day. Traditionally performed by a mohel. This ceremony is also called a bris.

CHAVURAH ("a fellowship," pl. *chavurot*): a small group or Bible Study in which a group of believers fellowship around common values

HAGGADAH ("telling," pl. *haggadot*): a booklet used to go through a Passover Seder, such as *The Messianic Passover Haggadah*.

HALAKHAH ("walking"): traditional Jewish law, the expression of Torah in daily life and conduct

HANUKKAH ("dedication"): Feast commemorating the rebuilding and dedication of the Temple after its desecration by Syrian invaders. Referenced in the extra-Biblical, historical books of "Maccabees," as well as in John 10:22. From the verb *hanakh* or "train;" used for a disciple.

HASHEM ("the Name"): a reverent and traditional way of referring to God. This term refers specifically to God's four-letter Personal Name, rendered in many English Bibles as "Lord;" also called the "tetragrammaton."

KAVANAH ("intentionality"): a traditional concept regarding how one is to pray. This word speaks of being focused and not distracted, purposeful and not haphazard, fervent and not apathetic, reverent and not insolent.

KIPPAH ("dome"): Hebrew term for traditional skullcap worn by men. In Yiddish, it is called a *yarmulke*.

KOHELET ("Preacher"): the main speaker of the Book of Ecclesiastes, as well as the Hebrew name of the book.

KOHEN GADOL ("High Priest")

MASHIACH ("Anointed," Greek *Christos* or "Christ"): Messiah, the Anointed of God to bring salvation to humanity.

MESSIANIC: a follower of Yeshua the Messiah, or a group of such followers. Though it has the same meaning, this word differs from the term, "Christian," in that it suggests a re-emphasis on the faithfulness of God in the Messiah, first to His people Israel and equally to all the nations.

MINYAN (lit. "to count"): traditionally a quorum of ten men. Traditionally, this is required for a corporate Jewish prayer service

OLAM HABA ("the world to come")

ONEG ("delight"): a time of refreshment with food after Shabbat services (*oneg Shabbat* can refer more broadly to various activities to enjoy Shabbat)

PASSOVER (Hebrew *Pesach*): foundational biblical holiday commemorating the rescue of the children of Israel from Egypt, and pointing to the sacrificial death of Messiah.

PURIM ("lots"): holiday based on the book of Esther, often celebrated by giving gifts, dressing in costumes, and a holding a dramatic reenactment of the book of Esther (a *Purim* play).

ROSH HASHANAH ("head of the year"): traditional Jewish New Year stemming from the Feast of Trumpets in Leviticus 23. See also *Zikhron Teruah*

RUACH HAKODESH (*Ruach*: "Spirit, breath, or wind," *Kodesh*: "holy," a.k.a "the Holy Spirit"): the third Person of the Tri-unity Who applies God's plan of redemption to the life of the believer.

SEDER ("order"): a structured meal usually celebrated on one of the first two nights of Passover.

SHAMASH ("servant" or "deacon," pl. *shamashim*): a level of servant-leadership found in Messianic congregations entailing responsibility for executing responsibilities within the congregation (see also *zaken*)

SHLICHIM ("apostles," sing. *shaliach*)

SHAVUOT ("weeks," Greek *Pentecost*): Holiday known as the "Season of the Giving of the Law," also when the spirit of God was given to believers in Yeshua (Acts 2).

SHEMA ("Hear"): the centerpiece of Jewish liturgy, the recitation of Deuteronomy 6:4. Frequently followed by the *V'ahavta* (Deuteronomy 6:5-9)

SUKKOT ("booths," sing. *sukkah*): Feast to remember God's provision and protection in the wilderness wanderings, celebrated by creating and living in makeshift dwellings for eight days.

TALLIT (lit. "cloak"): prayer shawl with *tzitzit* (fringes) traditionally worn at morning services and certain special times. Symbolizes being wrapped in God's Word.

TALMIDIM (lit. "students" sing. *talmid*): trained disciples

TALMIDUT ("discipleship"): the process of becoming a *talmid* (student or disciple). A similar concept, *hanukkah,* from *hanakh*; connotes "training" or "dedication."

TALMUD ("study"): The primary written corpus of the "Oral Law." Made up of the *Mishnah* and *Gemara*. There is both a Babylonian and Jerusalem Talmud, with the Babylonian Talmud being much larger and seen as carrying more authority. Compiled between 200-500CE.

TANAKH: Term for the Hebrew Scriptures, stemming from an acrostic of its parts: *Torah* (Pentateuch), *Nevi'im* (Prophets), and *Ketuvim* (Writings).

TEVILAH ("immersion"): the practice of plunging believers into water as a symbolic testimony of their identification with Messiah. Also called *mikveh* ("reservoir" or "collected water"), which refers to ceremonial cleansing for ritual purification, and thus became a word often used by believers to refer to immersion.

TORAH ("instruction"): Divine instruction, the Scriptures. Also refers to the Five Books of Moses (or Pentateuch), and sometimes called the Law due to the Mosaic laws in this portion of the Hebrew Bible.

YESHUA ("the Lord is salvation" or "the Lord saves"): the Hebrew name often transliterated through the Greek as "Jesus"

YOM KIPPUR ("Day of Atonement"): found in Leviticus 23:27-32, and simply called "the fast" in Acts 27:9, this close of the High Holy Days is considered the holiest day of the year in traditional Judaism. It points to the time of Israel's national repentance and acceptance of Messiah (Zechariah 12:10).

ZIKHRON TERUAH ("a reminder by blowing of trumpets" or the Feast of Trumpets): A mysterious holiday found in Leviticus 23:24. This day begins the High Holy Days and Fall Feasts, and prophetically points to the catching up (or "rapture") of believers.

Z'KEIN ("elder" pl. *Z'keinim*): the highest level of servant-leadership within the congregation. Those responsible for overseeing the teaching, preaching, prayer, worship, and administration of the congregation.

OTHER BOOKS BY SAM

Messianic Discipleship: Following Yeshua, Growing in Messiah - Messianic discipleship workbook designed for use in one-on-one discipleship in Messianic congregations, leads the reader through the essentials of Messianic faith

Messianic Wisdom: Practical Scriptural Answers for Your Life - a follow-up to *Messianic Discipleship*. Addresses various issues in the life of a Messianic Jewish or Gentile believer, and how to live out your faith through them

Messianic Foundations: Fulfill Your Calling in the Jewish Messiah - foundational teaching on the vision and core doctrine of the Messianic Movement, motivated by the testimony of Yeshua as God's faithfulness to Israel

The Messianic Answer Book - answers to 15 common questions that unbelieving Jewish people have about the faith, as well as the testimonies of several Jewish believers. Excellent tool for sharing with those seeking answers

Messiah in the Feasts of Israel - From Passover to *Sukkot*, and Hanukkah to Purim, this book addresses the prophetic purpose of the Feasts; how they point us to Yeshua, and much more. (6-session DVD Bible study also available)

The Messianic Passover Haggadah - a guide to be used in conducting your own Passover Seder with Yeshua at the center

Messianic Life Lessons from the Book of Ruth - a devotional commentary on the redemptive story found in the book of Ruth, demonstrating the Gentile believer's calling to reach out to the lost sheep of the house of Israel, and God's grace for all found in the Messiah (6-session DVD Bible study also available)

Messianic Life Lessons from the Book of Jonah - a devotional commentary on the book of Jonah, demonstrating Israel's calling to be a light to the Gentiles; written for those who seek to find and follow the will of God in their life

Even You Can Share The Jewish Messiah - a short booklet with key information on sharing Yeshua with friends and neighbors, even *"to the Jew first"* (Romans 1:16).

S.W.A.T. (Street Witnessing and Training) - a short booklet with hands-on, practical guidance in conducting evangelism by handing out Messianic literature in public

To contact Sam concerning leadership coaching
or assistance for your congregation, or to schedule a
"Developing Healthy Messianic Congregations" conference
in your area, contact us:

Word of Messiah Ministries
P.O. Box 79238
Charlotte, NC 28271

Email: info@wordofmessiah.org
Phone: (704) 544-1948
WWW.WORDOFMESSIAH.ORG

Find us on Facebook & Twitter

Made in the USA
Coppell, TX
17 July 2020